The Tate Gallery 1982–84

The Tate Gallery 1982–84

ILLUSTRATED BIENNIAL REPORT

front cover
Joan Miró
Message from a Friend 1964
T 03691

ISBN 0 946590 10 9
Published by order of the Trustees 1984
Copyright © 1984 The Tate Gallery
Designed and published by the Tate Gallery Publications Department,
Millbank, London SWIP 4RG
Printed by The Hillingdon Press, Uxbridge, Middlesex

Contents

Trustees' Foreword

We were delighted to welcome Her Majesty The Queen Mother to the Tate Gallery on 19 April 1983 to lay the Foundation plaque of the Clore Gallery for the Turner Collection, in the presence of Mrs Vivien Duffield and Mr Leonard Sainer of the Clore Foundation. Work has continued well on the building, which has now taken shape, straddling Bulinga Street (now closed) and adding a distinctive character to our Millbank front. We now await the opening, scheduled for early 1986.

In preparation, the Trustees of the National Gallery, with the approval of the Trustees of the British Museum, have agreed that the works on paper in the Turner Bequest will be transferred to the Tate Gallery. A total of over 19,000 sheets (many of them sketch book pages and rough sketches) of the Turner works on paper were lodged at the Tate Gallery until the flood of January 1928 prompted their removal to the higher ground of Bloomsbury. They have been well looked after, but we are very pleased to anticipate their return when the Print Room of the Clore Gallery is ready next year. When the Clore Gallery opens, the Turner Bequest will once again be reunited.

The Gallery has acquired another very important group of Turner paintings – namely, the twenty oils that were formerly in the collection of Lord Egremont at Petworth. Offered in lieu of duty some twenty years ago, they were accepted by the Treasury and

Her Majesty Queen Elizabeth, The Queen Mother with
Mrs Vivien Duffield, Arabella and George Duffield and the Chairman
at the unveiling of the Clore Gallery plaque on 19 April 1983

Charles Robert Leslie
Interior at Petworth
T 13789

are now in the care of the Trustees of the Tate Gallery. They will however stay at Petworth House – the property of the National Trust – and thus they remain in the house with which they have been associated and for which some of them were painted.

Another important bequest has come to the Gallery. When Mrs Anne Kessler died in 1983 at the age of ninety-three, the group of fourteen French paintings and drawings that she had given the Tate Gallery twenty-five years before came to Millbank. Mrs Kessler was the niece of Frank Stoop, whose bequest in 1933 of seventeen works by Cézanne, Matisse, Picasso and others forms the main starting point of our modern foreign collection as it is today. Mrs Kessler's Renoirs, her Degas pastel, and especially her fine Dufys make a most welcome addition to the early part of the Modern Collection.

The Gallery has also benefited from the late Marchioness of Downshire, who left part of her Estate to make a fund for the acquisition of modern works of art. Another major gift has come from Mrs Yulla Lipchitz, who gave us over fifty plasters and terracottas by her husband, Jacques Lipchitz, strengthening further the Tate Gallery's already considerable modern sculpture collection. We are also grateful to the Friends of the Tate Gallery for their continued help with acquisitions. In particular, we would like to record the legacy left to the Friends by Miss H. M. Arbuthnot, which has been used to purchase Peter Blake's 'The Meeting', and to make a substantial contribution towards the cost of Miró's 'Message from a Friend'. The first gifts to the Gallery have now come from the

Patrons of New Art, and we are delighted to have their support and their encouragement for our most adventurous acquisitions.

The Grant-in-Aid for acquisitions rose substantially in the seventies – from £265,000 in 1974–75 to £1,570,000 in 1979–80 – but since 1980 there has been no real improvement. Rising prices have outstripped the small increases in the grant. It becomes increasingly difficult for the Tate Gallery to compete for the limited number of outstanding works. The purchasing activities of the Getty Trustees, now required to spend $90m per annum, may not directly affect us yet, but they have affected the entire art market. By comparison with $90m the sums available to the Tate Gallery (and to the National Gallery) are unfortunately woefully inadequate.

Changes in the taxation system that would make giving to the national museums as easy and advantageous as it is in the United States would certainly help us. If this is not possible, then the level of grant must be urgently reconsidered.

We have also tried to press for changes in the way that Value Added Tax is applied to works of art. At present it operates against the living artist, and gives a direct advantage to the foreign buyer who is exempt from the tax. The Tate has to pay 15% V.A.T. on the full value of all works executed since 1973, or of unsold work that remained in the artist's possession at that time. Older paintings are subject to V.A.T. only on the dealer's commission but purchase of work by living artists brings this extra tax burden. This can hardly have been intended when the regulations were introduced. Even gifts of work to the Tate Gallery from abroad have been subject to 15% import V.A.T., though this most unfair of impositions is at the time of writing being withdrawn.

There have been changes in the Board of Trustees during the period of this report: Sir Richard Attenborough, C.B.E., Rita Donagh, Francis Graham-Harrison, C.B., Paul Huxley and the Hon. Sir John Sainsbury have all left the Board; we are most grateful to them for their invaluable and generous services. We also record with sadness the deaths of two former Trustees, Stewart Mason, C.B.E., who served from 1966 to 1973, and Sir Dennis Proctor, K.C.B., who became a Trustee in 1952 and served as Chairman during the difficult years of 1953–59. His contribution to the well-being and public esteem of the Tate Gallery today will not be forgotten.

Hutchinson   *Chairman*
Virginia Airlie
Anthony Caro
Patrick Heron
Caryl Hubbard
Peter Moores
Peter Palumbo
Rex Richards
Richard Rogers

Gifts, Bequests, Donations and Funds

The Trustees and Director would like to thank the following for their gifts and bequests of works of art, donations and funds to the Tate Gallery:

Archive Collection
Mr Ivor Abrahams
Mrs Ruth Boswell
Mrs Rosemary Butler
Mrs Nancy Carline
Mr Denis Clarke Hall
Mr Desmond Flower
Mrs Angelica Garnett
Mr Josef Herman
The Executor of the Estate of Frances Hodgkins
Mrs Olda Kokoschka
Mr Robert Lewin
Professor William Lipke
The London Group
Mr Robert Longo
Mr George Melly
Mrs Nora Meninsky
The Executors of the Estate of Sir Cedric Morris
Mr Julian Opie
Mr Ewan Phillips
Mr John Piper
Mr Kenneth Powell
Mr Crispin Rogers
The late Mrs Anstice Shaw
Mr Gilbert Silverman
Mr Stephen Willats

British Collection
Canon J. H. Adams
British Sporting Art Trust
The late Mrs F. Ambrose Clark (through the British Sporting Art Trust)
Miss V. N. Cross (through the British Sporting Art Trust)
The late Miss M. Deakin
The late Mrs Bessie Gornall
The Sue Hammerson Charitable Trust
The Kretschmer Family
Hugh Paget, C.B.E.

Modern Collection
The late Miss Helen Arbuthnot (through the Friends of the Tate Gallery)
Art and Language
Mrs Ruth Boswell
Mrs Nancy Carline
Mr Anthony Caro
The late Mrs Ernestine Carter
Mr David Cast
The Trustees of the Chantrey Bequest
Herr Gunther Demnig
Madame Souza Desnoyer
The late Evelyn, the Marchioness of Downshire
Mr & Mrs Eric Estorick
Mr Frederick Gore
Mr Stanley William Hayter
The Executor of the Estate of Frances Hodgkins
Dr J. P. Hodin
Mrs Gabrielle Keiller (through the Friends of the Tate Gallery)
Madame Madeleine Kemeny
The late Mrs A. F. Kessler
Mrs Olda Kokoschka
Mr John Lessore
The Jacques and Yulla Lipchitz Foundation
The Lisson Gallery
Lord McAlpine
Mercedes Benz (UK) Limited
Mr Richard Michelmore
Miss Nancy Morris
Mr Timothy Nicholson
Mr John Piper
The late Vivian Pitchforth
Mr E. J. Power
The Rayne Foundation
Sir John Rothenstein (through the Friends of the Tate Gallery)
The late Mrs M. J. A. Russell
Mr Paul Schupf
Madame Andrée Stassart
Mrs Jack Steinberg (through the Friends of the Tate Gallery)
The late Mrs E. A. West

Print Collection
Mr J. G. Cluff
Mr Paul Beldock
Mr Bill Jacklin
Mr Orde Levinson
Mr & Mrs David McKee (through the American Federation of the Arts)
Mr Henry Moore
Mrs Leslie Oliver (through the Friends of the Tate Gallery)
Miss Valerie Thornton

In addition the Trustees wish to express their gratitude to the following societies for their continued support which is most warmly welcomed:

The Friends of the Tate Gallery for their gifts of the following works: John Hill 'The Carpenter's Shop', Eileen Agar 'Angel of Anarchy', Peter Blake 'The Meeting' or 'Have a Nice Day, Mr Hockney', Meredith Frampton 'Marguerite Kelsey', David Jones 'Crucifixion', Peter Lanyon 'The Wreck', Bernard Meadows 'Lovers', Sir William Nicholson 'Harbour in Snow, La Rochelle' and for their contributions towards Sir George Clausen 'Winter Work', Atkinson Grimshaw 'Bowder Stone, Borrowdale', Tilly Kettle 'Mrs Yates as Mandane', Max Beckmann 'Carnival', Jacques Lipchitz 'Half Standing Figure', Joan Miró 'Message from a Friend', Jean Tinguely 'Débricollage', Edward Wadsworth 'Regalia'. The Friends also gave generously towards the Coffee Shop project.

The Patrons of New Art for their gifts of the following works: Julian Opie 'Making It', Robert Longo 'Sword of the Pig', Paula Rego 'Nanny, Small Bears and Bogeyman'.

The National Art-Collections Fund for their contribution towards Max Beckmann 'Carnival' and Abraham Solomon 'Waiting for the Verdict' and 'Not Guilty'.

The National Heritage Memorial Fund for their contribution towards William Hogarth 'The Dance (The Happy Marriage VI)' and Richard Wilson 'Westminster Bridge under Construction'.

The Contemporary Art Society for their gifts of Roger Ackling 'Five Sunsets in One Hour' and Anthony Gormley 'Natural Selection' to the Modern Collection and John Walker 'Pacifica' to the Print Collection.

The Trustees also wish to thank the following for their generous financial help:
Britoil
Capital Radio
Mars Limited
Mobil Oil Co. Ltd
The Monument Trust
Olympus Cameras
Pearson
The Robert and Lisa Sainsbury Charitable Trust
Sotheby's
Alec Tiranti Limited
Winsor & Newton

Extremely generous gifts have also been received from donors who wish to remain anonymous; for these the Trustees are very grateful.

Income for the two years under review from the Knapping Fund was £18,007, from the Gytha Trust £11,199 and from the Abbott Fund £2,478. The Grant-in-Aid for 1982–83 was £1,860,000 and for 1983–84 £2,021,000.

Director's Report

The attendance figures in the two years under review are the highest in the Gallery's history – evidence of growing public interest in art, and a tribute to the Tate Gallery, which is not the most accessible of public museums. When there is an exhibition as popular as *The Pre-Raphaelites,* we frequently have almost 10,000 visitors in the building on a Saturday or a Sunday, and this puts a great strain on our services and makes the galleries uncomfortably full.

The Tate urgently needs more space, not just for the works of art that should be on display, but for the people who come to see them. It is for this reason that our development plans are so important. Society is slowly realising that the public art gallery plays a central part in the lives of an increasing number of people. As world travel becomes easier,, as working hours shorten, as leisure, enforced or voluntary, becomes more vital, so does the importance of the art museum increase. We need to plan now for the year 2000, when we can be sure that double and treble the number of the visitors we have today will be wanting to come to Millbank.

The building of the Clore Gallery is proving a real stimulus to the Gallery: if the

Her Majesty Queen Elizabeth, The Queen Mother with Mr James Stirling surveying the Clore Gallery site on 19 April 1983

enormous success of the Paris Turner exhibition is anything to go by, there will be great public excitement when it opens. We are delighted with our architects, James Stirling, Michael Wilford and Associates, and have been happy to watch the international recognition that has come to them since they were appointed architects for the Tate Gallery development in 1978. In particular we congratulate them on their art gallery buildings – the Neue Staatsgalerie in Stuttgart, and the extension to the Fogg Art Museum at Harvard, both of which will be complete before the Clore Gallery opens.

Thanks to an anonymous private donation, we have now been able to press ahead with plans for the second phase of development on the hospital site. James Stirling is now preparing designs for two new museums, one devoted to Modern Sculpture (of which the Tate has a particularly rich collection) and the other to New Art. By New Art we mean the work of the last ten years or so – this has its own audience, which is generally young and very enthusiastic, and it poses particular problems in the way that it is collected and displayed.

After a period of time, works in the New Art Museum would be transferred to the main Tate collections, and this is why before very long we shall need the third and final component of the Tate development plan – a Museum of Twentieth Century Art, in other words the classic Museum of Modern Art such as we know from New York or Paris. This would include all the paintings and sculpture in the Tate by foreign artists, together with a representation of British work. Our much more comprehensive British twentieth-century collection would remain in the existing Tate building, which would become what it was founded to be – a museum of British painting, from the past to the present.

Though each component museum would have a distinct character, each would be an integral part of the Tate Gallery, sharing services and facilities in the most economic way. Just as the Clore Gallery will include a lecture theatre, classroom, paper conservation studio and print room, so the new museum buildings will be associated with, for example, a sculpture conservation studio, extended exhibition preparation area, an archive and a library that would offer greater public facilities than we can at present.

All this will require considerable funding, and we accept that much of this finance must come from private sources. Fortunately the Tate Gallery has many friends – and the success of such groups within the Friends of the Tate Gallery as the Patrons of New Art has been immensely heartening. The Henry Moore Foundation is already helping us to establish the sculpture conservation studio in temporary premises, and will pay the salary of the first conservator and the student who is to assist. We are deeply grateful to the Foundation for filling a surprising gap in the Tate Gallery's services, and we hope that the Conservation Studio will become an international centre for the conservation and care of twentieth-century sculpture. It should play an important educational role, and the development of training and research in the Tate's own conservation department (see p.71) shows just how vital this is.

The Tate's own sculpture collection has been extended, not only by the generous Lipchitz gift, but also by the transfer from the Victoria and Albert Museum of eighty sculptures, British and foreign, made since Rodin. Works will be lent back to the V & A when required for display, but this transfer tidies up an overlapping of the national collections.

Acquisitions in the two years under review are considerable, and are listed on pages 98-136. A full catalogue is in preparation, but this takes time. The catalogue of acquisitions for 1980–82 is published simultaneously with this Biennial Report for 1982–84. In the meantime, some major acquisitions for both Historic British and Modern Collections are singled out for mention and illustration in the pages that follow. A number of outstanding masterpieces have been acquired, and we continue to pursue our aim of making the collections of British painting and of twentieth-century painting and sculpture as rich and comprehensive as possible.

Though the Tate Gallery's holding of early modern art can never rival that of New York or Paris, we can be reasonably confident that, so far as art since 1940 is concerned, ours is a collection that is different but in no way inferior. Indeed such is the depth and quality of the collection in this field that we would like to show a substantial part of it elsewhere than in London. Our plans for a Tate in the North, based in the wonderful Albert Dock buildings in Liverpool, have not yet come to fruition, but we hope that it may prove possible to realise this imaginative and far-reaching scheme.

At Millbank, we have had a varied and successful exhibition programme, culminating in the enormously popular Pre-Raphaelite show. We provide three major exhibitions a year, together with small shows and displays which are often every bit as interesting as the blockbuster. The Gallery has many publics: it would be very surprising if anyone liked everything that we do - we attempt to cater for all of them.

The exhibition activities of the Tate Gallery and the work of the Conservation and service departments are described later in this report. The Print Collection, the Archive and the Library continue to grow - very satisfactory in all respects, except that their need for better accommodation becomes increasingly urgent if they are to serve the public as they should. The Education Department will be better housed when the Clore Gallery opens late in 1985: for the moment their invaluable work is being done in very difficult circumstances.

The contribution made to the educational programme by the Voluntary Guides should not be overlooked; it is only a part of our debt to the Friends of the Tate Gallery. The formation of the Patrons of New Art, under the chairmanship of Felicity Waley-Cohen, will be of great significance in fostering the new and the adventurous. In the meantime we welcome a new Chairman of the Friends Council and of the Executive Committee, and thank Lady Airlie and Mrs Patrick Allen for their devoted services to the Tate over so many years.

The Publications Department pursues an active supportive role, with exhibition catalogues becoming grander and more definitive than ever. A multi-volume series of catalogues of the collection is now in active preparation: our aim must be to have information that often exists in earlier publications brought up to date and made readily accessible to the public, as well as to publish for the first time the results of the original research that is the primary duty of our curators.

The Restaurant has seen a change of Manager: Tom Machen, who since 1970 had given the Tate Gallery Restaurant an international reputation for food and particularly for wine, left us in 1982. We are greatly indebted to him, and happy that he continues to buy wine for us and keeps an eye on the cellar he so astutely layed down. Paul King has taken over a flourishing business. The Coffee Shop in particular must be one of the most elegant in London: Jeremy Dixon's designs, described in the last Biennial Report, have been an enormous success and we are delighted to say that the Restaurant will next year also be completely refurbished to Mr Dixon's plans which include better lighting for the Rex Whistler mural paintings.

In the two years under discussion, the Gallery's staff was inspected by the Management team of the Department of Education and Science. Such an inspection had been promised when the Gallery was devolved in 1975 and given greater responsibility for its own management. It had been awaited with some trepidation as it involved a review of the work and responsibilities of every member of staff (conservation and uniformed staff excepted). In the event the management review proved both positive and helpful, and we have made certain changes in the running of the Gallery that are already bringing us benefits. Roger Aylward's arrival from the National Portrait Gallery as our Administration Officer has greatly helped to put these changes into effect.

Finally, let me record with pleasure the award of the B.E.M. to our Head Attendant, Mr Collier. He sets such a fine example to his staff, and is always such a welcome presence to everyone in the Gallery that we are very gratified to see that his services are publicly recognised. And let me also, but with much regret (tinged with a little envy), record the early retirement of Judith Jeffreys, my Assistant Director. Mrs Jeffreys gave almost a lifetime of devoted service to the Tate Gallery, from the time of her appointment as an acting Assistant Keeper in 1951 onwards. She had watched the Gallery grow and flourish in a quite remarkable way. In her time she seemed to have done almost every job in the Gallery; she knew every member of staff, old and new; she could always advise on precedent and practice. To a new Director like myself, coming to the Gallery from outside in 1980, her support was incalculable: I shall personally always remain deeply grateful to her. It is people like Judith who make the Tate Gallery the great institution that it is. Their devotion is quite unselfish, done without any wish for personal advancement or reputation but always for the good of the Gallery. Her contribution will long be remembered.

Alan Bowness
Director

Information Department

The number of visitors to the Tate Gallery during the period covered by this Report was greater than in any earlier biennial period. The significance of this fact in the context of the Information Department is twofold. The function of the department is, on the one hand, to inform the world at large of the multiplicity of Tate activities, and on the other to welcome and direct visitors on arrival at the Gallery.

In the fulfilment of these functions the department has intensified and rationalised the information service which it provides by telephone, by post, and in person. It has explored and established new avenues for information and publicity. Most significantly it has, as in the past, been splendidly supported by the Press, and not only in connection with controversial issues which naturally occur from time to time.

Changes have been made in the design of printed material issued by the department, in particular the monthly calendar of events. These herald a wide-ranging revision of similar material and of the information panels and signposting throughout the building.

Via the Information Desk and the Suggestions Box a watch has been kept on indications of approval or doubt regarding innovations or changes in the amenities provided for the public. The contribution made by visitors in conveying their views is always welcomed and valued.

The work of the Information Department has been extended through identification with the sponsorship of Tate events which has added a new dimension to Gallery activities in recent years. Involvement in the organisation or coordination of these events has been considerable and rewarding. Liaison with sponsors and with those considering sponsorship, as well as with agencies which act on their behalf, has led to the formation of a circle of friends whose commitment to the ideals of the Gallery provides invaluable support and encouragement.

Looking ahead to the opening of the Clore Gallery the department anticipates a substantial expansion of its services to the public.

A New Dimension

The history of sponsorship at the Tate Gallery is recent but dramatic. It follows an uninterrupted tradition of private patronage for buildings which embraces Sir Henry Tate, Joseph (later Sir Joseph) Duveen, Lord Duveen, the Gulbenkian Foundation, and currently the Clore Foundation. It also complements a longstanding tradition of assistance towards the purchase of works of art from trusts, societies, funds, corporations and private individuals.

In recent years the Tate programme of special exhibitions has been widened and intensified, and the part played by sponsors in reinforcing this programme is at present the most significant aspect of sponsorship at the Gallery. Since the earliest example of exhibition sponsorship in 1982 many events have been made possible or have been enhanced by generous outside help. Following their sponsorship of the Landseer exhibition early in 1982, Pearson renewed their support by sponsoring the Pre-Raphaelite exhibition in 1984. Mobil Oil Co. Ltd have similarly sponsored two major exhibitions by British artists, Graham Sutherland in 1982 and John Piper in 1983. We are immensely encouraged by the way in which the example of these organisations has already been followed by two companies who will be sponsoring exhibitions later in 1984 – United Technologies Corporation, and Gerald Metals Limited.

Paint and Painting – sponsored by Winsor & Newton in the summer of 1982 and opened by Her Royal Highness Princess Michael of Kent – combined an exhibition on the history of colour and technique in painting with a public painting studio. The studio, housed in a pavilion designed by Alan Stanton and Peter Rice, revived the tradition of events held on the Tate Gallery lawn. A pavement art competition, also sponsored by Winsor & Newton, attracted enthusiastic response. Members of the public were provided with chalks with which to create on the pavement around the Gallery a work on the theme of their choice. Vouchers for artists' materials were presented to the prizewinners by Lord Hutchinson, the Chairman of the Tate Gallery Trustees. For their imaginative support for *Paint and Painting* and its related activities – including a one-day symposium on the conservation of modern paintings – Winsor & Newton received a 1982 ABSA/Daily Telegraph Award. One hundred and sixty nominations for a total of ten awards had been received that year by the Association for Business Sponsorship of the Arts. A second award for *Paint and Painting* was made under the Museum of the Year Award Scheme set up in 1972 by National Heritage and the Illustrated London News. This was the Museum of the Year Award for the best temporary exhibition, sponsored by James Bourlet & Son.

In the summer of 1983 the pavilion housed two major events. The first of these, a successor to *Paint and Painting*, was entitled *Making Sculpture.* The event benefited substantially by sponsorship in the form of materials and equipment provided by Alec Tiranti Limited. Earlier that year an example of material help of this kind had been provided by Capital Radio whose contribution to the Peter Blake exhibition took the form of equipment and tapes of appropriate music relayed in various sections of the exhibition.

The second event held in the pavilion in the summer of 1983 was an exhibition of the best entries to the 'Summertime' painting competition jointly organised by BBC Woman's Hour, the Radio Times and the Tate Gallery. Thousands of entries were received from all over the United Kingdom and from abroad. During the exhibition television personality John Fitzmaurice Mills was available in the pavilion to give advice on painting techniques and materials. Glass bowls, engraved by Mack Lonnon, were presented by

Members of the public working with different media inside the Paint and Painting Working Studio sponsored by Winsor & Newton

Her Royal Highness Princess Michael of Kent to the two prizewinners, the painters of the outstanding works on canvas and on paper. The 151 entrants whose work had been selected for hanging each received a commemorative certificate.

Sponsorship for publications associated with Tate events has made it possible to produce, at a low cost to the public, booklets such as those on artists' materials and on making sculpture. The catalogue for the Richard Wilson exhibition, shown in 1982, was sponsored by Britoil who have again offered substantial sponsorship for printed material related to a forthcoming Tate exhibition. Assistance has also been given towards the cost of the growing volume of leaflets which are an integral part of the activities arranged by the Education Department. In the series of Gallery Trails, which direct young people towards particular works and encourage close scrutiny in the context of an entertaining game, the Mars chocolate company financed a leaflet on the theme of 'Work, Rest and Play'.

The 13th Triennial Conference of ICOM (the International Council of Museums), held at the Barbican Centre in the summer of 1983, provided an opportunity for the Trustees and Director to welcome colleagues from museums in all parts of the world to an evening reception for which sponsorship was provided by Sotheby & Co. A similar opportunity was offered to the Trustees and Director in the same year by Olympus Cameras who sponsored a reception for Peter Blake to celebrate the opening of his exhibition.

The interest which the Association for Business Sponsorship of the Arts has always shown in the work of the Tate has been most encouraging. It was with the greatest pleasure that in 1983 we welcomed a group of twenty members of the Association to a behind-the-scenes tour. This included visits to the departments of Conservation, Photography, and Technical Services, with opportunities to meet members of staff from many departments and to discuss activities and future plans.

Abundant evidence of goodwill and generosity has already been shown towards the Gallery and we are encouraged by the growing number of friends in the industrial and commercial fields who share our concern for the enhancement of the range and quality of Tate activities. Their support has created a new dimension in our planning and we anticipate a continuing programme of jointly organised, exciting, enlightening and entertaining events.

The Historic British Collection

There have been no radical departures in policy from the lines set out in our report for 1978–80. Again, just as in the years 1980–82, there have been no dramas in the field of acquisitions, though, in our quiet way, we have continued to build up the representation of the Historic British Collection. We have acquired major works by Hogarth and Richard Wilson as well as an important example of the British pioneers of neo-classicism working in Rome in the second half of the eighteenth century, Gavin Hamilton's 'Agrippina with the Ashes of Germanicus'. Two 'hits' of the mid-nineteenth century Royal Academy have been bought: Abraham Solomon's 'Waiting for the Verdict' and, delayed for two years, 'Not Guilty'. Two interesting religious paintings of the first half of the nineteenth century, by Joseph Severn and William C. T. Dobson, have been added, and our representation of later nineteenth-century realism has been strengthened by pictures by Atkinson Grimshaw, Sir George Clausen, La Thangue, Sir James Guthrie and Edward Walton. The most important of these works have been singled out for special attention on the pages immediately following, while all the acquisitions of the Historic British Collection are listed with abbreviated catalogue information on pp. 98–103. As usual, full catalogue information will be published in due course in a separate volume.

Members of the Historic British Collection staff continue to be increasingly involved in major exhibitions. Leslie Parris had the task of co-ordinating the efforts of a remarkable team of experts on the Pre-Raphaelite Movement; as is reported elsewhere, their efforts have been rewarded with near-record attendance figures. Judy Egerton is busy on the major George Stubbs exhibition to be held later in 1984; this too promises to be a great success with the general public, as well as full of scholarly revelations. Looking further ahead, Elizabeth Einberg is collecting material for an exhibition of painting in the Age of Hogarth.

The Tate Gallery's own collection of paintings in the Age of Hogarth is to be the subject of the first of a series of scholarly, detailed catalogues covering the Historic British Collection. Work is far advanced, though it would be presumptuous to promise a publication date. Other volumes will cover the preceding period, that is works from the sixteenth and seventeenth centuries; the 'high' eighteenth century, centring around the work of Reynolds and Gainsborough; Romantic painting (though separate catalogues have already been issued of the major contributors, Turner, Constable and, in his own personal way, William Blake); the new realism and anecdotal painting of the earlier nineteenth-century, ranging from Wilkie to Frith; and High Victorian painting. The number of works to be covered in each volume will range widely, but it is hoped to bring some unity to the series by similarities in presentation.

A considerable amount of thought and preparation is being devoted to the rearrangement of the Historic British Collection that will result from the opening of the Clore Gallery for the Turner Collection. Ideally one would like to plan the necessary changes in conjunction with the work of physically refurbishing the galleries concerned, but there are practical difficulties about this. To begin with at least, the presentation of British art in the earlier years of the nineteenth century will be rather a case of Hamlet without the Prince, but, once the Clore Gallery is fully established with its own Curator of the Turner Collection, and the first dramatic presentation of the Turner Collection as a whole has lost its initial impact, ways will no doubt be found to relate Turner in some way to the main chronological sequence of the British School.

Inside Two 'Carpenter's Shops'

'The Carpenter's Shop at Forty Hill, Enfield' by John Hill, an almost forgotten artist, was acquired for the Tate Gallery chiefly because its subject-matter is unusual and the picture very convincingly painted. Hill was self-taught as an artist, but there is nothing naive about the fresh and direct style which he displays here. This picture was in fact probably exhibited at the Royal Academy in 1813 under the title 'Interior of a Carpenter's Shop'.

John Hill was himself a carpenter and builder at Forty Hill. This scene probably represents his own workshop, and the figure of the master of the shop (seen at its farther end), whose moleskin hat and dark jacket distinguish him from his assistants in their white caps and shirtsleeves, may be a self-portrait. But although this picture depicts a particular carpenter's shop early in the nineteenth century any modern spectator who has experienced the traditional techniques and customs of a carpenter's training will recognise every detail of the scene. And the closer you look at this painting, the more detail you will see in it. None of these details are picturesque props; all of them are painted from first-hand knowledge of the carpenter's trade.

JOHN HILL

The Carpenter's Shop at Forty Hill, Enfield

T 03668

The three men at work in this interior are not posing for the artist. Each of them is absorbed in his work and in command of the task to which he is putting his skills. Every one of them is evidently a fully qualified carpenter, for each has his own tool-box close at hand. These tool-boxes were (and still are) usually begun in the last years of a carpenter's apprenticeship, and might take several years to finish. On the outside these tool-boxes looked plain and serviceable; they were usually painted green, as these are. When opened they revealed the finest workmanship of which the craftsman was capable; they usually consisted of twelve drawers, the whole elaborately inlaid and veneered. Tool-boxes served two chief purposes; they enabled a carpenter to keep his own personal tools safely and tidily, and they could be shown to a prospective employer as evidence of a carpenter's skill. Within a workshop they also served an everyday practical purpose in giving the carpenter somewhere to sit and eat his midday meal.

The white caps worn by the master carpenter's two assistants were traditional for several centuries, and were worn also by tradesmen such as plasterers and house-painters. They were made of stout paper, folded into a box-like shape. A similar paper cap is worn by the Walrus's friend the Carpenter in Tenniel's illustrations to *Alice: Through the Looking-Glass.*

For those who would like to know more about the picture but are not familiar with the carpenter's trade, it may be a help to state just what can be seen in it. We are looking into the interior of a small joinery shop, made chiefly of timber but with one brick wall. The floor is made of flagstones, which in winter would probably have been covered with wooden pallets. The windows on either side of the shop are glazed with small panes of bottle-glass; broken panes have been stopped by the time-honoured custom of stuffing bundles of wood-shavings into the cracks. At the farther end of the shop is a large unglazed opening, big enough for large pieces of work to go through; this opening gives ventilation and maximum light (and, incidentally, a charming view of the countryside outside), and it is at this vantage point that the master of the shop has chosen to station himself. This opening could be closed by outside shutters.

In the centre of the foreground, an axe and a cross-cut log lie on the flagstones, probably to symbolise the first and most basic step in carpentry; this is the only slightly unrealistic note in the picture, for no carpenter would leave an axe on the floor like that. On the left is a wicker basket used for carrying tools between the shop and work outside it; from it protrude a hand-saw, an adze, a gauge and what is either an unfinished staircase baluster or the template for it. Behind the basket is a sash-cramp, used (still) in the making of sash windows to glue or 'cramp up' their frames. Between the windows on the left hang hand-saws, a bow-saw and various templates; beneath the furthest window is a metal-working vice, which would extend the sort of work this workshop can undertake.

The carpenter on the left, with his back to the spectator, is working at a carpenter's bench, the basic design of which has remained unchanged for centuries; on it lie several planes, a wooden mallet, various dividers and pincers, a bradawl and a gimlet. This man is using a square to mark out a piece of timber for cutting; two pieces of wood which he has already stripped, planed and squared lie on the bench at his right. His fellow-assistant, on the right of the picture, is sawing a piece of marked-out timber on a wooden trestle or saw-horse.

At the farther end of the shop, the master is planing timber. The wooden beams of the wall in front of him are hung with various tools, including several brass-backed tenon saws and a coffin-maker's saw (used, not only in coffin-making, for sawing long joints) and with various templates, mostly for making heavy mouldings. One or two objects on this wall specifically refer to work carried out in this particular shop: for instance, a picture frame made of dark wood, or stained dark, perhaps made for one of Hill's own paintings, and a carved eagle, perhaps a small version of a carving made for a church pulpit. Chalked numbers on the wall on the master's right are presumably calculations for the work at present in hand.

The array of tools continues across the brick wall on the right, and includes several spare vices, boxes of pegs and nails and, at the extreme right, a mitre-block for cutting corners. The only indispensable items missing from this view are glue-pots; they must have been kept at the end of the workshop which is (as it were) occupied by the spectator and which probably gave approximately one-third more space to the workshop. Everything else which should be here is here; everything in this workshop has a practical function and is accurately depicted.

John Everett Millais's representation of a carpenter's shop, in the painting called

JOHN EVERETT MILLAIS

Christ in the House of his Parents (The Carpenter's Shop)

N 03584

'Christ in the Carpenter's Shop' or 'Christ in the House of His Parents', of 1849-50, is very different to John Hill's. On the surface, Millais's picture depicts the Holy Family at Nazareth, with Joseph practising his trade as a carpenter. As Malcolm Warner explains in his entry on this picture in *The Pre-Raphaelites* exhibition catalogue, 1984 (No. 26, pp. 77-9), Millais made regular visits to a carpenter's shop in search of reality. According to Holman Hunt, this carpenter's shop was in Oxford Street. Millais began work there a few days after Christmas 1849, arranged to have a bed installed there so that he could work on his background early in the morning, and by 12 January 1850 was suffering from a cold caught in the carpenter's shop (his sufferings were very minor compared with those of Holman Hunt when painting 'The Scapegoat', but they were undergone in the same spirit).

Millais included only such details as he wanted. His carpenter's shop is not so much a place of work as a stage for a few carefully selected props. The most realistic detail is the carpenter's bench, which is of the same timeless design as the bench in Hill's carpenter's shop, and as my own bench in the Tate carpenter's workshop today. The piece of work on it, on which Joseph and his assistant had been engaged, appears to be a braced door, or possibly a table-top. There is no earthly reason why the long nail on which the boy Christ has wounded himself should ever have been driven into it, except of course that the whole point of Millais's picture is to use this wound to foreshadow the wounds Christ received in His crucifixion. The same wish to symbolise or prefigure the instruments of Christ's Passion leads Millais to select only a few oddly assorted tools, which in fact would be ludicrously inadequate for any actual construction. The two large nails which lie on the work-bench are cut nails, of the sort used in fixing floorboards in a house; there are only two of them, and both are bent, presumably to intensify the feelings of foreboding for Christ's future suffering. The tools on the wall at the back of this workshop include a bow-saw of the type peculiar to the cooper's trade of barrel-making and a hammer of the type used by upholsterers. There is no plane, yet that tool is of course indispensable in a carpenter's shop. The most realistic tool here is the auger.

Millais's picture is a semblance of reality rather than reality itself. In his carpenter's shop, a set-square is not so much a set-square as a symbol of the Trinity. There are no symbolic overtones in Hill's picture. Its realism is, literally, almost artless; but there is, and should be, room for Hill's picture as well as Millais's in the national gallery of British Art.

Jack Warans

I should like to acknowledge Judy Egerton's help in our discussions of the two pictures. Anyone interested in finding our more about the tools mentioned can find descriptions and illustrations in R. A. Salaman, *Dictionary of Tools*, 1975.

Acquisitions of the Historic British Collection

MARCUS GHEERAEDTS THE YOUNGER

**Portrait of a Man in Masque Dress, probably Philip Herbert,
4th Earl of Pembroke** *c.*1610

T 03466

There are good reasons for believing that this unusual portrait, and what is obviously its pair, the 'Unknown Man' in identical costume in the Stanford University collection in California, represent William Herbert (1580-1630), 3rd Earl of Pembroke, and his younger brother Philip (1584-1650), later 4th Earl of Pembroke. The 'incomparable pair of brethren', to whom the editors dedicated the first folio of Shakespeare's works in 1623, rose to high positions at court both under James I and Charles I, but were better known in their younger days for their surly temper, womanising, and determination to shine at masques and tournaments. Philip was a particular favourite of James I, who created him Earl of Montgomery in 1605.

The portrait's conception in the style of a cameo of a Roman emperor's head suggests a connection with one of the innumerable court masques on classical themes performed throughout the early years of the seventeenth century. The sensitively but strongly modelled head appears typical of Gheeraedts' best work at this period, when he was the favourite painter of the Queen, Anne of Denmark. The provenance of the paintings before their appearance on the art market in the late 1960s is as yet unknown.

RICHARD WILSON

Westminster Bridge under Construction 1744

T 03665

The building of Westminster Bridge began in 1738 and was nearly completed in 1746, although engineering difficulties delayed its opening until 1750. The growing edifice soon became a favourite subject of London view-painters, including the young Wilson, who painted the subject at least twice; a smaller version, dated 1745, is in the Philadelphia Museum of Art, and shows an additional arch nearing completion. Compared with his contemporaries Canaletto and Scott, who based memorable compositions on this subject, Wilson treats the structure much less as an architectural centrepiece. Instead he emphasises its landscape setting and its relationship to the flat muddy banks of the Thames.

From a viewpoint just to the right of Parliament Stairs on the Westminster side of the river, we look north towards St Stephen's Chapel on the left with Westminster Hall behind, and the dome of St Paul's in the distance on the right. In the foreground an elegant couple approach a ferry with its gesticulating boatman, who is shown wearing the distinctive uniform and badge of his profession. Its long narrow shape suggests that the painting was meant for an overmantel.

The work is a particularly fine example of Wilson's hitherto little-known early period, and shows his considerable achievement in the traditional genre of view-painting before his departure for Italy in 1750 turned him towards landscape painting in a more heroic mould.

'Westminster Bridge' was acquired with the assistance of the Miss M. Deakin Bequest and the National Heritage Memorial Fund.

WILLIAM HOGARTH

The Dance (The Happy Marriage VI) *c*.1745

T 03613

Hogarth's popular success in 1745 with the engravings after his 'Marriage A-la-Mode' led him to contemplate painting a contrasting set called 'The Happy Marriage'. The project was never completed, and all that remains of it are a number of swift oil-sketches plausibly thought to be his first thoughts on the theme. Outstanding among them is this superbly assured rendering of a dance in a country mansion after the wedding. A work of astonishing painterly virtuosity and verve, it shows Hogarth's range from remarkably free brushwork to almost finished detail. Shown almost completed are the two sources of light which define the balance and depth of the scene: a majestic chandelier floating above the frenetic action on the dance-floor, and the still, silvery moonlight seen through a window thrown open by a perspiring reveller. By contrast, the dancers are lightly touched in, yet every one exhibits strong individual characteristics, from the stately and graceful to the buffoonishly grotesque. Above all, it is one of the most masterly studies of rapid action produced in the early eighteenth century.

After being on loan to the Tate Gallery for the last fifteen years, the painting has now entered the permanent collection, to be paired with Hogarth's 'The Staymaker', an interior in the intimate domestic mood thought to come from the same series.

'The Dance' was acquired with the assistance of the National Heritage Memorial Fund.

THOMAS JONES

The Capella Nuova, Naples 1782

T 03545

The most remarkable of all Thomas Jones's paintings are his first-hand impressions of buildings in Naples and Rome. This is an excellent example, showing the spontaneity of Jones's view-making and the individuality of his chosen angle of vision from an upper window at roof-top level. The small shuttered back window with its discoloured sill invokes, rather as Canaletto's flower-pots do, the realities of ordinary life behind the grand façades of public buildings. On the other hand the absence of figures gives the picture an exceptionally still – indeed still-life – quality.

'The Capella Nuova, Naples' is one of three works by Jones presented to the Tate Gallery by Canon J. H. Adams.

THOMAS WEAVER

Ram-Letting from Robert Bakewell's Breed at Dishley 1810

T 03438

Robert Bakewell (1725-1795), of Dishley Grange, near Loughborough, Leicestershire, was one of the most important breeders of farm livestock of his day. In particular, he produced a new Leicestershire breed of sheep, whose measurements were published in 1770 as a remarkable example of careful breeding; contemporaries noted that within half a century his sheep 'spread themselves over every part of the United Kingdom and to Europe and America', and thus England 'had 2 lbs. of mutton where there was only 1 lb. before'. Bakewell founded the Dishley Society to ensure the purity of the breed. He also produced new breeds of Dishley longhorned cattle and of black draught-horses.

Bakewell was the first to carry on the trade of ram-letting on a large scale; his rams commanded increasingly high fees. This picture, painted fifteen years after his death, shows eminent breeders and agriculturists at Dishley during bidding for a season's use of rams from Bakewell's breed. A key to the picture identifies the chief figures as Thomas Bates; Humphry Davy, the celebrated chemist; Sir Joseph Banks; Captain Barclay of Ury; H. Stafford; John Richardson; Sir John Sinclair; Arthur Young, Secretary to the Board of Agriculture; William Wetherell; Thomas Booth; Thomas William Coke, M.P.; Sir Charles Knightly; Charles Colling; Robert Colling; Mr. Waters of Durham; and John Maynard of Eryholme, Darlington.

'Ram-Letting' is one of a large group of paintings bequeathed to the British Sporting Art Trust by Mrs F. Ambrose Clark and presented by the Trust to the Tate Gallery.

Francis Danby

Children by a Brook *c.*1822

T 03667

Born in Ireland, Danby spent the early part of his career in Bristol, where he worked as a drawing-master and made topographical watercolours for local collectors. While there, he also painted several small poetic landscapes with figures, the latter shown reading, talking or absorbed in some other quiet activity. The intimate character of these subjects, sometimes (as here) involving children, is matched by the artist's close attention to natural detail and to subtle lighting effects. Danby painted such works for a short time only in the early 1820s, before turning to more spectacular subjects aimed at London audiences. His exhibit at the 1824 R.A., 'Sunset at Sea after a Storm', was bought by the President, Sir Thomas Lawrence, and Danby found himself being adopted as the Academy's answer to John Martin whose work was attracting great public attention outside the Academy.

Joseph Severn

The Infant of the Apocalypse Saved from the Dragon *c*.1827–31/1843

T 03364

A religious picture by a British artist is rare enough, an altar-piece painted for a church in Rome even more so. This picture is the half-sized *modello* for an altar-piece commissioned by Cardinal Weld for the church of San Paolo fuori le Mure, Rome. Equally surprising, perhaps, is the fact that the *modello* was purchased from the artist by the statesman W. E. Gladstone. It shows part of the vision of St John the Divine on the Isle of Patmos, with the child of the woman clothed in the sun being saved from the great red dragon. In style it shows parallels with the German Nazarene painters working in Rome at that time and also such British artists as Charles Eastlake and William Dyce; in its reliance on early Renaissance models it anticipates to some extent the Pre-Raphaelites.

WILLIAM CHARLES THOMAS DOBSON

The Child Jesus Going Down with his Parents to Nazareth 1856

T 03448

Taking the final verses of the second chapter of St Luke as its source, this picture depicts the twelve-year-old Jesus being carried back to Nazareth after Joseph and Mary had returned to Jerusalem and found him with the elders in the temple.

W. C. T. Dobson was an artist whose paintings represent a particularly successful aspect of the revival in religious art in nineteenth-century England. Much of their popularity was undoubtedly due to the fact that though Dobson's work showed a rigorous handling of gesture and design similar to that which can be seen in pictures by the Pre-Raphaelites, his characterisation was imbued with a certain degree of sentimentalism.

'The Child Jesus' was originally acquired by the philanthropist Baroness Burdett Coutts. The subject and its first owner are powerful reminders of a Christian piety which today we regard as quintessentially 'Victorian'.

T 03614

T 03615

ABRAHAM SOLOMON
Waiting for the Verdict 1857 **'Not Guilty'** 1859
T 03614–5

From the mid-1840s until his early death in 1862 Abraham Solomon was considered one of the most original painters of genre of his generation, inventing his own subjects rather than relying on well-worn scenes from familiar books and plays. Both 'Waiting for the Verdict' and 'Not Guilty' were recognised during the artist's lifetime as his finest achievements, containing thought-provoking ideas as well as painterly skill. As such, the two works represent one of the high points in the treatment of modern-life subject matter by Victorian artists. It is thus particularly appropriate that Solomon should be represented for the first time in the British Collection by these paintings.

'Waiting for the Verdict', with its heightened atmosphere of pathos and carefully sustained air of uncertainty, was enthusiastically received when it was first exhibited at the Royal Academy in 1857. Solomon, recognising his sucess in making his audience speculate about the outcome of the trial which is the subject of the picture, produced the sequel 'Not Guilty' which appeared at the Academy in 1859.

The narrative detail in both pictures is particularly strong and provides a very good example of the sort of story-telling that nineteenth-century audiences found so attractive and which is still popular with gallery visitors today.

From the setting, the costumes and other accessories – all painted with great attention to detail – the drama seems to be set in a provincial town during the Assizes. The hero, an agricultural labourer, is up before the judge on a serious charge, perhaps for poaching. Though the spectator is encouraged to puzzle out what the circumstances are and though an answer is found in 'Not Guilty', the spectator's imagination is still allowed some play. There is a clear hint in the presence of a man leaving the court-house, followed by the accusing finger of a bystander, that the original charge against the innocent man was malicious rather than mistaken and that the truly guilty man is escaping. Nevertheless, the all important feeling, that the road to ruin has been avoided, triumphs.

'Waiting for the Verdict' and 'Not Guilty' were acquired with the assistance of the National Art-Collections Fund and the Sue Hammerson Charitable Trust.

ATKINSON GRIMSHAW
Bowder Stone, Borrowdale *c.*1864
T 03683

Grimshaw is still best known for the moonlit suburban landscapes and dock scenes which first made him popular with northern collectors in the 1870s. His earlier work in land-scape is a comparatively recent rediscovery, the present picture, for example, being unknown until it appeared at auction in 1983. Grimshaw painted several Lake District scenes in the 1860s, using photographs of the area as well as visiting it. 'Bowder Stone' is probably close in date to 'Nab Scar' of 1864, another recent rediscovery. Grimshaw's work of this period reflects the influence of Pre-Raphaelite landscape painting, particularly that of J. W. Inchbold who, like Grimshaw, was a native of Leeds.

This work was acquired with the help of the Friends of the Tate Gallery.

H. H. LA THANGUE
The Return of the Reapers 1886

T 03413

La Thangue was one of the leaders of the generation of English artists which turned for inspiration in the 1880s to the open-air realism of the French painter Bastien-Lepage. It was while studying in Paris in the early 1880s (and painting in Brittany with Stanhope Forbes) that La Thangue developed the square-brush technique and bright palette seen in 'The Return of the Reapers'. This picture also shows his characteristic device of placing figures on ground that slopes steeply towards the spectator and consequently flattens the picture space. A striking example of La Thangue's 'French' style at its freshest, 'The Return of the Reapers' represents a phase in English painting which has been comparatively neglected until recently.

The Modern Collection

The Tate Gallery's Modern Collection consists of all the Gallery's works by British artists born in or since 1860 and also all the works by foreign artists (starting nowadays with the generation of the French Impressionists). The modern British section therefore forms a continuation of the Historic British Collection and has been assembled on the same comprehensive scale. Although the coverage of the period 1900–70 is now nearing completion in many areas, we are constantly on the watch for works which would fill the remaining gaps and enable us to achieve the ideal balance. At the same time we have a responsibility to keep abreast with the latest developments in art and acquire many works which were painted or sculpted within the last two or three years, including some by quite young artists.

In an ideal situation the Tate Gallery would serve as the principal showcase for modern British art, the place where visitors, both British and foreign, could count on seeing a comprehensive display of twentieth-century British painting, sculpture and drawings right up to the present day. But although the Gallery certainly has the potential to do this, there has so far never been the space to show more than a fraction of the collection at any one time and its full riches remain hidden from view. We are very conscious that this situation is unsatisfactory and that it is discouraging to the artists themselves, who often find that their works have disappeared into store for indefinite periods. During this particular biennium the problem of space has been even more acute than usual, because several of the largest galleries have been closed for months at a time for repairs to their roofs. The opening of the Clore Gallery early in 1986 will improve matters a little, as the rehang of the collections planned to follow the emptying of the original Turner rooms will allow the downstairs galleries to be used for twentieth-century British art; but the only fully adequate solution would be the construction of further buildings on the hospital site.

The new purchases of foreign works include several major additions to the Surrealist collection, which is now becoming exceptionally strong. These include four works by Miró (two large paintings of different periods and two small sculptures), a painted cork relief by Max Ernst, a painting by Delvaux and a collage by the poet André Breton, who was the official founder of the Surrealist movement. The representation of post-war European art has been greatly strengthened by the purchase of a number of examples of influential movements which were hitherto very poorly represented in the collection, if at all: outstanding among these were works by the Nouveau Réaliste artists Arman, Spoerri, Raysse, Niki de Saint Phalle and Tinguely; also one of the finest COBRA paintings by Constant, and works by the Austrians Rainer, Nitsch and Brus, who have made a very distinctive contribution to Expressionism and body art. Special mention must also be made of the purchase, in the field of new art, of a group of works by the Germans Baselitz and Kiefer, the Italians Clemente and Chia, and the Americans Schnabel and Salle, who are pioneers of the new wave of figurative painting which is currently attracting widespread international attention.

The Tate Gallery has always owed a great deal to gifts from private collectors and artists, and in 1982–84 we were fortunate to receive three of particular importance to the Modern Collection. The first was the bequest from Mrs A. F. Kessler of fourteen paintings and drawings by Daumier, Degas, Renoir, Toulouse-Lautrec, Matisse, Raoul

Dufy, Picasso and Modigliani. Mrs Kessler had made over this splendid group of works to the Tate Gallery by Deed of Gift in 1958, but happily she continued to live for a further twenty-five years until she died in 1983 at the age of 93. Her gift follows a family tradition, as she was a niece of C. Frank Stoop, whose bequest in 1933 of works by Cézanne, van Gogh, Matisse, Picasso, Braque and others forms the main starting-point for the Tate's modern foreign collection as it is today. To mark the importance of this bequest, the works were put on show in February–April 1984 as a special exhibition with a catalogue. The second, from an anonymous benefactor, was of a collection of forty-two paintings and drawings, mainly small landscape studies by English Impressionist artists such as Paul Maitland, Arthur Studd and the little-known but interesting William Evelyn Osborn.

The other particularly exceptional gift was that of no less than 57 plasters and terra-cottas by Lipchitz presented by the Jacques and Yulla Lipchitz Foundation. The plasters, which came from the artist's studio, were all of sculptures from which the full edition of bronzes had been cast, and between them these works cover almost every phase of his development, including his Cubist period.

1983–84 also saw the gift from the newly formed Patrons of New Art of their first three purchases: paintings by Robert Longo and Paula Rego, and a sculpture by Julian Opie. We hope that the Patrons will become an increasingly important source of acquisitions of the most avant-garde new art, and enthusiastically welcome their help in building up this part of the collection. As a first step in the process that will lead eventually to the construction of a separate building specially for the most recent art, the part of the central hall known as the North Duveen Gallery has been set aside for the display of new art. It will be used both to show works from the permanent collection and to mount small supporting exhibitions.

Finally we should like to draw attention to the transfer from the Victoria and Albert Museum in 1982 of 70 twentieth-century sculptures from their collection, all but a few by British artists but including a sculpture by Schwitters and the superb stone 'Head' by Modigliani which has been at the Tate Gallery on loan for many years. This transfer of all the V&A's twentieth-century sculptures, apart from certain works by Rodin, was made as a step towards rationalising the division between the two museums, and in return we transferred to the V&A six of the earliest sculptures in our collection, including four by Carpeaux.

During this two-year period every member of the curatorial staff of the Modern Collection was actively engaged in organising exhibitions, in addition to his or her usual duties.

Acquisitions of the Modern Collection

EDGAR DEGAS
Woman in a Tub *c.* 1885
T 03563

Degas's exhibits at the 8th Impressionist Exhibition of 1886 included ten pastels of female nudes 'bathing, washing, drying, wiping themselves, combing their hair and having it combed', and this became one of his favourite themes. This picture, with its carefully modelled forms set in space and relatively great amount of detail (the figure lit by a window on the left), is among the earliest. One of the great attractions of this theme for Degas was that it gave him the opportunity to depict the female nude in an ordinary domestic setting, engaged unselfconsciously in an habitual, instinctive action. However, despite the apparent casualness, the figure and her surroundings are locked into a close-knit, rhythmical design.

Bought by Mrs A. F. Kessler in 1938, it is one of several fine French Impressionist works included in her bequest to the Gallery.

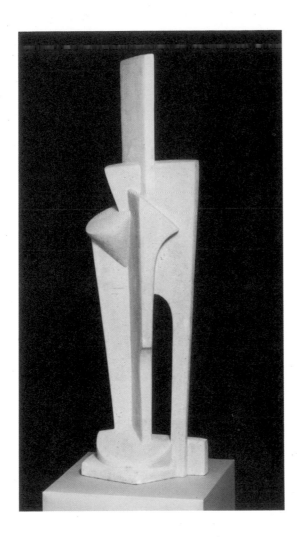

JACQUES LIPCHITZ
Half Standing Figure 1915
T 03397

Lipchitz was one of the two most important sculptors to join the Cubist movement (the other being Henri Laurens). This piece, one of his rare Cubist stone carvings, is a major work of the period and was chosen for inclusion in the exhibition of *The Essential Cubism* at the Tate Gallery in 1983. Made in 1915, it resembles Cubist pictures of about 1914–15 by Picasso and Juan Gris in the way the image of a half-length figure is constructed out of a number of overlapping, tilted and interpenetrating planes; but, instead of being simulated on a flat surface, these are rendered in three dimensions and in the round. One of his most nearly abstract works of this time, it is architectural and classical in character.

The collection of fifty-seven terracottas and plasters by Lipchitz presented by the Lipchitz Foundation in 1982 covers his entire development, including his later, very different and much more expressionist works, which have allegorical subject-matter, more naturalistic anatomy and an emphasis on knotted, writhing forms.

The 'Half Standing Figure' was acquired with the help of the Friends of the Tate Gallery and of Mrs Jack Steinberg and the Rayne Foundation.

C. R. W. Nevinson
A Bursting Shell 1915
T 03676

In the years just before the First World War C. R. W. Nevinson was almost alone among British artists in responding wholeheartedly to the paintings and sculpture of the Italian Futurists, and in June 1914 he and Marinetti, the founder of the Futurist movement, issued a joint manifesto, *Vital English Art*. He painted a number of pictures in 1913 and 1914 of such subjects as railway trains and dancers in vigorous motion.

Soon after the outbreak of war in August 1914 Nevinson joined the Red Cross and was posted to the Western Front. He also found time to paint a few pictures, mainly of soldiers marching or resting. 'A Bursting Shell', painted in 1915, is probably the most original and most Futurist of all these: a violent, cataclysmic image of a shell exploding in a confined space between houses, and sending out a spiral of flash waves, with thick black shafts splintering out towards the corners of the picture.

ANDRÉ DERAIN

Portrait of Madame Derain in a White Shawl *c.*1919–20

T 03368

Although André Derain first made his reputation as one of the leading Fauve painters, working with a brilliant colour range of reds, yellows, pinks and blues, he later gradually reverted to a more traditional way of painting and to a palette in which earthy brown and black tend to play a major role. This large and stately portrait of his wife was painted about 1919–20, shortly after he had resumed painting after four years of war service in the French Army, and it still has a rather stylised Byzantine character like some of his works of 1912–14. The handling of the paint is characteristically rich and succulent.

One of Derain's last paintings of this type, it remained in his possession, and that of his family, until it was bought by the Tate Gallery.

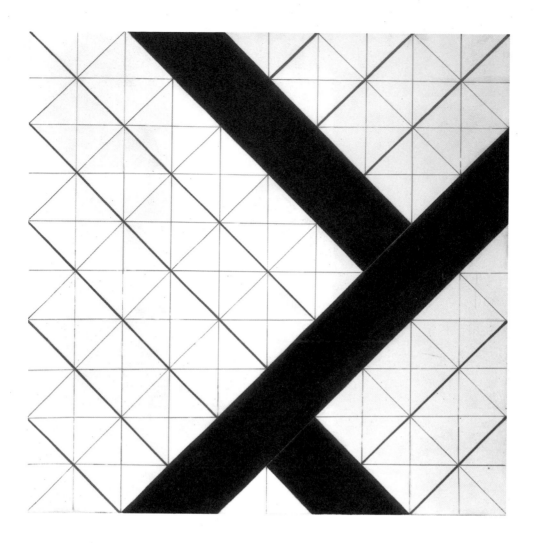

THEO VAN DOESBURG

Counter-Composition VI 1925

T 03374

As co-founder and editor of the magazine *De Stijl,* Theo van Doesburg was one of the seminal figures in modern art. The picture bought by the Tate is one of the 'Counter-Compositions' which he began making at the end of 1924 and in which he broke away from the exclusive use of the verticals and horizontals previously characteristic of De Stijl, and turned the compositions at an angle of forty-five degrees to create a more dynamic effect – an innovation which led Mondrian to leave the De Stijl group in protest. Rather unusual in being executed in black and white, without any of the three primary colours, it is based on a regular grid of intersecting vertical, horizontal and diagonal lines. As well as the heavy black stripes, set diagonally so that they appear to collide with the edges of the picture, there are delicate variations in the width of the other lines which suggest contrasting diagonal emphases. It is a particularly subtle and graceful work of this period, and was reproduced in *De Stijl* in 1927.

EDWARD WADSWORTH
Regalia 1928
T 03398

After his brief Vorticist period Wadsworth's principal subject until his death remained the maritime scene as observed from the coast. Arguably his greatest achievements were the marine still-lifes of the late 1920s. With the acquisition of 'Regalia' the Gallery now represents this theme at its most magnificent. The works of this phase show a concern with extreme orderliness, precision and clarity. Their classical spirit and organisation make them leading examples of the 'return to order' which occurred internationally in the 1920s in reaction against the experimentation of the previous decade. Wadsworth returned too, as here, to the traditional medium of tempera, which he was helping at this time to revive.

But in 'Regalia' the beautiful and strange array of objects seems to pass beyond the explicit into the realm of the enigmatic. Its very stillness seems paradoxically to hint at movement, while the curious nature of the shapes and instruments suggests lives and functions quite other than the severely practical. There is a link here with the metaphysical paintings of de Chirico, which is reinforced by Wadsworth's emphasis on the measurement of time and space.

'Regalia' was acquired with the help of the Friends of the Tate Gallery.

RAOUL DUFY
Cornfield 1929
T 03564

Like the Degas 'Woman in a Tub', this picture was included in the bequest from Mrs A. F. Kessler. It is one of nineteen oils by Dufy of harvest scenes in Normandy painted at intervals over a period of some years, and apparently depicts fields in the neighbourhood of Couliboeuf, a village to the east of Falaise. One of Dufy's largest and finest landscapes, it is executed in the lively calligraphic style characteristic of his later work, with patches of brilliant saturated colours.

Mrs Kessler bought this landscape several years after Dufy had finished the large group portrait of the Kessler family on horseback, which is also included in her bequest to the Tate Gallery but with a life interest to a cousin.

W. R. SICKERT
Miss Earhart's Arrival 1932
T 03360

Originally a pupil of Whistler, Sickert had by the 1930s largely abandoned making careful preparatory drawings in favour of using photographs. The Tate Gallery owns several major portraits derived in this way, but 'Miss Earhart's Arrival' is one of those late paintings which Sickert based unashamedly on contemporary newspaper photographs, with all their qualities of immediacy and pictorial chance. His painting shows the disembarkation from her aeroplane, in pouring rain, of the first female aviator to make a solo trans-atlantic flight. By the standards of his day, Sickert's composition was astonishing. Almost all the figures' backs are turned to the spectator, Miss Earhart and her machine are difficult at first to distinguish, and the scheme is dominated by long, irregular but parallel strokes of white paint. However, this surprising image has qualities which new developments in painting today enable us to discern perhaps more clearly than at any time since it was painted. These include the absolute painterly assurance always characteristic of Sickert but here applied with exuberant directness, and an insistence on the eloquence of a moment of human drama, which Sickert, for all his ruthless simplifi-cations, intensifies far beyond its mundane documentary source.

MAX ERNST
Dadaville *c.*1924
T 03707

The Gallery now owns three of the greatest early Surrealist paintings by Ernst ('Celebes' of 1921 and 'Of This Men shall know Nothing' and 'Pietà or Revolution by Night', both of 1923). These are all painted in a style which grew out of his use of collage, with bizarre combinations of images to produce a dream-like and disturbing effect. 'Dadaville' is one of the first examples of a quite different approach to Surrealism in which the image was originally suggested by a rough surface or rubbing. It would seem, from its title, to date from the Dada period before the official foundation of the Surrealist movement in October 1924. Made out of pieces of cork on a plaster background, and partly painted, it is the only relief of its kind.

Following his discovery of the technique of *frottage* (rubbing) in 1925, Ernst worked for several years on a series of paintings of haunted forests which are related to this image.

JOAN MIRÓ

A Star caresses the Breast of a Negress (Painting-Poem) 1938

T 03690

Of all the Surrealist painters Miró was the one most closely associated with Surrealist poetry. He called this picture a painting-poem, and used as title the poetic inscription on the picture itself. Whereas some other paintings of the same year have a violence which reflects his horror at the barbarities of the Spanish Civil War, this work is gentle, playful and erotic, with rhythmical calligraphy and brightly coloured contrasting shapes against a black background. Apart from the comic little figure and the ladder-like form on the right, all the shapes are abstract, and the forms are detached from one another and floating, dancing in space.

PAUL DELVAUX
Leda 1948
T 03361

The work of the Belgian Surrealist painter Paul Delvaux represents quite a different approach to Surrealism from that of Ernst or Miró, and is closer to the tradition of Old Master painting. But his nudes in their twentieth-century settings have a gentle dream-like character as though they are in the act of sleep-walking. Although this picture alludes to the erotic myth of Leda and the Swan, both girl and swan are passive, as in a trance; and the painting has been known both as 'Leda' and as 'The Dream'.

OSKAR KOKOSCHKA
The Crab 1939-40
T 03834

In 1938 Kokoschka came to Britain as a refugee from Nazism and spent almost a year in Cornwall (summer 1939 – summer 1940), living in a block of flats high above the sea at Polperro. Since painting in the open air was, after the outbreak of war, forbidden on security grounds, he worked mainly in coloured pencils. Four oil paintings, however, are known to exist: 'Polperro I' (Courtauld Institute Galleries), 'Polperro II' (Tate Gallery), 'The Crab' and 'Private Property'. The two Polperro pictures are straight landscapes. 'The Crab' and 'Private Property' have a more allegorical intent, and were succeeded in Kokoschka's work by five sarcastic political pictures, three of which are on loan to the Tate Gallery.

'In front of our house at Polperro I painted a large foul-smelling crab someone had given me', Kokoschka wrote in his autobiography. '. . . I was astonished at the sheer phlegm of the English, who remained heedless of the war, while on the Continent people were letting the Führer drive them over the edge of an abyss like panic-stricken sheep.' In her monograph of 1947, Edith Hoffmann quotes Kokoschka to the effect that the monstrous crustacean with semi-human expression represents Chamberlain after Munich, while the comparatively tiny figure of the swimmer is the artist struggling to reach the English coast.

Constant

Après Nous la Liberté 1949

T 03705

The Dutch artist Constant Nieuwenhuys was, with Karel Appel, Asger Jorn and others, one of the original members of the group known as COBRA (short for Copenhagen, Brussels, Amsterdam) which was founded in Paris in 1948. Although short-lived – COBRA lasted only until 1951 – the movement gave European art fresh impetus after the disillusion and deprivation brought by world war, and has recently been the subject of a revival. This renewal of interest in COBRA coincides with a marked return among younger artists to a kind of painting which is loosely figurative, expressionistic and spontaneous.

In Constant's 'Après Nous la Liberté' various human and animal figures emerge from a black void suggesting darkness or night. It is larger than most COBRA works, and its imagery goes beyond the simple zoomorphic fantasies which occasionally make COBRA painting seem too evocative of child art. The playful is tempered by the threatening and grotesque, while the introduction of the French *tricolore* adds a political note which looks forward to Constant's terrifying anti-war pictures of 1950 51.

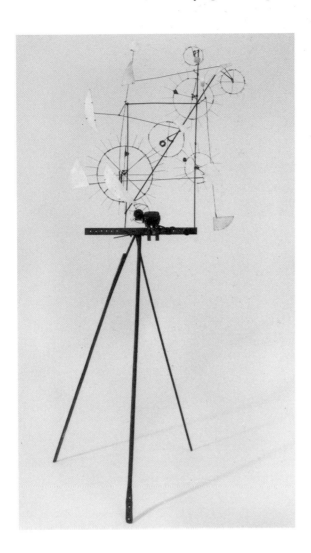

JEAN TINGUELY
Metamechanical Sculpture with Tripod 1954
T 03823

This is one of two sculptures acquired after the tremendously successful *Tinguely* exhibition at the Tate in the autumn of 1982. In Tinguely's early work, cut-out geometric shapes, painted usually black or white, are attached to thin wire wheels with protruding spokes and set in motion by means of an electric motor. Their nervous, jerky movements have a gentle irony somewhat reminiscent of Klee's drawings. Movement and sound are an integral part of Tinguely's work but in his early sculptures image plays an equally important role. As with more 'serious' kinds of kinetic art, they are essentially moving abstract pictures.

JOAN MIRÓ

Message from a Friend 1964

T 03691

The second newly acquired painting by Miró is this picture 'Message from a Friend' of 1964. The friend mentioned in the title is the American sculptor Alexander Calder, noted for his mobiles which often incorporate Miró-like forms. The exceptionally large size of this work, nearly nine feet square, is similar to the mural-like scale of American Abstract Expressionist painting of the 1950s and 1960s, but the shapes (such as the bulbous form like a whale, the criss-crossed 'star' and the irregular discs) are very much part of Miró's personal vocabulary. Exhibited at the Salon de Mai in 1964, it is one of the grandest and most ambitious of all his later paintings.

   'Message from a Friend' was purchased with the help of a substantial contribution from funds bequeathed by Miss H. M. Arbuthnot through the Friends of the Tate Gallery.

PABLO PICASSO
Reclining Nude with Necklace 1968
T 03670

Hitherto the Gallery owned no canvas of Picasso's principal subject, the human figure, from his last forty-one prolific years. Till recently, the work of his last decade, at least, was widely regarded as marking a sad decline. Now, however, it is increasingly recognised that to the very end Picasso continued to open up new territory in terms of both style and content, and his late work is proving increasingly influential on new art.

'Reclining Nude with Necklace' 8 October 1968 exemplifies the immensely free and at first sight more casual use of paint, often (as here) brilliantly coloured, which is characteristic of his late years. Its effect is at once strikingly decorative and emotionally intense. The scribbling and swift patterning in paint convey urgency both as acts in themselves (especially where the paint cascades upwards like fireworks or sea spray) and in defining human anatomy. With great boldness and vitality Picasso has radically re-ordered the body and its proportions to create a staring, displayed presence which is almost grotesque but extremely powerful – at once defiant and vulnerable, monster and siren.

JEAN DUBUFFET
The Ups and Downs 1977
T 03679

Dubuffet has been the most inventive and influential French artist of the post-war period, and the Gallery now owns nine works from different phases of his career.

The particular series to which this belongs grew out of making a large number of paintings on paper which were allowed to accumulate in disorder on the floor of the studio. Their chance arrangements and overlappings gave the artist the idea of cutting up the pieces and using them to make assemblages to which he gave the collective title 'Théâtres de mémoire' (Theatres of memory) because of the way they combined evocations of a number of different places and scenes. This painting, which is one of the largest, dates from January 1977 and incorporates as many as thirty-five pieces, some with Dubuffet's characteristic lively hobgoblin-like figures and some with contrasting patterns.

PHILIP GUSTON
Black Sea 1977
T 03364

Philip Guston shocked the art world in 1970 when he exhibited a group of paintings with grotesque, heavily outlined cartoon figures, which marked a radical departure from his previous Abstract Expressionist style. The 'late' paintings, as they became known, introduced a personal, angry or humorous vocabulary, a raw depiction of the artist's habits both in the studio and at home. 'Black Sea' (1977), bought from David McKee, the dealer who encouraged and supported Guston in his final decade, has a more contemplative subject than most, and the central image, though similar to the theme of boots which is one of the recurrent images of this period, is the outline of the head of the artist's wife Musa: she is shown with the covers pulled up in bed as in 'Red Blanket' of the same year. Nevertheless the setting also suggests a vast landscape or sea, and the picture is painted with a sensuous richness still akin to the works of Guston's abstract period.

Already several years before his death in 1980 these late pictures had begun to be re-assessed and widely admired, and they have been among the works which have inspired the new wave of figurative artists.

Arnulf Rainer
Wine Crucifix 1957–78
T 03671

Until 1982, the Viennese expressionist body-language movement of the 1960s was un-
represented in the collection. Since then the Gallery has acquired important works by
Arnulf Rainer, Hermann Nitsch and Günter Brus, all of which throw light on the
different ways each has approached the essential notion of art as suffering and catharsis.

'Wine Crucifix' is one of the first in the series of cross pictures which Rainer began in
the mid-1950s and which he has returned to at moments throughout his career. In 1978,
as is his practice, he painted over part of the image. The act of painting has for him
affinities with the Abstract Expressionism of New York and Paris artists of the early
1950s, although the distinguishing feature of Rainer's art is an intensive worrying over the
same point or path, building up a dark, impenetrable area or shape until most of the

individual marks are submerged in the whole. The cross has an additional appeal as a symbol of pain and suffering. In 'Wine Crucifix', red paint seems to drip from the heavy black crucified figure like blood, suggesting an extension of the practice of drip painting for figurative purposes, as in the work of Nitsch. The German title of the painting, *'Weincruzifix'*, is a play on the German words for 'weep' and 'wine', evoking the equation of blood and wine in Christian symbolism.

T 03825

T 03826

JOSEPH BEUYS
Two **Untitled Vitrines** 1983
T 03825 and T 03826

One of the most influential figures in post-war European art is the German sculptor Joseph Beuys. Although he began his career after the war as a sculptor in the traditional sense, Beuys's main achievement dates from the 1960s, when he succeeded in widening the definition of sculpture to include multi-media actions and environments.

Beuys has also restored to German art a sense of identity by constructing a myth around his own biography, that of the survivor endowed with almost magical powers. Images of injury and healing are frequent in his work, the latter usually expressed through the use of materials such as felt, evoking insulation, warmth and absorption, and various kinds of fat which suggest a more fluid, less earthbound state.

The two *Vitrines,* or showcases, contain small sculptures or symbolic objects covering the whole of Beuys's career, from the early 1950s to the present. They have been chosen for their striking contrasts of form, colour and material. While the one containing fat is predominantly soft and pale in tone, the other is darker and includes hard shapes with cutting edges such as a length of tramrail. The latter *Vitrine* explores different kinds of energy (another Beuysian theme) and juxtaposes ideas of conduction and insulation.

It is difficult to convey in words the unique flavour of Beuys's art – its basis in elemental human experience, its multiple associations, sense of tragedy and peculiarly old or used quality. With this new acquisition, visitors to the Tate can now see a small but impressive group of his work.

T 03403

left
T 03405
far left
T 03404

ANSELM KIEFER
Parsifal I, II & III 1973
T 03403–5

The paintings of Anselm Kiefer explore sensitive themes in an attempt to exorcise the trauma of Germany's violent and troubled past. A tragic sense of loss at his country's corrupted cultural heritage and an ironic awareness of the artist's ambiguous place in historical events are the principal concerns of Kiefer's art.

The 'Parsifal' cycle comprises four pictures, three now belonging to the Tate Gallery and the fourth in the collection of the Kunsthaus, Zurich. All four depict the wooden attic of Kiefer's home, a former schoolhouse, which assumes a mythical character, suggesting a stage-set for some dark, archetypal drama. Inspired by a mixture of Teutonic myth and Wagner's opera *Parsifal* about the legend of the Holy Grail (evoked in the names and phrases inscribed on each picture), Kiefer's imagery is nevertheless not a literal illustration of his sources. His world is a romantic fusion of past and present, fact and imagination, personal memory and collective experience.

GEORG BASELITZ
Adieu 1982
T 03672

Of the German painters who have risen to international prominence in the last few years, Georg Baselitz is one of the most distinguished. His career began in the late '50s, when he left East Berlin to continue his art schooling in the West. At that time tachism and its American variant, action painting, were becoming widely accepted as the natural style of the post-war era. It was in opposition to such an art that he developed his own special brand of figuration.

By 1969 Baselitz started to paint the motif, now restricted to the simplest kind of figure, still-life or landscape, on its head or side. He has observed this practice ever since, as can be seen in 'Adieu', in which two figures are depicted against a chequer-board background of yellow and white squares suggesting an urban or architectural setting. Street scenes were popular with the German Expressionists, and in the late 1970s Baselitz painted a series of pictures of people at windows. In 'Adieu', the waving, doll-like figure on the right resembles his own monumental limewood sculptures, which also recall German Expressionist carvings, though they are more roughly hewn.

By overturning the image Baselitz hopes that the spectator will see the picture as a painted surface first and foremost. Picture-making, as opposed to telling a story or devising symbols, is what interests him, but it is typical of his desire to challenge the conventions of painting that he has sought to create an abstract art without getting rid of the figure or object.

Jannis Kounellis
Untitled 1979
T 03796

This installation which occupies the corner of a room or gallery consists of an outline drawing in charcoal of an empty industrial townscape, whose blank fortress-like walls, and sharp perspectives, are reminiscent of de Chirico's dreamlike urban imagery, also inspired by the industrial cities of Northern Italy. Above the town, on either side of a smoking chimney, a jackdaw and a hooded crow, apparently arrested in flight, are impaled on arrows. To the right, five sheets of paper, heavily worked in a soot or charcoal based medium, have been incised with images, of Madonna heads, birds and an Italian landscape. This theatrical arrangement, mixing illusion and real objects, and contrasting classical or mythological themes with industrial images, is typical of Kounellis's work. He frequently refers to fire in its creative and destructive capacities (here symbolised by the charcoal and smoke), and it has been suggested that the executed birds signify both the end of idealism and the artist's Romantic endeavour.

PETER BLAKE

'The Meeting' or 'Have a Nice Day, Mr Hockney' 1981–3

T 03790

This picture is an updating of Courbet's 'The Meeting' alias 'Bonjour Monsieur
Courbet', in a Los Angeles setting. David Hockney is Courbet, Blake is Monsieur
Bruyas, Courbet's patron, and Howard Hodgkin plays the role of Bruyas's servant.
Hockney's staff has become a brush, an echo of Daumier's cartoon of the battle of styles.
The background is the boulevard near the beach where roller skaters abound. Some
figures were drawn from photographs especially taken on a later visit. It was exhibited in an
unfinished state in Peter Blake's very successful retrospective at the Tate Gallery in
February–March 1983; he continued to work on it afterwards for several more months,
and added various features such as the three trees on the left and the dog (which he based
on one in the Tate's painting by Stubbs).

It was presented by the Friends of the Tate Gallery, who bought it out of funds
generously bequeathed by Miss Helen Arbuthnot.

STEPHEN COX
Gethsemane 1982
T 03794

In the early 1970s the young British sculptor Stephen Cox was making Minimal sculpture, but by the end of the decade he had come to feel that Minimalism had reached an impasse and in 1979 he went to Italy 'to rebuild my sculptural language'. He started to work there in stone and marble, and in 1981 decided to make a series of carvings using all the different types of stone described by Vasari in the technical introduction to his *Lives of the Most Eminent Italian Architects, Painters and Sculptors.*

'Gethsemane' is one of the works he made in Rome. In it he wanted to combine the green quality of the material (peperino stone) with an allusion to the South Italian landscape where it was quarried and therefore introduced olive trees into the imagery, carved in low relief. The title was suggested by the red staining of part of the stone, a natural defect caused by oxidation, which may call to mind the bloodshed at the Crucifixion, subsequent to Christ's agony at Gethsemane. The fragmentation of the stone, arranged in the form of a Roman arch, can be interpreted both as a reference to antique art and as a way of drawing attention to the character of the material.

ROBERT LONGO
Sword of the Pig 1983
T 03782

Robert Longo, one of the foremost young artists in New York, describes his work as his 'response to being a man in this re-birth of neo-machismo in the culture now'. The form of the work, that of a sword with blade, shield and handle, was chosen because of its aggressive masculinity, while the ironic use of 'pig' in the title denotes derision of male chauvinism. At the same time the masculinity of each part is undermined by the way it is treated: the relief on the left is similar both to a church and to a man on his back with an erection, the blade of the sword bears an image of inert, and therefore impotent, missile silos, and the muscular central figure, like a flayed piece of meat, is rendered sickly by the yellow perspex which covers it.

The Print Collection

This biennium has seen the steady development of the Print Collection. Though still housed in temporary accommodation in the Garden Room, it has been consolidating its position in relation to the rest of the Modern Collection as an additional but far from peripheral collection. During 1982 a series of three related showings selected from the collection were mounted in Gallery 61 (each accompanied by a leaflet). These comprised prints by British, European and American artists, and one, for which Catherine Lacey collaborated, also included some recently acquired works on paper in other media. Besides the main showings we began an intermittent series of small displays highlighting a particular technique and showing widely different uses of that medium. From March 1983 Richard Francis showed two large-scale paper works by German artists: Klaus Rinke's 'Mutations' and Hanne Darboven's 'Construction 19 × 42/60', with works by Bernd and Hilla Becher and Joseph Beuys. Later that summer there was a special showing of James Stirling's drawings for the Turner Gallery and, in September, Gallery 61 was used for part of Michael Compton's 'New Art' exhibition. This included works by Daniel Buren, Luciano Fabro and Cindy Sherman which either were or are now in the Print Collection. After the close of the exhibition a small group of recently acquired prints was added to the remaining 'New Art' works, including Jennifer Bartlett's six-part woodcut and screenprint 'At Sea Japan'.

In December 1983 'Image and Process', an exhibition of prints by Richard Hamilton, opened. It had been assembled by Hamilton himself, taking seventeen prints dating from 1953 to 1981 and showing them with working drawings, trials and proofs. The Hamilton exhibition was followed by a small showing of paintings, prints and drawings by Edward Burra, Paul Nash, William Roberts and Edward Wadsworth.

The Print Collection concentrates on artists' prints in the period since 1945 with particular emphasis on contemporary works, though we also seek to increase the strength of the collection in the post-war decades. To this end, small groups of prints dating from the 1950s to the present were purchased from Prunella Clough and Terry Frost; a hand-coloured linocut of 1949 by Peter Lanyon and a group of etchings of 1949 to 1951 by Richard Hamilton were also bought. Some important European acquisitions were made: a portfolio of all the etchings made by Wols, a lithograph of 1953 by Jean Dubuffet and a hand-coloured etching from 'Series II', 1952 by Joan Miró. Extending our representation of major American prints from later years, Robert Ryman's 'Seven Aquatints', Robert Rauschenberg's 'Preview' (on silk) from the 'Hoarfrost' series, and a monotype on the 'Savarin' theme by Jasper Johns were bought. A complete portfolio by Philip Guston was generously presented by David McKee through the American Federation for the Arts. Guston had not made many prints but in a productive burst of work not long before he died he made a remarkable series of lithographs at Gemini in Los Angeles.

Among other outstanding works acquired were a group of prints by Georg Baselitz including etchings from the mid to late 1960s and two monumental linocuts, one from the series he made between 1977 and 1979 when he first began to work on a large scale, and one from a more recent series. Baselitz has always made prints reiterating the themes of his paintings and has been a prolific and influential printmaker. A further list of artists by whom we have acquired portfolios could vividly illustrate the breadth of different styles and tendencies reflected in contemporary artists' use of graphic art and printing:

ROBERT RAUSCHENBERG
Preview 1974
P 07715

JOAN MIRÓ
Untitled
from **Series II** 1952
P 07900

among 'new' European painters, Sandro Chia and Martin Disler; among artists who have used action and performance, Günther Brus and Arnulf Rainer; among artists using a conceptual framework, John Baldessari and Jonathon Borofsky; and among artists using text, Jenny Holzer.

During 1983 the final parts of Tom Phillips' 'Dante's Inferno' were completed. This *tour de force* contains the artist's own translation of Dante's thirty-four cantos with four prints to illustrate each one. The prints were made in a special printing workshop Phillips had set up in his own studio and the whole project took the best part of seven years to complete. A group of prints was bought from Colin Self which included a number of rare or unique impressions and trial proofs, the earliest dating from the early 1960s. Among other British artists' prints acquired were etchings by Lucian Freud and John Walker, lithographs by Harry Holland, lino-cuts by Barry Flanagan and screen-prints by Ian Hamilton Finlay.

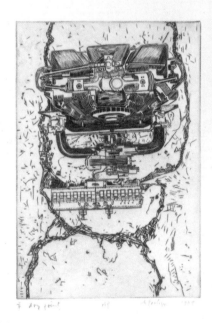

EDUARDO PAOLOZZI
Head 1979
P 07680

Despite the restrictions of the Garden Room, where viewing area and offices must perforce share the space, the number of visitors using the Print Room appointments system has steadily increased. The Reference Catalogue is now complete to date and visitors use it to see what the collection contains. A number of art schools now regularly send students in to see prints under study conditions and Print Collection curators also liaise with the Education Department for visits by organised groups of secondary school students and art teachers in training. Early in 1984 plans were made to provide a new Print Room and further gallery space for prints and works on paper downstairs in Gallery 62. This will allow Gallery 61 to be used for showing works on paper, sometimes with paintings as well, while a changing programme of small exhibitions can be accommodated in Gallery 62, thus giving us a better opportunity to show the collection properly. It will also enable all the prints to be stored together and will give much better viewing conditions for visitors to the Print Room.

GEORG BASELITZ
Head 1980
P 07780

PHILIP GUSTON
Painter 1980
P 77009

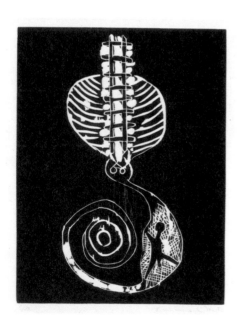

FRANCESCO CLEMENTE
High Fever 1982
P 07834

LUCIAN FREUD
Head of a Woman 1982
P 07782

Conservation Department

RESEARCH PROJECTS

For many years the staff of the Conservation Department have been responding to new conservation problems created by the wide range of materials and techniques used by modern artists. Frequently we are presented with an ethical or technical decision for which there is no precedent. The nature of the Tate Gallery collection has therefore obliged us to carry out our own research and development in order to cope with some pressing problems.

An ideal conservation treatment should be reversible, the materials used should be stable and not have any harmful effects on the complicated structure which is the work of art. Great caution is therefore necessary when introducing any new material and, in the past, conservation practice has evolved slowly. But for modern works, when traditional solutions are not appropriate new ones must be sought and applied promptly.

Fortunately we have occasionally been able to call on the facilities of the National Gallery Scientific Department which is well equipped for the analysis of pigments, oils and resins. Cooperation with the Technology Department of the Courtauld Institute has also enabled us to research more efficiently into conservation methods by directing the talents of the students in our joint training scheme and by pooling the resources of both departments. The role of the department in training students has encouraged us to expand the section of the Tate library devoted to conservation. Photographic slides to illustrate particular aspects of conservation have been collected for teaching purposes. An archive containing interesting examples of historical material and information on the colourmen's trade has slowly been accumulated. In addition guidelines to students and bibliographies have been, and continue to be, written. All the results of specific research projects are kept in reference files and some have been published in conservation journals.

Since works of art are expected to be suitable for exhibition and loan whenever possible, much effort has gone into the assessment of structural stability and into improving methods of consolidation and support. The need to protect works of art at present in good condition from the deterioration and damage which are likely to occur has led us to devise improved framing methods. The benefits of glazing and backboards have been accurately quantified and damages caused to inadequately framed works have been recorded. Further work has been done to measure the effects of shock, vibration, temperature and relative humidity changes in packing cases used when lending works of art.

Improvements to the structure of paintings on canvas brought about by the replacement of stretchers, relining of canvases and consolidation of paint films are a major investment in time and effort. There has been much reappraisal of conservation practice in recent years and many new adhesives and structural materials have become available. Before they can be employed on a regular basis their ageing and handling properties must be assessed. Both controlled experiments with the material and practical experience on actual paintings are required before a new material can be considered safe for use.

In cooperation with the Courtauld Institute, assessments have been made of the adhesives commonly used in conservation treatments, the ageing of beeswax/resin mixtures, the properties of microcrystalline wax/ketone resin mixtures and the ageing of polymer dispersions. Such research has aided development work on lining materials and

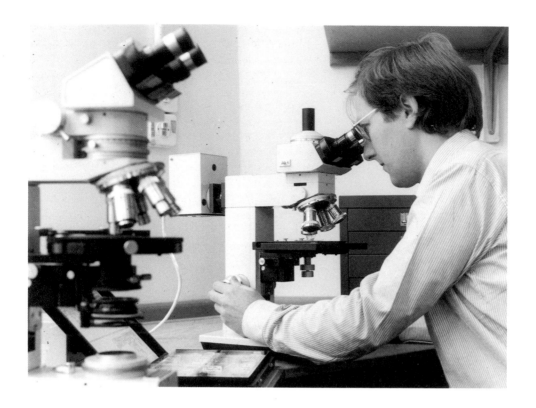

techniques in recent years and progress in this area will continue with the acquisition of a new lining table capable of moisture treatments. Auxiliary rigid supports made from aluminium honeycomb laminates and linings of woven polyester cloth are now used regularly and with confidence. To achieve this state of affairs many other initially promising materials have been assessed and rejected.

A study of the ageing process in linen canvas and of methods of controlling its rate of deterioration is beginning to have positive benefits. Thus a clearer picture is emerging of the behaviour of canvas when exposed to light, ultra-violet radiation, air pollution and other contaminants. A survey of sulphur dioxide and nitrogen dioxide air pollution within the gallery has enabled us to appreciate the advantages of air-conditioning and to make accurate and attainable specifications for future systems, and we have been able to assist some other institutions in identifying the extent of air pollution within their museums.

Students' projects are a mainstay of our research effort. Useful studies have been undertaken on stretcher design, and on the conservation aspects of plywood and hardboard painting supports. Projects on acrylic and modern tempera painting have improved knowledge of the use of these materials by artists. Another project to assess the practical potential of microscopy for paint analysis has helped to extend the range of facilities available for the routine examination of works of art. The students are allocated a full term to complete the work and consequently are able to explore their chosen subject in some depth.

The exhibition *Paint and Painting* to celebrate 150 years of Winsor & Newton provided an incentive for members of the Conservation Department to collect together information on the painting technique of selected artists (as illustrated by a chosen picture for each artist). A book, *Completing the Picture,* was published by the Gallery in 1982 to accompany the exhibition. Much of the information for the book and exhibition was drawn from conservation records and examinations.

The painting techniques of living artists can be investigated most easily by interview or questionnaire and this is now done on a regular basis. The forthcoming Francis Bacon exhibition catalogue will contain information on the artist's techniques based on this type of research. It is hoped that it will provide a useful precedent for further cooperation with curators and artists.

The Conservation Department continues to make a significant contribution in the field of practical conservation and technical art history by maintaining an active programme of research and development. Most of our routine problems are unlikely to be solved by anyone else.

SCULPTURE CONSERVATION

Sculptures in the Tate Gallery collections have been rather sparingly displayed until recent times, though they comprise 14% of the total holding of art works. Similarly the sculptures have not been systematically conserved to the same extent as easel paintings and works on paper. It has been accepted for some time that there is a need to re-establish a more equitable balance in the display of three-dimensional works, echoing the increasing proportion of works of this type being acquired by the Modern Collection. The low key response to sculpture conservation needs has had to be adopted by the Department because of the lack of facilities and specialist staff. Simple treatments have been carried out to meet the needs for loan and display by paintings conservators with advice from colleagues in the V & A; more involved problems being undertaken by freelance specialists, commissioned by the Department, for which there has been very little funding.

In the past two years there has been limited activity in sculpture conservation as a result of two particular gifts. Firstly at the Barbara Hepworth Museum in St Ives in Cornwall, where a long needed survey was carried out in 1982. Condition reports were made by a consultant conservator, Michael Eastham, with recommendations for treatment needed to ensure the well-being of the sculptures in their original outdoor setting. This resulted in money being allocated in 1983 for Michael Eastham to carry out his recommendations as well as a reconstruction of the plinths by the P.S.A. for safety and security. The other unexpected commitment resulted from a gift of 57 sculptures and maquettes in terracotta and plaster from the studio of Jacques Lipchitz. On arrival they had to be identified, examined so that condition reports could be made, cleaned and have minor repairs carried out before photography and cataloguing could proceed. This was done by existing staff but in certain cases more extensive treatment will require the expertise of a qualified sculpture conservator.

Investigations into the possibility of establishing a sculpture section within the Department had previously foundered for lack of suitable space and funds, for equipment and staff. Proposals to transfer a painting conservator post to sculpture had to be resisted as existing staffing levels were only just adequate to meet the workloads imposed by acquisitions, loans and the continuing training programmes, as well as the conservation of the paintings in the collections.

In 1982 it was accepted by the Director that, regardless of such obstacles, a way would have to be found to establish a sculpture conservation studio staffed by an experienced conservator and a student. Space could be found in the Queen Alexandra Hospital building but money for upgrading and fitting out such an area seemed beyond the resources of the P.S.A. Coincidentally financial limitations were imposed on the Gallery by the reduction of the Vote so the establishment of a new conservator post seemed un-realistic. The transfer of a painting student post to sculpture remained a possibility but a student without a qualified supervising conservator or working area was no solution to our dilemma and bold intentions.

At this moment, as rarely happens, a benefactor appeared, who had been told of our problem and promptly offered to fund the equipping of a studio, a fellowship for the salary of the conservator for two years and a scholarship for the student for four years. So by the autumn of 1984, thanks to the generosity of the Henry Moore Foundation, the selected sculpture conservator, supported by a student, when not involved in training at the Courtauld Institute or elsewhere, will begin to survey the condition of the thousand works of sculpture in the collection. Once an assessment of priorities has been established, conservation work and treatment will start in an improvised studio space. At the same time the area in the old hospital building will have to be planned and adapted by the new conservators to serve as an interim studio for the next few years until purpose-built accommodation is available.

Museum Services

Archive

In November 1982 the Archive moved from the basement of the Tate Gallery to first floor premises of No.20 John Islip Street, which have since been expanded by three further rooms. It is now possible to separate storage from sorting areas, and offices from research rooms while keeping the whole operation on one floor. The light and airy workrooms have raised morale, and the compact layout offers an efficient and convenient unit.

In January 1984 Mrs Jennifer Booth joined the Department. She comes with a long experience as an archivist as well as a knowledge of twentieth-century art through her work at the Central School of Art. Mrs Booth's extensive knowledge of records management, together with the availability of new storage space, has given us the ideal opportunity to collate and sort the Tate Gallery's own records. However, it will be some little while before the listing can be brought up to date. The appointment of Tamsyn Woollcombe as secretary and assistant in February 1983 has made a significant contribution to the organised running of the department. A temporary post was filled by Alun Grafton, who in the time has achieved a complete listing of the Archive photograph collections and two other important and extensive projects. These were the copying of Reg Butler's press-cutting collection kindly loaned by Mrs Rosemary Butler, amounting to approximately 2,000 items, and the documenting and listing of John Piper's collection of negatives which are being printed by the Gallery photographers. These are likely to amount to 6-7,000 contact prints. In the two years under review, accessions to the Poster Collection have amounted to 300 items, 15,600 press-cuttings have been added to the files, 7,250 private view cards were collected, 2,500 photographs and colour transparencies were listed and some 37 sound tapes were catalogued. Cataloguing of the more complex archival collections was slowed down by the move and revisions to the Index, but 2,000 entries for the Artists International Association have now been completed, along with a number of small groups of papers.

Another watershed, inspired by the move, is the forthcoming publication of the Archive Index on Microfiche. The preparation for this has involved work on the standardisation of all entries, something which could only be contemplated at this early stage in the life of the Archive and before the entries rose to more than the current 25,000. We hope that the Index on Microfiche will be available in the autumn of 1984. The move has also made it possible to arrange talks and conducted tours for approximately 60–70 people at a time. Both the fifty members of the Thames Region of the Society of Archivists and the seventy Friends of the Tate (our early benefactors) expressed their interest in, and enjoyment of, their visits.

The strengthening of our major collections by purchase and gift has continued with important additions to material about Richard Carline, Stanley Spencer, Claude Rogers, Vanessa Bell and Paul Nash. It is with warmth and gratitude that we wish to pay tribute to the work Mrs Anstice Shaw accomplished on behalf of the Paul Nash Trust. We were inspired by her devotion to her task and enjoyed a long and fruitful collaboration with her. Shortly before she died in November 1983 she gave the Archive the last and most precious of Paul Nash's personal belongings which she had cherished and cared for since Margaret Nash's death in 1960. Stanley Spencer letters to Gwen Raverat and Daphne Charlton were purchased at separate auctions, and with the sale of Claude Rogers' house in Suffolk more of his papers were generously donated by Crispin Rogers. Angelica Garnett made a gift of 1,552 negatives and photographs taken by her mother, Vanessa Bell, which has added a fascinating visual dimension to the considerable correspondence already in the collections.

Gifts of new mixed collections have come from Ewan Phillips, and consist of records and documents from his art gallery; from the Executors to Sir Cedric Morris, including the papers of Arthur Lett-Haines; records from 1973 to 1981 from the London Group; and the *7 & 5 Society* Minute Book from John Piper, who was its last Secretary. Among the artists or their families who have presented fine collections of drawings, watercolours, sketchbooks, prototypes and printing proofs are Ivor Abrahams, James Boswell, Edna Clarke Hall, Josef Herman, Frances Hodgkins and Steve Willats. Ken Powell presented the prototype for 'Light Screen 1954' by Adrian Heath, a luminous construction made of coloured semi-transparent plastics. Mrs Olda Kokoschka presented a small but interesting collection of papers about the Tate Gallery's Oskar Kokoschka portrait of Ambassador Maisky 1942–43.

Important purchases consist of a fine collection of self-portrait drawings and gouaches by 125 different artists between 1949 and 1958 as commissioned at the time by 'Arts Reviews'; papers from Dr Charles Harrison; correspondence with Sir Michael Sadler; drawings by David Jones; a fine photograph album of Parkhill, Streatham, home of Sir Henry Tate; papers from the Goupil Gallery which also included documents relating to the Walter Greaves/James Abbot McNeill Whistler controversy.

Archive Display 29 March – 22 June 1984, shown in conjunction with Cedric Morris retrospective exhibition – Dress and blouse by Cresta Silks Limited, loaned by Patrick Heron – Fabric design by Cedric Morris *c*.1935

Tate Archive Poster 652 ' "Be attention Be" eine
neue Arbeit von Bruce McLean' Bergmanstrasse 2,
1 Berlin 61 Agentur für kulturelle Angelegenheiten
n.d. (April 1982)

Following a two-year gap, due partly to the reconstruction of the Coffee Shop and the Archive move, only two Archive displays have been mounted. The collection of twenty letters from Jean Tinguely to members of the Tate Gallery staff during preparations for his exhibition were framed and shown upstairs in the Sculpture Hall as a graphic prelude to the main exhibition. In February 1984 we once again occupied the far from ideal area next to the Coffee Shop and displayed a selection of photographs and documents from the Cedric Morris/Arthur Lett Haines Archive. The spectacular loan by Patrick Heron of Delia Heron's wedding dress (the fabric having been designed by Cedric Morris for Tom Heron of Cresta Silks) gave the display an altogether different dimension.

Loans to outside exhibitions have increased during this period, the most important group being the fifty-eight items which accompanied the Artists International Association exhibition for a period of two years and five venues, starting at MOMA Oxford and ending at the Camden Arts Centre, London. To the Arts Council's *Omega* exhibition at the Crafts Council Gallery we lent one item, and to the Grey Art Gallery, New York University, for their exhibition *A Sense of Place: The Paintings of Edward Burra and Paul Nash*, we lent a superbly illustrated letter from Paul Nash to Edward Burra.

Donations of time and money are of great importance to the continuing work of the Archive and without them we would be a lot poorer. A donation towards cataloguing the Fluxshoe collection was generously made by Gilbert Silverman of Detroit, Illinois – this we hope to follow up by the appointment of a specialist researcher to carry out the work.

We are deeply grateful to the twenty volunteers who have helped us throughout the years. Over the years the two groups of ladies from NADFAS and CDFAS have made it possible for the Archive to create collections of press-cuttings and private view cards that otherwise would not have been collected. Since 1975 Mrs Juliette Shaw has helped with the press-cuttings collections and Mrs Marlene Burston has been working on checking transcripts since September 1983.

Our great hope for the near future is to be able to increase the facilities for researchers. The Archive Collection has never been in greater demand, and since January 1983 when the Archive reopened in its new premises, 237 bookings have been taken. So, matching the demand for research to our new facilities will be the aim during the next two years.

Education

This biennium has been a testing and taxing but exciting time for the Education Department. Demand for our services generally has been strong and steady, pushing constantly at the limits of our capacity to meet it and occasionally exceeding them. This has been particularly the case with our services for visiting school parties where pressures have been intense; one may speculate that this is partly due to the steady campaigning of the various organisations, national and international, now devoted to the development of museums' education. During the calendar year 1982, for example, 2,000 educational groups were recorded visiting the Gallery, mostly from secondary schools. Of these we taught 300 and gave advice and worksheets to an estimated 200 more. Six hundred of these groups came to visit a special exhibition, and were booked in through the Education Department.

Another major factor has certainly been the generally raised public profile of the Tate Gallery due to such spectacular exhibitions as *The Essential Cubism* or, at the very end of this biennium, *The Pre-Raphaelites*. To these pressures the staff of the Education Department have responded with great commitment and energy and this in spite of considerable disruption to our accommodation, first in the latter half of 1982 from the building work on the much needed extension to the Coffee Shop, and then from our move in the summer of 1983 to temporary offices. This, however, is in preparation for an eventual move back into rebuilt and new premises linking the existing building to the Clore Gallery.

Face to face teaching, in the galleries, of schoolchildren, is the single most demanding aspect of the department's work and, in mid 1983, it was decided to implement a shift of policy towards dealing with school groups more by means of the provision of advice and information to teachers, printed study sheets for children's use in the galleries and courses for teachers in the use of the gallery. Looking back, it may be said that the Tate Gallery Education Department since its foundation in 1971 has developed an exceptional, and even leading, expertise in the practice and theory of introducing children to art and the art museum. The Tate's unique and stimulating mix of old and new art may be partly responsible for this. This expertise continues to be applied direct but it is also increasingly being passed on to teachers and educators through the development of our courses. During the period under review, well established courses for teachers in training, such as the annual joint National Museums Institute of Education course, have continued. New structures have been developed and new audiences tapped in courses run with regional museum (Brighton), courses for lecturers in education and museum education officers (*A New Look* run jointly with the British Museum, National Gallery and Victoria and Albert Museum) and, most recently, courses for inservice teachers. These include one-day briefings on special exhibitions, a new departure for us.

We now also provide advance information and briefing material for teachers planning to bring groups to special exhibitions, together with materials for children to work with in the exhibitions. Finally in connection with teaching we are pursuing a policy of increasing the work we do with primary school teachers and children.

The public lecture, public film and other audio-visual programmes have continued to be major spheres of activity. In the calendar year 1982 for example, we provided, as in previous years, a public lecture every weekday lunchtime and every Saturday and Sunday afternoon, together with twenty-one special evening lectures and thirty-three evening introductory lectures to exhibitions. These last, together with the weekend public lectures, were provided by our long-serving part-time lecturer, Laurence Bradbury. We are grateful to the voluntary guides who further enabled us to provide four tours every weekday and a fifteen-minute Picture of the Month talk every Saturday and Sunday afternoon. In the same year we ran almost 300 film shows.

The lecture programmes generally have been stimulating and sometimes exciting as in the case of the artist Steve Willats' evening lecture 'The New Reality', also something of a multi-media event. The special lecture programme has indeed been notable for successful contributions by artists speaking on their own work, usually in connection with a recent acquisition or an exhibition. Both the evening and lunchtime lecture programmes have also been enlivened by 'research in progress' contributions from young art historians outside the Tate. Among the most memorable of these was Mary Cowling's fascinating decoding of Frith's 'Derby Day'. Evening lecture series were organised for the major exhibitions of Richard Wilson, James Barry, *The Essential Cubism*, and John Piper.

In the film section this period has seen the continuing development of a pattern of lively seasons of films relating to specific areas of the Tate's collections or, especially, to major temporary exhibitions. These have been accompanied by increasingly substantial published programme notes. Perhaps particularly notable among many were 'Hans Richter's film work', 'Peter Blake and the Pop Image', 'Cubism and the Cinema' and 'New Art'.

The Education Department has also continued to produce introductory tape-slide programmes to accompany major exhibitions. Here the acquisition of new computerised equipment and the appointment of a Curator grade G in 1983 has enabled us to produce a vastly more sophisticated type of programme which can be transferred on to video-tape to form permanent educational material. So far programmes have been made on six exhibitions and one on the framing and packing of pictures.

During this biennium the Education Department has staged, or been largely responsible for, a variety of special events. Some of these were aimed at breaking new ground in relating works in the Tate Gallery to other arts. Three short plays by the American artist, poet, playwright and museum curator Frank O'Hara were performed in the large gallery containing works by his Abstract Expressionist contemporaries; there were two dance events, one based on the Songs and Proverbs of William Blake by Benjamin

Members of the public modelling heads in clay during the exhibition *Making Sculpture* – summer 1983

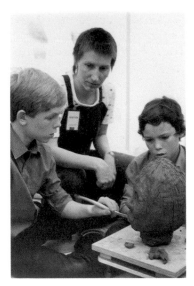

79

Britten, performed by dancers from the Ballet Rambert, and the other in collaboration with the Laban Centre on works by Anthony Caro, John Hoyland and Bridget Riley. A remarkable performance at the Bloomsbury Theatre of two unperformed plays by Wyndham Lewis was organised by us on the occasion of the Lewis Centenary Symposium.

On National Arts Day, 24 June 1984, we organised a competition of pavement art. Participants worked on the paving stones all round the perimeter of the Gallery and filled nearly every one. Winners were chosen at the end of the day by a panel of judges including Tony Banks of the GLC (now M.P.) and one of the Tate Gallery's Trustees, Rita Donagh. The summers of 1982 and 1983 were marked by two major didactic projects – *Paint and Painting*, a celebration of the bicentenary of Winsor & Newton, and *Making Sculpture* mounted with help from the sculpture materials firm of Alec Tiranti Ltd. The basis of both was a working studio. Members of the Education Department contributed to the original conception of *Paint and Painting* and organised lecture and film programmes to accompany it. *Making Sculpture* was conceived and organised by the Education Department in collaboration with the Information Department and a curator each from the Modern and Print Collections, who were responsible for its two main aspects, demonstrations of sculpture making by professional sculptors working in public on the lawn, and the studio operation in the pavilion. *Making Sculpture* took place during six weeks of the glorious summer of 1983. For the first three weeks the studio served mainly groups of schoolchildren and for the second mainly an adult public. Each participant made a head in clay. The best of these were cast and at the end judged by a panel including the Director and the sculptor Barry Flanagan, who was so delighted with the work of one child that he generously made it possible to cast all three winners in bronze. These were subsequently displayed in the Gallery. The completed works of the professional sculptors were displayed on the lawn and one was subsequently acquired for the Gallery. *Paint and Painting* and *Making Sculpture* were an enormous success, generating much goodwill, and there is no doubt that public participation events of this kind produce a very strong response.

During this biennium our holiday programmes for children have also developed, with increasingly well conceived and well produced children's 'trails' as well as imaginative competitions. Outstanding were the 'Looking into Colour' trail at Christmas 1982 and the poetry competition at Easter 1983. The voluntary guides have continued to provide their very successful holiday tours for children. Mention should also be made of the voluntary guides special tour service for the handicapped which has been steadily developing since the Tate's Sculpture for the Blind exhibition in the Year of the Disabled, 1981. The Tate's voluntary guides now possess a considerable body of expertise and experience in this area.

The Department is now beginning to prepare for the challenge of animating the new education facilities being built as part of the Clore Gallery project.

Exhibitions

There has been no great change in exhibition policy during the period under review but we may boast, nevertheless, that it has been a very successful two years with a programme of exhibitions that have been intelligently conceived, feelingly organised and attractive to the public. In addition there have been some that have broken new ground.

The Landseer exhibition was still in the Gallery in April 1982. The next large British Old Master show was that of Richard Wilson, selected by Professor David Solkin of the University of British Columbia and shown subsequently at the National Museum of Wales and the Yale Center for British Art. We presented at the same time a kind of exhibition that we do more rarely - a complete study of James Ward's 'Gordale Scar', exhibited with drawings, sketches and contemporary photographs. This was selected and catalogued by Edward Nygren of the Corcoran Gallery in Washington.

Another unusual exhibition was that devoted to Lionel Constable, selected and catalogued by Leslie Parris and Ian Fleming Williams. This show was the culmination of several years research, which has resulted in the separation of Lionel Constable's oeuvre from that of his father, John Constable, and in a much greater understanding of the relationship between John Constable and those of his descendants who were painters. The effect has been reciprocally to clarify the achievement of John himself. Some of the organisers' results had been published beforehand and the exhibition aroused keen interest.

The strange Anglo-Irish history painter of the eighteenth century, James Barry, was the subject of an exhibition by Dr William Pressly of Yale University, the third American scholar of a British artist cited in this report. There was no really large British Old Master show in 1983. The exhibition of the Pre-Raphaelites opened early in 1984 at the end of the biennium and has been drawing great crowds. It was sponsored by Pearson. This exhibition, selected by a committee of experts, co-ordinated by Leslie Parris and the Director, had the advantage of being based on the work of a group of great artists which was not the creation of art historians or critics but a self-selected and fruitful personal association. The selectors were careful not to go too far beyond this nucleus, but later, often more luxuriant, works of the principal artists were included as well as those by less famous artists during the period when they were close to the first protagonists. The result was virtually the definitive Pre-Raphaelite exhibition.

Such an exhibition, comprising many very rare and vulnerable works, cannot travel (in spite of the urgent solicitations of colleagues in other galleries here and in other countries) and is unlikely to be repeated for a long time. The exceptional educational effort accompanying this show is described in the section on the Education Department.

The principal and most successful modern exhibition was *The Essential Cubism* selected by Douglas Cooper with the assistance of Gary Tinterow, formerly of the Fogg Museum, and now a curator at the Metropolitan Museum. We were sad to learn that Mr Cooper, a great collector and scholar in the field of modern art, died in April 1984. The exhibition may be considered his last splendid achievement. Its style and theme were at the core of his lifelong commitment to the greatest art of his period.

The exhibition was selected with rare connoisseurship and, at the same time, with unusual clarity of concept and structure - it proved to fulfil precisely the promise of its title. We had many visitors and a quite outstanding response from those most attached to the art of painting. This was certainly one of the greatest exhibitions the Tate Gallery has ever presented.

The De Chirico exhibition, selected and circulated by the Museum of Modern Art,

New York, was even more stringently selected, to the extent that it provoked complaints about the near exclusion of work after about 1920. The image it presented so clearly, however, was that of one of the most original artists of that amazing period, the second decade of this century.

The large exhibition of the great Swiss contemporary artist, Jean Tinguely, was again exceptionally popular and was re-exported to his own country. Credit must be given to M. Caillat, lately the Ambassador of Switzerland in London, who was determined to bring off an exhibition of a Swiss artist during his term of appointment. He was able to contribute much to the ease and pleasure of organising such an exhibition but, of course, the star in every way was the artist himself: the humour, ingenuity and brilliance of his work is matched exactly by his correspondence, manner and personality.

Two of the most highly respected British artists of the mid-twentieth century had retrospective exhibitions – Graham Sutherland and John Piper. Both artists are affectionately regarded as characteristically British in theme and sensibility and yet both have drawn on the wider inheritance of Europe and the world. The exhibitions were selected by Tate curators, Ronald Alley and David Fraser Jenkins respectively. These two exhibitions may be considered as part of a series. They followed those devoted to Ben Nicholson, Henry Moore, Barbara Hepworth, Ceri Richards and David Jones, so that the Gallery will have presented all the most renowned artists of one celebrated generation when the Francis Bacon exhibition opens next year.

Peter Blake is of course a much younger artist but his retrospective in February 1983 confirmed in the most conspicuous way the strong appeal of his work and its own high craft and exuberant inventiveness. Blake, like many artists, contributed not only his paintings to the exhibition but his own sense of how to present them to best effect. In addition, with Chrissy Wilson, he created and assembled the witty and extravagantly detailed 'Sculpture Park' that fascinated crowds in the Duveen Gallery.

Alongside these major exhibitions, there have been a sequence of small-scale shows, many of them just as interesting and definitive as the larger manifestations. The Tate Gallery's contribution to the great Festival of India in 1983 was an exhibition of six modern Indian artists, Tagore, Roy, Sher Gil, Subramanyan, Husain and Khakhar. This was selected by a British painter who has often travelled in India, Howard Hodgkin, and was followed by an exhibition of Hodgkin's own *Indian Leaves*, evoking his personal experiences in the subcontinent.

Another small-scale exhibition was devoted to the long career of the abstract artist Paule Vézelay. It was a great pleasure to welcome her to the exhibition in her 91st year, and we much regret her recent death.

An exhibition of Reg Butler's last series of figure sculptures was enlarged to become a compact retrospective memorial exhibition.

This series of smaller exhibitions included, in addition, two such diverse figures as the politically active German-American conceptual artist, Hans Haacke, and the gardening, teaching painter (hardly less socially sensitive), Sir Cedric Morris, who stood for so many years apart from the hotbeds of the *avant-garde*. Another show was not so much *avant-garde* in style as a manifestation of the 'state of the art': Harold Cohen has developed computer hard- and soft-ware so as to create an artificial intelligence that is itself creative in terms devised by the artist.

Two further small exhibitions formed part of the prologue to the programme of purchasing and exhibiting New Art – both of successful American artists: Julian Schnabel and Jennifer Bartlett. A much larger manifestation was the *New Art* selected by Michael Compton with a large element of works already in the collection. This was the largest survey of contemporary art at the Tate for twenty years. It was a deliberately partial selection of art considered new in spirit by young or old artists, mostly unfamiliar in London. The Trustees acquired several further works from this exhibition.

An exhibition of quite a different character was the complex *Paint and Painting*, sponsored by Winsor & Newton in honour of their 150 years of activity. It comprised two parts: an exhibition within the Tate of the practical and technical development of artists' materials (especially pigments) and, in the garden at the front of the Tate, a pavilion in which visitors could try out with expert help a full range of materials. This opportunity was enjoyed by so many that in the following summer, 1983, a sculpture studio was set up in the same pavilion where members of the public could model a head in clay, again with skilled advice if required. A series of young sculptors practised their art in a shelter close by. One of the works so created, 'Making It' by Julian Opie, was later purchased by the Patrons of New Art and presented to the Gallery.

The number of exhibitions shown in the period under discussion was again very high, as this report shows, but thanks to the great popularity of some and to the generosity of sponsors the net cost has been very low. This is a state of affairs which it will be difficult to maintain after the year 1984-85.

Library

The scope and coverage of the Library's stock continued to expand during the period under review. Notable acquisitions by purchase included: Ambroise Vollard's *Tableaux, pastels et dessins de Pierre-Auguste Renoir* (2-volume reprint, 1954, of the largely destroyed 1918 edition); Sigurd Willoch's *Edvard Munch: raderinger* (Oslo, 1950); *Das Werk von Gustav Klimt* by Hermann Bahr and Peter Altenberg (Vienna, 1918); and a long-needed run of the exhibition catalogues of the *Society of Artists of Great Britain* for 1760-90. The Library has always attracted a steady flow of donated material from a wide variety of sources and the period 1982-84 was no exception. Among numerous individual items, there were groups of exhibition catalogues from Mrs Nora Meninsky, Sir Norman Reid and John Skelton; artists' books from David Jarvis, Media Space (Perth, Western Australia) and Richard Roehl; monographs on Italian artists from Dr G. P. Peloso of Genoa; and books and catalogues from Timm Ulrichs. A particularly welcome donation, an unbound copy of Sir Thomas Browne's *Urne Buriall, and The Garden of Cyrus* (1932; with Paul Nash illustrations), was generously presented by Desmond Flower.

All in all, despite a levelling-off in purchase funds compared with earlier years, 11,529 items were accessioned. The bookstock reached 25,753 volumes, bound periodicals 3,463 volumes, and exhibition catalogues 92,297 items

By the end of 1981 existing shelf accommodation had become alarmingly congested; both the Rotunda area and the adjoining stackroom were virtually full and it was necessary to disperse some material to temporary shelving in nearby curators' offices. The most important event, therefore, for the Library in 1982-84 was the fitting-up of a Reserve Stack on the upper floor of one of the remaining ward blocks on the Hospital Site. This additional accommodation, providing some 2,500 linear feet of shelving, was occupied in August 1982 and filled to about half capacity. As a result, immediate, if relatively short-term, relief was available for shelf space in the Rotunda area, adjacent offices and the stackroom, mainly by the removal of holdings of non-art material, a number of general works on art, and runs of less frequently used periodicals and group exhibition catalogues. The material consigned to the Reserve Stack was and remains reasonably accessible from the main building by means of day-to-day collection of items on request. In spite of this, by the end of the period under review, the Reserve Stack was approaching two-thirds capacity and the shelving in the Rotunda area and the stackroom could be estimated to have little more than a further two years' capacity, beyond which the Reserve Stack would have to absorb growth. This, too, will be filled in no more than five years and complete saturation will be reached. Thus even the short-term position remains critical and the urgent need for planning for and implementation of new library premises incorporated in a Study Centre is paramount if the Library is to be able to develop as a unified and accessible collection and ultimately to fulfil a national role.

Although the working environment of the Library remained far from ideal for both staff and users, some modest improvements were managed in the cramped and congested Rotunda area. Catalogue card cabinets were regrouped and staff positions were altered to give a little more seating and desk space and to provide a better sequence for the work-flow. Interim up-grading of the very poor lighting was achieved by the simple expedient of increasing the power of the chandelier lights and by directing them downwards; tubular desk lamps were also installed at staff desks. In spite of the restrictions imposed on service by the premises and in spite of the necessity of limiting external use to a 'library of last resort' basis, attendances at 2,203 were some 19% up on the previous period reported.

There was one change in the staff of the Library during 1982–84: Sheila Wells left after nine years' service and was replaced as Clerical Officer by Caron Galbraith. Don Gillett served as a temporary cataloguer for five months during the absence of Beth Houghton on maternity leave. A significant innovation was the compiling of bibliographies for Tate Gallery exhibition catalogues by the Library's staff; contributions included bibliographies for Peter Blake by Beth Houghton and Krzysztof Cieszkowski, for John Piper by Beth Houghton and Hilary Gresty, for Reg Butler by Meg Duff, and for Cedric Morris by Krzysztof Cieszkowski. Active participation in UK art librarianship development was maintained by the Library's representation on the ARLIS (Art Libraries Society) Committee for National Co-ordination of Art Library Resources, on the British Library's Working Party on the Provision of Materials for the Study of Art (later British Library Interim Committee on Art Documentation), and on London University's Library Resources Co-ordinating Committee (Subject Sub-Committee on the History of Art). Finally, the Library continued to help with professional library training by receiving library school visits from two parties from Robert Gordon's Institute, Aberdeen, as well as a visit from library staff at Brighton Polytechnic, and by providing fieldwork training for student librarians from the College of Librarianship, Wales.

Technical Services

The management of loans from the collections

Technical Services performs a central role in the management of the collections, both administratively and physically: nowhere are its several functions more inextricably linked than in dealing with requests to borrow works of art from the Gallery's collections. This is a growing responsibility; during the period covered by this Report the Gallery received requests to borrow 803 works of art of which 589 (71%) were lent.

The Registrar's Office acknowledges all such requests and coordinates a complex vetting procedure: the Gallery must be sure that works of art are not required for its own displays during the proposed period of the loan, that the works of art requested can withstand the rigours of the journeys involved and that the institution is suitably equipped to provide adequate security, environmental control and handling for the works of art that it wishes to borrow.

The standards of care afforded to works of art in transit are being improved all the time: cases are being more robustly constructed, better insulated and shock-protected. They are fitted out so that repacking does not require the provision of new or additional materials by the borrower. The improved cases lessen the risk of damage in transit and their design means that repacking for return is much less dependent upon the expertise of the borrower. However, their complex construction involves Technical Services in much additional work. Case designs which are clear and correctly dimensioned must be produced, and when packing cases are received they must be checked and their interiors tailored to the needs of individual works of art. The Gallery's commitment to the improvement of standards of care in transit is also a time-consuming activity: Technical Services is amassing technical data on the various forms of transport available, keeping abreast of developments in packing technology and is involved in a programme of scientific measurement of conditions encountered in transit.

Some methods of transport are improving: air-conditioned and better sprung road vehicles are becoming available. But in transport by air, additional difficulties are being encountered: the world economic recession has led to a contraction and a rationalisation of air freight operations. Direct transatlantic flights are not available as often as needed and often routes involving stopovers must be used. Such arrangements expose works of art in transit to the possibility of trans-shipment and arrangements for suitable climate control en route and for an uninterrupted flight and a guaranteed time of arrival are compromised. Sending an authoritative and suitably qualified escort appears to be the only solution to the problem.

Unlike many museums and galleries, the Tate Gallery does not have a policy of escorting every loan. Escorts are only sent when there is a compelling practical reason. Generally this has been when the value of the consignment is very high, or the works of art were unusually fragile or their handling and installation were likely to pose unusual problems. To these criteria, it has been necessary to add the possible complexity of the journey. Although the Gallery is fortunate in having a number of staff who are specialists in one or other of these areas of concern, it is now often necessary to cope with several different kinds of problem on any one assignment. The sheer scale of the loans operation also means that specialists cannot always be available. Technical Services is developing a training programme for couriers. In addition, they will in the future be provided with a dossier on their journey which will include local maps, telephone numbers to contact in various kinds of emergency and details of any local conditions which may affect them.

In order to maintain up-to-date information, they will be expected to complete a questionnaire which is provided with their dossier and which acts as a checklist of all their duties. Questions include details of transport, standards of handling and environmental control en route and in the borrowing institution. Escorting can no longer be regarded as a restful break from the rigours of normal gallery existence!

During the forthcoming two-year period, the opening of the Clore Gallery will increase Technical Services' workload in other areas and it is likely that the number of loans made will be somewhat curtailed. This will enable the development of methods and procedures to continue at a more leisurely pace and it is hoped that by the end of that time much of the routine paperwork will be handled by computer.

Photographic

During the past two years the department has continued to play a major supporting role in every area within the Gallery. The demands upon its facilities steadily increase and it has been fortunate enough to increase its staff by one photographer, bringing its strength up to a total of seven.

This moderate expansion in staff has allowed the department to cooperate in some of the new ventures within the Tate, such as the tape slide programmes, which now supplement many of the current exhibitions, and for which it produces all the photographic and titling material. It has also taken on the responsibility for the supply of photographic prints to the public through the Publications Department.

The growing trend of professionals within institutions to be more involved in the education of their younger colleagues has prompted the department to offer facilities to schools and colleges. It now provides places for students to gain short period industrial and commercial experience in photographic techniques, with particular emphasis in the field of fine art. It is also hoped that, in the near future, a more formal training programme may be offered as a support to the existing college courses in photographic sciences.

The department continues to offer a comprehensive graphic service for the production of posters and signs for display within the gallery and has helped to standardise a style using the new Millbank typeface.

The department looks forward to new trends – in particular it welcomes the possible introduction and setting up of soft X-ray techniques which would be most useful as a diagnostic tool in conservation and as an aid to research for the collections.

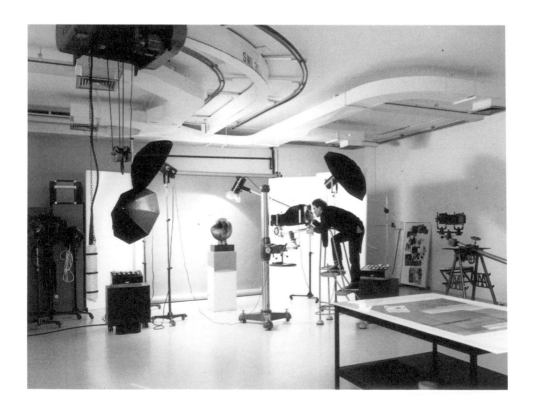

The Friends of the Tate Gallery

The Friends of the Tate Gallery raise funds to supplement the Gallery's annual purchasing grant from Government, and generate interest in all aspects of art. Visitors who join have the opportunity of being directly associated with the Tate Gallery and enlarging their artistic knowledge, while making a contribution towards the purchase of paintings, sculpture and prints for the collections. Thus the Friends act as an important link between the general public and the Tate Gallery itself.

The Friends is governed by a Council which meets twice a year, and by a smaller Executive Committee which meets more frequently. Council and Executive Committee members generously give of their time and interest to further the aims of the society. In January 1984 a change of officers took place: Judge Stephen Tumim succeeded the Countess of Airlie as Chairman, and Mrs William Morrison became Chairman of the Executive Committee in place of Mrs Patrick Allen. Lady Airlie and Mrs Allen have given long and devoted service and we are most grateful for the contribution they have made to assist the growth of the Friends.

The years 1982–84 have seen further steady expansion. General funds have been utilised to purchase outright, or assist with the purchase of, 14 works:

for the Historic British Collection

Sir George Clausen, *Winter Work*
Atkinson Grimshaw, *Bowder Stone, Borrowdale*
John Hill, *The Carpenter's Shop at Forty Hill, Enfield*
Tilly Kettle, *Mrs Yates as Mandane in the 'Orphan of China'*

for the Modern Collection –

Eileen Agar, *Angel of Anarchy*
Max Beckmann, *Carnival*
Meredith Frampton, *Marguerite Kelsey*
David Jones, *The Crucifixion, Capel-y-ffin*
Peter Lanyon, *Wreck*
Jacques Lipchitz, *Half Standing Figure (1915)*
Bernard Meadows, *Lovers*
Sir William Nicholson, *Harbour in Snow, La Rochelle*
Jean Tinguely, *Débricollage*
Edward Wadsworth, *Regalia*

In addition a number of works of art were presented to the Gallery through the Friends:

Sir Matthew Smith, *Winter in Provence* – presented anonymously in memory of Sir Robert Adeane
Sir Roland Penrose, *Last Voyage of Captain Cook* – presented by Mrs Gabrielle Keiller
Felix Rozen, 10 prints: *Uncertain Opus* – presented by Mrs Leslie Oliver
Eduardo Paolozzi, 53 prints – presented anonymously

Sir William Rothenstein, study of the attendant for *The Princess Badroulbadour* – presented by Sir John Rothenstein
Mrs Jack Steinberg also generously supported the purchase of *Half Standing Figure* by Jacques Lipchitz

The number of works with which the Friends are associated has been enlarged still further as a result of an important bequest of money under the terms of the will of Miss H. M. Arbuthnot. Her interest was primarily in modern art; consequently funds from her legacy have been utilised to facilitate the purchase of two important works for the Modern Collection:

Peter Blake, *'The Meeting'* or *'Have a Nice Day, Mr Hockney'*
Joan Miró, *Message from a friend*

As it was judged important for support to be given to Jeremy Dixon's excellent new design for the Tate's Coffee Shop, the Friends made a donation from general funds. Further support was given to this project through the Friends by the Monument Trust and the Robert & Lisa Sainsbury Charitable Fund; the Tate Gallery exhibitions programme has also benefited from a donation given anonymously through the Friends.

Meredith Frampton, **Marguerite Kelsey**
T 03145 Presented by The Friends of the Tate Gallery

Subscription rates are modest and have remained unchanged since January 1981, although an increase is envisaged during the latter part of 1984. Visitors have been increasingly attracted by the advantages of joining and the total membership is currently in excess of 7,000. This figure is conservative as any membership can include husband and wife, but the increased volume of members has been assimilated without difficulty as a result of the computerisation of membership records in May 1982. The number of Benefactor life members has also enlarged and special acknowledgement must be made to Sir Richard & Lady Attenborough, Dr & Mrs J. D. Cohen, Mr & Mrs Gilbert de Botton, Mr & Mrs Alan Driscoll, Mrs Sue Hammerson, Mr & Mrs Alex Herbage, Mr William A. McCarty-Cooper, Mr Simon Sainsbury, The Hon. Mrs Quentin Wallop, Mr & Mrs William E. Wiltshire, Miss Elizabeth Willson and Mr & Mrs Terry Willson. Generous donations have also been received from the Bankers Trust Company and the Tramman Trust.

During 1982 the Patrons of New Art were established within the Friends' organisation. Limited to 200 individual members, this group aims to encourage a lively and intelligent interest in new developments in art, and in particular its collection, both private and public. Subscriptions and donations from members assist the acquisition of works by younger artists for the Tate Gallery's collection of contemporary art, and during the period under review funds have been used to purchase the following works:

Julian Opie, *Making It,* 1983
Robert Longo, *Sword of the Pig,* 1983
Paula Rego, *Nanny, small bears and bogey-man,* 1982

Early in 1984 a member of the Patrons of New Art anonymously donated generous funds to establish the Turner Prize; an award which it is hoped will become an annual prize awarded to the person considered to have made the greatest contribution to art in Britain during the previous twelve months.

A greatly appreciated advantage of membership is the facility for members of the Friends and their guests to enter the Tate on Sunday mornings, and on some Monday evenings, to view special exhibitions or sections of the permanent collections in un-crowded conditions. As they have become popular, an increasing number of associated lectures are now arranged during these viewing times.

A wide choice of other activities is also organised, and recently groups of members have visited Paris and Zürich; had the opportunity to join a cruise to the Mediterranean; spent days at Henry Moore's studios in Hertfordshire and in Warwickshire and Surrey viewing public or private collections, and enjoyed private views of major exhibitions at the other galleries or museums. Further high points have been pre private-view parties at the Tate Gallery for *The Essential Cubism* and *The Pre-Raphaelites* exhibitions. A full list of activities, both for Friends and Young Friends, is printed in the Friends' Annual Report.

Membership rates at time of going to press

Any membership can include husband and wife

Benefactor £1,500. Life membership.
Patron of New Art £325 annually or £250 if a Deed of Covenant is signed.
Patron £150 or over annually. Five fully transferable guest cards.
Corporate £75 or over annually. For corporate bodies and companies. Two fully transferable guest cards.
Associate £40 or over annually. Two fully transferable guest cards.

Member £10 annually or £9 if a Deed of Covenant is signed.

Educational & Museum £8 annually or £7 if a Deed of Covenant is signed. For the staff of museums, public galleries and recognised educational bodies.

Young Friends £7 annually. For persons under twenty-six.

Advantages of membership

1 *Free Admission* to the Gallery, when closed to the public, on Sunday mornings between 11.00 and 13.00 hours, and during *major* special exhibitions, on the first Monday evening of the month between 18.30 and 21.00 hours. The exceptions are Bank Holiday weekends and the whole of the months of August and September. (The Atterbury Street entrance should be used.) *Members may bring two guests.*

Please Note

a. The British and Modern collections of the Gallery will be open on alternate Sunday mornings.

But b. During major special exhibitions the exhibition only will be open on both Sunday mornings and Monday evenings.

2 *Free Entry* to all exhibitions at the Tate Gallery.

3 *Catalogues* at reduced prices.

4 *Private Views* of all special exhibitions at the Tate Gallery.

5 *The Tate Gallery Reference Library* may be used by members, but only by appointment made through the Friends' Office, for enquiries not answered by the National Art Reference Library at the Victoria & Albert Museum.

6 *Opportunities to attend* lectures, private views at other galleries, films, parties and other activities.

7 *Visits* to exhibitions abroad, and British and foreign private collections.

8 *Publications.* Information about the Tate Gallery and the Friends' Annual Report are sent free to members. A minimum discount of ten per cent is available on Tate Gallery publications, and subscriptions at a reduced rate are available on some art magazines.

9 *The Members' Room* is always open.

Secretary General: Ms Cherry Barnett MA

Barbara Hepworth Museum

Since 1980, when the Barbara Hepworth Museum in St Ives became the first outstation of the Tate Gallery, knowledge of the museum has spread considerably. Publicity emanating from the Tate Gallery has done much to help, in particular the display of posters on the London Underground. Many visitors have expressed approval that a small provincial museum should be part of the National Collection, administered by a leading gallery for the benefit of those living in, or visiting, a part of the country remote from the Metropolis, and have said they would like to see this policy developed further.

Attendance figures show a small but steady increase each year. Most visitors are holidaymakers, so the popularity of the museum in terms of tickets sold relates directly to the state of the West Country tourist industry, which shows signs of resurgence after recent bleak years.

During 1983 the Property Services Agency began the first stage of a three-year programme of improvements in the museum garden. The first, and most important, operation was the pruning of overgrown trees and lopping of branches that had become dangerous. This resulted in more sunlight reaching other plants growing near the trees, and which were in danger of becoming stunted due to lack of light. Because of limited public funds the Trustees of the Hepworth Estate have generously provided money to buy more plants which, added to what the PSA can do, will within the year improve the garden's appearance enormously without in any way changing its original character.

Following a visit from Lord Dunluce, Keeper of Conservation, concern was expressed about the condition of many plinths supporting the sculptures in the garden. In many cases these were insecure, foundations were lacking and rising damp affected each to some degree. On the advice of an independent conservator of monuments and sculpture, Michael Eastham, it was decided to rebuild the plinths incorporating damp-proof membranes. This work was carried out during October and November 1983.

Interior gallery
upstairs at the
Hepworth Museum

Restaurant

During 1970 the Trustees decided to run the Gallery catering services themselves, taking over from the concessionaires who had been operating up until then. Staff were appointed and the Department was established. In 1972 a new Coffee Shop and a new waitress service Restaurant were opened, offering a much wider range of facilities than had previously been available. The present organisation of the Department thus became established and, since then, a fine reputation has been gained for the quality of food and service offered to customers. With the facilities that had become available the Department was also able to cater for any special entertainment requirements for the Gallery, particularly for such events as exhibition previews or other special occasions.

Credit for the successful establishment and the international reputation of the Tate Gallery Restaurant must go to Tom Machen who was Manager from 1970 until his departure in 1982. He personally gave the Restaurant its excellent wine cellar, and we are delighted to say that he has agreed to continue advising us on the purchase of wines. He was succeeded as Manager by Paul King.

The start of the period covered by this Report coincides with the opening of the new Coffee Shop during December 1982. It had become necessary after ten years for the Coffee Shop to be completely refurbished and improved. It had also become possible to incorporate a circular storage room and a corridor into the Coffee Shop area, thus greatly improving the facilities. The increased number of seats has helped to alleviate the problems of overcrowding, particularly during busy exhibition periods which had previously caused some difficulties. The new designs by Jeremy Dixon incorporated, as before, a self-service counter offering a wide variety of food and drink ranging from light snacks to full lunches from the cold buffet selection. In September 1983 an extension of the licence held by the Restaurant was granted to include the Coffee Shop, making wine available for sale with meals during lunch. This extension of the licence has enabled the Coffee Shop to remain open during the exhibition Private Views, and for late Gallery openings, offering a much wider selection than had previously been possible for such occasions.

With the new Coffee Shop successfully established, the needs of the Restaurant have now come to the fore. It is twelve years since the Restaurant was established in its present form and a full redesigning programme is now in hand for January 1985. As with the Coffee Shop, the scheme has been designed by Jeremy Dixon, and the excellent plans will focus attention towards the Rex Whistler mural and away from the centre of the room. The ceiling will be replaced, bringing much needed improvements to the air-handling system. This, together with the new furnishings and other proposed alterations, will bring about a completely fresh look to the Rex Whistler room, whilst enhancing the established style of the Restaurant itself.

Publications

For the first time the Department's annual turnover has exceeded £1 million. In the second of the two years under review, shop sales amounted to £883,107, with mail order and exhibition sales at £194,550 and £202,128 respectively – giving a total of £1,279,785 which is an improvement of 397,643 on the previous year. This is a figure well in advance of inflation and has been helped particularly by two very successful exhibitions: *The Essential Cubism* and *The Pre-Raphaelites*. In the accounts published by the auditors Price Waterhouse, it is recorded that while Gross Profit has fallen from 40.33% (1982-3) to 36.75% (1983-4), Net Trading Profit has risen from 7.8% (£68,789) to 13.15% (£168,343) in the second year. At the end of the period cash reserves stood at £389,795, with debtors at 83,354. Outstanding liabilities of £258,692 were well covered by the reserves, and stock valuation after firm depreciation amounted to £461,369. The Department's contribution to the Gallery's activities in goods and services continues to be substantial and totalled £127,597 in the two-year period.

The catalogues produced for the Gallery's exhibitions are almost invariably substantial contributions to the literature of their subjects. Among those published since our last report, *The Essential Cubism, The Pre-Raphaelites, John Piper, Richard Wilson, Graham Sutherland, James Barry, Peter Blake, Reg Butler,* and *Cedric Morris* have all been favourably noticed. Sales of *The Essential Cubism* and *The Pre-Raphaelites* have been particularly good at 19,000 (£9.50) and 46,000 (£8) respectively. Both the *John Piper* and *The Essential Cubism* have been selected for the British Book Design Exhibition of 1984. Our regular printers, Balding and Mansell of Wisbech, and The Hillingdon Press of

THE ESSENTIAL CUBISM 1907-1920

Uxbridge, deserve unstinted praise for the reliability of their service and the quality of their work which is often produced under the most taxing conditions.

Distribution arrangements abroad continue to perform satisfactorily. Particular attention has been given to the sales of colour reproductions and posters in North America where warehousing facilities have now been established. Desk diaries, wall calendars and address books remain very popular and editions of ten to fifteen thousand are sold every year to provide lasting publicity for the Gallery. The increased level of trading in the Gallery shop has been much assisted by successful exhibitions and the decision to provide some of these with their own specialist sales points has paid substantial dividends.

The healthy reserves now built up will provide a useful foundation for the long-term publishing of comprehensive, fully illustrated collection catalogues, the first volume of which, devoted to the age of Hogarth, should appear before the end of 1985. This period will also see the establishment of a series of monographs on modern masterpieces in the Tate collections.

A new display letter has been produced for the Gallery's exclusive use by the distinguished letter cutter and designer Michael Harvey. It is to be used in the galleries for signing and general notices, and has been adapted for display use on stationery and other ephemeral printing. The coat-of-arms has been remodelled by Douglas Coyne under the direction of Dr Herbert Spencer RDI of the Royal College of Art, who is at present supervising the re-styling of the Gallery's printed matter.

Acquisitions 1982–84

The fully documented and illustrated
catalogue of acquisitions is to be issued separately.

The Historic British Collection

HENRY ANDERTON *c.*1630–1665

T 03543
Mountain Landscape with Dancing Shepherds *c.*1650–60
Inscribed 'Anderton Fecit' on rock c. foreground
Oil on canvas, $18 \times 23\frac{1}{2}$ (45.7×59.7)
Bequeathed by Hugh Paget CBE 1983

JAMES BARRY 1741–1806

T 03784
A Grecian Harvest Home first published 1792
Etching and engraving, $16\frac{1}{4} \times 19\frac{7}{8}$ (41.3×50.5) on paper, $18\frac{1}{2} \times 24\frac{5}{8}$ (47×62.5)
Purchased from Christopher Mendez (Grant-in-Aid) 1983

T 03785
The Thames first published 1792
Etching and engraving, $16\frac{7}{16} \times 20\frac{1}{16}$ (41.8×51) on paper, $18 \times 22\frac{1}{8}$ (45.7×56.2)
Purchased from Christopher Mendez (Grant-in-Aid) 1983

T 03786
The Distribution of Premiums at the Society of Arts first published 1792
Etching and engraving, $16\frac{1}{2} \times 20\frac{1}{16}$ (42×51) on paper, $16\frac{5}{16} \times 20\frac{3}{4}$ (43×52.8)
Purchased from Christopher Mendez (Grant-in-Aid) 1983

T 03787
Elysium & Tartarus first published 1792
Etching and engraving, $16\frac{1}{2} \times 36\frac{3}{8}$ (43.2×92.5) on paper, $20\frac{5}{8} \times 36\frac{3}{8}$ (52.4×92.5)
Purchased from Christopher Mendez (Grant-in-Aid) 1983

T 03788
Detail of the Diagorides Victors 1795
Etching and engraving, $28\frac{7}{8} \times 18\frac{1}{2}$ (73.3×47) on paper, $30\frac{5}{16} \times 20$ (77×50.8)
Purchased from Christopher Mendez (Grant-in-Aid) 1983

THOMAS CHURCHYARD 1798–1865

T 03618
Windmills
Inscribed 'January 25. 18 [..]/Between 10 & 11 [...]' on back
Oil on panel, $6\frac{7}{16} \times 4\frac{13}{16}$ (16.4×12.2)
Presented anonymously in memory of Terence Rattigan 1983

T 03619
A House by a River
Inscribed 'T.C.' and 'Harriet Churchyard' on back
Oil on panel, $5\frac{9}{16} \times 7\frac{7}{8}$ (14.2×20)
Presented anonymously in memory of Terence Rattigan 1983

T 03620
The Garden Tent
Inscribed 'T.C' and 'Bessy' on back
Oil on panel, $7\frac{1}{16} \times 6\frac{7}{16}$ (18×16.4)
Presented anonymously in memory of Terence Rattigan 1983

T 03621
Aldeburgh Beach
Inscribed 'Emma –' and 'Harriett.' on back
Oil on board, $4\frac{3}{4} \times 6\frac{1}{16}$ (12×15.4)
Presented anonymously in memory of Terence Rattigan 1983

SIR GEORGE CLAUSEN 1852–1944

T 03666
Winter Work 1883–4
Inscribed 'G CLAUSEN 1883–4./ CHILDWICK' b.l. and 'WINTER WORK./ G.CLAUSEN./1883.' on back
Oil on canvas, $30\frac{1}{2} \times 36\frac{1}{4}$ (77.5×92)
Purchased from the Fine Art Society Ltd (Grant-in-Aid) with help from the Friends of the Tate Gallery 1983

JOHN CONSTABLE 1776–1837

T 03607
Study of a Girl in a Cloak and Bonnet 1810
Inscribed 'E Bergholt 1810 –' b.l. and 'Minna. Dc^{r} 27th 47' on back
Oil on board, $12\frac{7}{16} \times 6\frac{7}{8}$ (31.6×17.5)
Purchased from Sotheby's (Grant-in-Aid) 1983

THOMAS COOK *c.*1744–1818
after William Hogarth 1697–1764

T 03827
Dr. Benjamin Hoadly, Bishop of Winchester
Writing-engraving: 'Painted by Wm Hogarth/Engraved by T. Cook./The Right Reverend Father in God/DR BENJAMIN HOADLY, LORD BISHOP OF WINCHESTER/Prelate of the Most Noble Order of the Garter/London: Published by G. & L. Robinson, Paternoster Row, & F. Cook, N° 38, Tavistock Street, Covent Garden'.
Engraving, $16\frac{11}{16} \times 11\frac{1}{2}$ (42.4×29.2)
Transferred from the reference collection 1984

ABRAHAM COOPER 1787–1868

T 03422
The Day Family 1838
Inscribed 'AC [monogram] 1838' b.l. and from b.l. to b.r. 'Mrs Anne Day', 'Mrs Day/John Day Junr', 'John Day', 'Venison ridden by Saml Day', 'Chapeau d'Espagne ridden by Willm Day'
Oil on canvas, $38\frac{1}{8} \times 50\frac{1}{8}$ (96.8×127.3)
Bequeathed to the British Sporting Art Trust by Mrs F. Ambrose Clark from the collection of the late F. Ambrose Clark; presented to the Tate Gallery 1982

FRANCIS DANBY 1793–1861

T 03667
Children by a Brook *c.*1822
Oil on canvas, $13\frac{9}{16} \times 18\frac{1}{8}$ (34.5×46)
Purchased from Spink and Son Ltd (Grant-in-Aid) 1983

PETER DE WINT 1784–1849

T 03669
Study of Burdock and Other Plants
Oil on board, $10\frac{3}{8} \times 13\frac{1}{4}$ (26.2×33.5)
Purchased from Andrew Wyld (Grant-in-Aid) 1983

WILLIAM CHARLES THOMAS DOBSON 1817–1898

T 03448
The Child Jesus Going Down with his Parents to Nazareth 1856
Inscribed 'WCTD [monogram] 1856' b.l.
Oil on canvas, $46\frac{7}{8} \times 35\frac{3}{8}$ (109 × 90)
Purchased from the Fine Art Society Ltd (Grant-in-Aid) 1982

JOHN FERNELEY 1782–1860

T 03423
John Burgess, Esq., of Clipstone, Nottinghamshire with his Harriers 1838
Inscribed 'J. Ferneley/Melton Mowbray/1838' b.c.
Oil on canvas, $37\frac{3}{4} \times 55$ (95.9 × 139.8)
Bequeathed to the British Sporting Art Trust by Mrs F. Ambrose Clark from the collection of the late F. Ambrose Clark; presented to the Tate Gallery 1982

T 03424
Sir Robert Leighton after Coursing with a Groom and a Couple of Greyhounds 1816
Inscribed 'J. Ferneley/Melton Mowbray/1816' b.r.
Oil on canvas, $41\frac{3}{8} \times 55$ (105 × 139.7)
Bequeathed to the British Sporting Art Trust by Mrs F. Ambrose Clark from the collection of the late F. Ambrose Clark; presented to the Tate Gallery 1982

T 03425
Mr Power and his Son with 'Norton', a Grey Hunter 1819
Inscribed 'J. Ferneley/Melton Mowbray/1819' b.l.
Oil on canvas, $34 \times 42\frac{1}{2}$ (86.1 × 107.5)
Bequeathed to the British Sporting Art Trust by Mrs F. Ambrose Clark from the collection of the late F. Ambrose Clark; presented to the Tate Gallery 1982

T 03426
'Defiance', a Brood Mare, with 'Reveller', a Foal 1833
Inscribed 'J. Ferneley/Melton Mowbray/1833.' b.c. and 'Reveller' b.l.
Oil on canvas, 28 × 37 (71.2 × 94)
Bequeathed to the British Sporting Art Trust by Mrs F. Ambrose Clark from the collection of the late F. Ambrose Clark; presented to the Tate Gallery 1982

T 03439
Colonel Healey of Morris Grange, Wearing Raby Hunt Uniform, Riding with the Sedgefield Hunt *c.*1832
Inscribed 'John Fernley [sic]/Melton Mowbray' b.l.
Oil on canvas, $29\frac{1}{2} \times 37\frac{3}{4}$ (74.9 × 95.9)
Presented by Miss V. N. Cross through the British Sporting Art Trust 1982

JOHN FERNELEY JNR *c.*1815–1862

T 03427
Hunt Scurry 1832
Inscribed 'J. Ferneley Jr./1832' b.r.
Oil on canvas, 17 × 35 (43.2 × 88.9)
Bequeathed to the British Sporting Art Trust by Mrs F. Ambrose Clark from the collection of the late F. Ambrose Clark; presented to the Tate Gallery 1982

MARCUS GHEERAEDTS THE YOUNGER active 1561–1635

T 03456
Portrait of a Woman in Red 1620
Inscribed '1620' above hand c.r.
Oil on wood, $44\frac{15}{16} \times 35\frac{1}{2}$ (114.2 × 90.2)
Purchased from O. & P. Johnson Ltd (Grant-in-Aid) 1982

T 03466
Portrait of a Man in Masque Dress, probably Philip Herbert, 4th Earl of Pembroke *c.*1610
Oil on octagonal oak panel, $21\frac{7}{8} \times 17\frac{9}{16}$ (55.6 × 44.6)
Purchased at Christie's (Grant-in-Aid) 1982

SAMUEL HIERONYMUS GRIMM 1733–1794

T 03603
The Glacier of Simmenthal 1774
Inscribed 'S.H. Grimm fecit 1774' lower right, and with a lengthy description of the glacier on the back
Watercolour on paper, $11\frac{5}{8} \times 14\frac{5}{8}$ (29.5 × 37.1)
Purchased from Thos. Agnew & Sons Ltd (Grant-in-Aid) 1983

ATKINSON GRIMSHAW 1836–1893

T 03683
Bowder Stone, Borrowdale *c.*1864
Inscribed 'Atkinson Grimshaw/[?Borro'dale]' b.r.
Oil on canvas, $15\frac{3}{4} \times 21\frac{1}{8}$ (40 × 53.6)
Purchased at Sotheby's (Grant-in-Aid) with help from the Friends of the Tate Gallery 1983

SIR JAMES GUTHRIE 1859–1930

T 03446
The Wash 1883
Inscribed 'J.Guthrie/ -83-' b.l.
Oil on canvas, $37 \times 28\frac{15}{16}$ (94 × 73.5)
Purchased from the Fine Art Society Ltd (Grant-in-Aid) 1982

GAVIN HAMILTON 1723–98

T 03365
Agrippina Landing at Brindisium with the Ashes of Germanicus 1768–71
Oil on canvas, $71\frac{3}{4} \times 100\frac{3}{4}$ (182.5 × 256)
Purchased from P. & D. Colnaghi Ltd (Grant-in-Aid) 1982

JAMES TURPIN HART 1835–1899

T 03396
A Rustic Timepiece 1856
Inscribed 'Jas. T. Hart/1856' b.r. and on the back of the canvas 'The Rustic Time-/Piece/J.T. Hart/Upper Talbot St/Notting Hill'
Oil on canvas, 21 × 17 (53.3 × 43.2)
Purchased at Phillips, Son & Neale (Grant-in-Aid) 1982

WILLIAM HAVELL 1782–1857

T 03393
The Thames Valley 1807
Inscribed 'WHAVELL 1807' b.r.
Oil on board laid on panel, $19 \times 24\frac{1}{2}$ (48.2 × 62.3)
Purchased from Spink and Son Ltd (Grant-in-Aid) 1982

T 03394
Windsor Castle ?1807
Inscribed 'Windsor -/ 31/ Windsor Castle/ in the distance/ WHavell' on back
Oil on card, $4\frac{9}{16} \times 8\frac{5}{8}$ (11.6 × 21.9)
Purchased from Spink and Son Ltd (Grant-in-Aid) 1982

JOSEPH HAYNES 1760–1829
after William Hogarth 1697–1764

T 03828
The Stay-Maker 1782
Writing-engraving: 'From an Original Sketch in Oil by Hogarth in the Possession of Mr Saml Ireland/Etch'd by Jos. Haynes Pupil to the late Mr Mortimer /Publish'd as the Act directs Feby 1 1782 at No 3 Clements Inn.'
Etching, 12⅛ × 15⅛ (30.8 × 38.4)
Transferred from the reference collection 1984

CHARLES COOPER HENDERSON 1803–1877

T 03428
Sportsmen in Scottish Shooting-Dress Driving to the Moors *c.*1845
Oil on canvas, 13 × 24⅛ (33.1 × 61.2)
Bequeathed to the British Sporting Art Trust by Mrs F. Ambrose Clark from the collection of the late F. Ambrose Clark; presented to the Tate Gallery 1982

T 03429
Mail Coach in a Snowstorm *c.*1843
Oil on canvas, 17⅞ × 30⅛ (45.4 × 76.4)
Bequeathed to the British Sporting Art Trust by Mrs F. Ambrose Clark from the collection of the late F. Ambrose Clark; presented to the Tate Gallery 1982

JOHN FREDERICK HERRING 1795–1865

T 03430
The Hunting Stud 1845
Inscribed 'J.F. Herring Senr 1845' b.r.
Oil on canvas, 17⅞ × 27⅞ (45.5 × 70.8)
Bequeathed to the British Sporting Art Trust by Mrs F. Ambrose Clark from the collection of the late F. Ambrose Clark; presented to the Tate Gallery 1982

JOHN HILL ?1779–1841

T 03668
The Carpenter's Shop at Forty Hill, Enfield ?exh.
Oil on canvas, 18½ × 27⅛ (47 × 68.8)
Presented by the Friends of the Tate Gallery 1983

WILLIAM HOGARTH 1697–1764

T 03613
The Dance (The Happy Marriage VI) *c.*1745
Oil on canvas, 26⅞ × 35⅛ (68.3 × 89.2)
Purchased from Southwark Borough Council (Grant-in-Aid) with assistance from the National Heritage Memorial Fund 1983

THOMAS JONES 1742–1803

T 03367
In the Road to Santa Maria de' Monti, Naples 1781
Inscribed 'In the Road to Sa Ma de' Monti by Naples/10th May 1781' and 'morng' ('morning', twice), with a pencil sketch of the direction of the sun's rays, at top
Watercolour on paper, 8 5/16 × 10 15/16 (21.1 × 27.8)
Purchased from Morton Morris & Co. (Grant-in-Aid) 1982

T 03544
An Antique Building Discovered in the Villa Negroni 1779
Inscribed 'T. Jones' lower right and 'An Antique Building discovered in a Cava in the Villa Negroni at Rome in ye year 1779' on back
Oil on paper, 16 × 21¾ (40.7 × 55.2)
Presented by Canon J. H. Adams 1982

T 03545
The Capella Nuova, Naples 1782
Inscribed 'The Capella nuova fuori della porte di Chiaja, Napeoli May 1782' and 'TJ' on back
Oil on paper, 7⅞ × 9⅛ (20 × 23.2)
Presented by Canon J. H. Adams 1982

T 03546
A Scene in the Colosseum, Rome ?1777
Inscribed 'A Scene in the Collo*f*seo at Rome' on back
Oil on paper, 17 × 11⅜ (43.2 × 28.9)
Presented by Canon J. H. Adams 1982

CHARLES KEENE 1823–1891

T 03840
Two Artists Working by Lamplight in a Studio
Pen and brown ink on paper, 7⅜ × 5 (18.7 × 12.7)
Purchased from the Fine Art Society Ltd (Grant-in-Aid) 1984

TILLY KETTLE 1734 or '35–1786

T 03373
Mrs Yates as Mandane in 'The Orphan of China' exh. 1765
Inscribed 'Mrs. Yates' b.l.c.
Oil on canvas, 75¾ × 51 (192.4 × 129.5)
Purchased from Anthony Dallas & Sons Ltd (Grant-in-Aid) with help from the Friends of the Tate Gallery 1982

SIR EDWIN LANDSEER 1803–1874

T 03395
The Harper 1821–2
Inscribed 'EL' on the top of the harp
Oil on canvas, 35⅞ × 28 (91.2 × 71)
Purchased from Mrs P. E. Bustin (Grant-in-Aid) 1982

HENRY HERBERT LA THANGUE 1859–1929

T 03413
The Return of the Reapers 1886
Inscribed 'H·H·LATHANGUE' b.l.
Oil on canvas, 46⅞ × 27⅜ (119 × 69.5)
Purchased from Mr Arthur Grogan (Grant-in-Aid) 1982

CHARLES ROBERT LESLIE 1794–1859

T 03789
Interior at Petworth *c.*1845
Verso: slight sketch of a seated male figure in costume
Inscribed 'N' and 'Dec 4th/1844'
Oil on panel, 13⅞ × 11 13/16 (35.2 × 30)
Purchased from Thomas L. Twidell (Grant-in-Aid) 1983

WILLIAM MARLOW 1740–1813

T 03602
A Post-House near Florence
Inscribed 'W Marlow' lower left
Watercolour on paper, 10 × 14 (25.2 × 35.6)
Purchased from Thos. Agnew & Sons Ltd (Grant-in-Aid) 1983

BEN MARSHALL 1768–1835

T 03431
James Belcher, Former Heavyweight Champion of England ?1803
Oil on canvas, $35\frac{5}{8} \times 27\frac{5}{8}$ (90.6 × 70.2)
Bequeathed to the British Sporting Art Trust by Mrs F. Ambrose Clark from the collection of the late F. Ambrose Clark; presented to the Tate Gallery 1982

T 03433
Portraits of Cattle of the Improved Short-Horned Breed, the Property of J. Wilkinson, Esq., of Lenton, nr. Nottingham 1816
Inscribed 'B. Marshall 1816' b.c.
Oil on canvas, 40 × 50 (101.5 × 127.1)
Bequeathed to the British Sporting Art Trust by Mrs F. Ambrose Clark from the collection of the late F. Ambrose Clark; presented to the Tate Gallery 1982

BEN MARSHALL 1768–1835
(? and **LAMBERT MARSHALL**)

T 03432
Rural Courtship ?*c.*1830
Oil on canvas, $34\frac{1}{2} \times 40\frac{7}{8}$ (87.7 × 104.1)
Bequeathed to the British Sporting Art Trust by Mrs F. Ambrose Clark from the collection of the late F. Ambrose Clark; presented to the Tate Gallery 1982

JAMES POLLARD 1792–1867

T 03434
Coursers Taking the Field at Hatfield Park, Hertfordshire 1824
Inscribed 'J Pollard' b.c.
Oil on canvas, $41 \times 56\frac{15}{16}$ (104.2 × 147.2)
Bequeathed to the British Sporting Art Trust by Mrs F. Ambrose Clark from the collection of the late F. Ambrose Clark; presented to the Tate Gallery 1982

T 03435
The Manchester and Liverpool Coach Passing Whittington College, Highgate 1836
Inscribed 'J Pollard 1836' b.r.
Oil on canvas, $14\frac{1}{2} \times 18$ (36.9 × 45.7)
Bequeathed to the British Sporting Art Trust by Mrs F. Ambrose Clark from the collection of the late F. Ambrose Clark; presented to the Tate Gallery 1982

T 03436
Fly Fishing at Tottenham Mills 1831
Inscribed 'J. Pollard 1831' b.c.
Oil on canvas, $14 \times 17\frac{9}{16}$ (35.6 × 44.6)
Bequeathed to the British Sporting Art Trust by Mrs F. Ambrose Clark from the collection of the late F. Ambrose Clark; presented to the Tate Gallery 1982

T 03437
Trolling for Pike in the River Lee 1831
Inscribed 'J Pollard 1831' b.r.
Oil on canvas, $14 \times 17\frac{9}{16}$ (35.6 × 44.6)
Bequeathed to the British Sporting Art Trust by Mrs F. Ambrose Clark from the collection of the late F. Ambrose Clark; presented to the Tate Gallery 1982

GEORGE ROMNEY 1734–1802

T 03547
John Howard Visiting a Lazaretto *c.*1791–2
Graphite and iron gall ink on paper, $13\frac{1}{2} \times 19\frac{1}{4}$ (34.3 × 49)
Purchased from Christopher Powney (Grant-in-Aid) 1982

DANTE GABRIEL ROSSETTI 1828–1882

T 03817
Sketch of an Angel's Head
Chalk, $17\frac{7}{16} \times 19\frac{11}{16}$ (44.3 × 50), on canvas, $20\frac{5}{16} \times 22\frac{5}{16}$ (51.5 × 56.7), formerly attached to the stretcher of N 05064, 'Proserpine'
Presented by W. Graham Robertson 1940

ALEXANDER RUNCIMAN 1736–1785

T 03604
Fingal Encounters Carbon Carglass *c.*1771–3
Etching, $5\frac{7}{8} \times 9\frac{5}{8}$ (14.9 × 24.5) on paper, $6\frac{1}{4} \times 10$ (15.8 × 25.4)
Purchased from Christopher Mendez (Grant-in-Aid) 1983

T 03605
Fingal Encounters Carbon Carglass (smaller upright version) *c.*1771–3
Etching, $5\frac{3}{4} \times 3\frac{3}{8}$ (14.6 × 8.7) on paper, $6 \times 4\frac{7}{8}$ (15.2 × 12.3)
Purchased from Christopher Mendez (Grant-in-Aid) 1983

T 03606
Agrippina with the Ashes of Germanicus ?*c.*1771–3
Etching, $5\frac{5}{8} \times 4\frac{3}{16}$ (14.4 × 10.6) on paper, $6\frac{3}{8} \times 4\frac{7}{8}$ (16.1 × 12.3)
Purchased from Christopher Mendez (Grant-in-Aid) 1983

SIR WILLIAM SEGAR,
attributed to
active 1580 or 5–1633

T 03576
Portrait of a Man in a Slashed Black Doublet *c.*1595–1605
Oil on oak panel, $39\frac{3}{8} \times 31\frac{3}{4}$ (92.4 × 80.6)
Purchased from Wilkins & Wilkins (Grant-in-Aid) 1983

JOSEPH SEVERN 1793–1879

T 03357
The Infant of the Apocalypse Saved from the Dragon *c.*1827–31
Oil on canvas (arched top), 88 × 50 (223.5 × 127)
Purchased at Sotheby's (Grant-in-Aid) 1982

WILLIAM HENRY SIMMONS
1811–1882 after Abraham Solomon 1824–1862

T 03616
Waiting for the Verdict
Published 1866
Mezzotint, $21\frac{3}{4} \times 27\frac{1}{2}$ (55.2 × 69.9)
Presented anonymously by the former owner of T 03614–15

T 03617
Not Guilty published 1866
Mezzotint, $21\frac{13}{16} \times 27\frac{5}{8}$ (55.4 × 69.4)
Presented anonymously by the former owner of T 03614–15

FRANCESCO SLETER
1685–1775

T 03465
A Representation of the Liberal Arts: Ceiling Design for the State Dining Room at Grimsthorpe Castle, Lincolnshire *c.*1724
Oil on canvas, $24\frac{1}{8} \times 30$ (61.3 × 76.2)
Purchased from Harari and Johns (Grant-in-Aid) 1982

ABRAHAM SOLOMON
1823–1862

T 03614
Waiting for the Verdict 1857
Inscribed 'A Solomon 57' b.l.
Oil on canvas, $40\frac{1}{8} \times 50\frac{1}{8}$ (102 × 127.3)
Purchased from a private owner through Albion Fine Art (Grant-in-Aid with the assistance of the National Art-Collections Fund and the Sue Hammerson Charitable Trust) 1982

T 03615
'Not Guilty' (Companion Picture to 'Waiting for the Verdict') 1859
Oil on canvas, 40 × 50 (101.6 × 127)
Purchased from a private owner through Albion Fine Art (Grant-in-Aid with the assistance of the National Art-Collections Fund and the Sue Hammerson Charitable Trust) 1982

SIMEON SOLOMON 1840–1905

T 03702
A Youth Relating Tales to Ladies 1870
Inscribed 'SS/ 1870' at right (initials in monogram)
Oil on canvas, 14 × 21 (35.5 × 53.4)
Presented by the Kretschmer family in accordance with the wishes of William Kretchmer 1983

SIDNEY STARR 1857–1925

T 03643
A Study 1887
Inscribed 'A STUDY/Sidney Starr/38 Abercorn Place/Abbey Road,/N.W.' on back
Oil on canvas, 18 × 14 (45.5 × 35.5)
Presented anonymously in memory of Terence Rattigan 1983

GEORGE STUBBS 1724–1806

T 03778
Reapers Published 1791
Mixed method engraving, $18\frac{15}{16} \times 26\frac{3}{4}$ (48.2 × 68) on paper, $20\frac{3}{8} \times 27\frac{3}{4}$ (51.7 × 70.5)
Transferred (as duplicate) from British Museum 1983

T 03779
Labourers Published 1789
Mixed method engraving, $20\frac{5}{8} \times 27\frac{1}{2}$ (52.3 × 69.7) on paper, $21\frac{5}{8} \times 28\frac{1}{2}$ (54.9 × 72.4)
Transferred (as duplicate) from British Museum 1983

T 03780
Foxhound Published 1788
Mixed method engraving, $3\frac{5}{8} \times 4\frac{1}{2}$ (9.2 × 11.5) on paper, $6\frac{9}{16} \times 8\frac{1}{16}$ (16.9 × 20.6)
Transferred (as duplicate) from British Museum 1983

T 03781
Foxhound Viewed from Behind Published 1788
Mixed method engraving, $3\frac{5}{16} \times 4\frac{1}{8}$ (8.4 × 10.7) on paper, $7\frac{1}{16} \times 10\frac{1}{4}$ (18 × 26)
Transferred (as duplicate) from British Museum 1983

T 03843
A Horse Attacked by a Lion Published 1788
Mixed method engraving, $9\frac{13}{16} \times 13\frac{3}{16}$ (24.8 × 33.4) on paper, $11\frac{3}{8} \times 14\frac{15}{16}$ (28.3 × 38)
Transferred (as duplicate) from British Museum 1984

T 03844
A Lion Resting on a Rock Published 1788
Mixed method engraving, $8\frac{7}{8} \times 12\frac{5}{16}$ (22.6 × 31.2) on paper, $9\frac{7}{8} \times 12\frac{7}{8}$ (25.2 × 32.6)
Transferred (as duplicate) from British Museum 1984

J.M.W. TURNER 1775–1851

The ownership of the following twenty oil-paintings has been transferred from H.M. Treasury to the Tate Gallery; they will however continue to remain at Petworth House, Sussex, with the rest of the collection administered by the National Trust.

T 03868
Ships Bearing up for Anchorage ('The Egremont Seapiece') exh.1802
Inscribed 'JMW Turner pinxit' b.r.
Oil on canvas, 47 × 71 (119.5 × 180.5)

T 03869
Narcissus and Echo exh.1804
Oil on canvas, 34 × 46 (86.5 × 117)

T 03870
Windsor Castle from the Thames *c.*1805
Inscribed 'JMW Turner RA ISLEWORTH' b.r.
Oil on canvas, 35 × 47 (89 × 119.5)

T 03871
The Thames near Windsor ?exh.1807
Oil on canvas, 35 × 47 (89 × 119.5)

T 03872
The Thames at Weybridge *c.*1807–10
Oil on canvas, 35 × 47 (89 × 119.5)

T 03873
The Thames at Eton exh.1808
Oil on canvas, $23\frac{1}{2} \times 35\frac{1}{2}$ (59.5 × 90)

T 03874
The Confluence of the Thames and the Medway exh.1808
Inscribed 'JMW Turner RA fe' b.r.
Oil on canvas, 35 × 47 (89 × 119.5)

T 03875
The Forest of Bere exh.1808
Inscribed '. . . Turner RA' b.r.c.
Oil on canvas, 35 × 47 (89 × 119.5)

T 03876
Margate exh.1808
Oil on canvas, $35\frac{1}{2} \times 47\frac{1}{2}$ (90 × 120.5)

T 03877
Near the Thames' Lock, Windsor exh.1809
Inscribed 'JMW Turner RA' b.r.
Oil on canvas, $35 \times 46\frac{1}{2}$ (89 × 118)

T 03878
Tabley, Cheshire, the Seat of Sir J.F. Leicester, Bart.: Calm Morning exh.1809
Inscribed 'JMW Turner RA' b.r.
Oil on canvas, 36 × 46 (91.5 × 117)

T 03879
Cockermouth Castle exh.1810
Oil on canvas, $23\frac{3}{4} \times 35\frac{1}{2}$ (60.5 × 90)

T 03880
Petworth, Sussex, the Seat of the Earl of Egremont: Dewy Morning 1810
Inscribed 'JMW Turner RA 1810' b.l.
Oil on canvas, $36 \times 47\frac{1}{2}$ (91.5 × 120.5)

T 03881
Hulks on the Tamar ?exh.1812
Inscribed 'JMW Turner RA' b.r.
Oil on canvas, $35\frac{1}{2} \times 47\frac{1}{2}$ (90 × 120.5)

T 03882
Teignmouth exh.1812
Inscribed 'JMW Turn . . .' b.l.
Oil on canvas, $35\frac{1}{2} \times 47\frac{1}{2}$ (90×120.5)

T 03883
The Lake, Petworth: Sunset, Fighting Bucks *c.*1829
Oil on canvas, $24\frac{1}{2} \times 57\frac{1}{2}$ (62×146)

T 03884
The Lake, Petworth: Sunset, a Stag Drinking *c.*1829
Oil on canvas, 25×52 (63.5×132)

T 03885
Chichester Canal *c.*1829
Oil on canvas, 25×52 (63.5×132)

T 03886
Brighton from the Sea *c.*1829
Oil on canvas, 25×52 (63.5×132)

T 03887
Jessica exh.1830
Oil on canvas, 48×36 (122×91.5)

Nos. T 03868–87: The Tate Gallery and the National Trust (Lord Egremont Collection) Petworth House; transferred from H.M. Treasury 1984.

JOHN VANDERBANK ?1694–1739

T 03539
A Young Man of the Lee Family, possibly William Lee of Totteridge Park, Herts. 1738
Inscribed 'Jno Vanderbank Fecit 1738' b.l.c.
Oil on canvas, $66\frac{1}{8} \times 42\frac{1}{16}$ (167.9×106.8)
Purchased at Sotheby's (Grant-in-Aid) 1982

JOHN WAINWRIGHT fl.1860s

T 03378
Flower-Piece 1867
Inscribed 'John Wainwright 1867' b.l.
Oil on canvas, $26\frac{1}{16} \times 22$ (66.2×55.9)
Bequeathed by Mrs Bessie Gornall 1982

JAMES WARD 1769–1859

T 03440
The Moment 1831
Inscribed 'J WARD [monogram] RA. 1831' b.r.
Oil on panel, $14\frac{7}{16} \times 18\frac{5}{16}$ (36.7×46.6)
Purchased at Sotheby's (Grant-in-Aid) 1982

T 03577
Study for 'Gordale Scar': Detail of Rocks near a Waterfall 1811
Inscribed 'Gordale/Augt 19th 1811' and 'JWD RA' lower right of centre
Pencil on paper, $10\frac{3}{4} \times 14\frac{1}{4}$ (27.3×36.4)
Purchased from Mme E. Arnold (Grant-in-Aid) 1983

T 03578
First Compositional Study for 'Gordale Scar' 1811
Inscribed 'Malham water/Augt 15th 1811 /JWD.' and 'Gordale' lower left of centre
Pencil on paper, $11 \times 15\frac{1}{2}$ (28×39.4)
Purchased from Mme E. Arnold (Grant-in-Aid) 1983

THOMAS WEAVER 1774 or 1775–1843

T 03438
Ram-Letting from Robert Bakewell's Breed at Dishley, near Loughborough, Leicester 1810
Inscribed 'T. Weaver Pinx^{t} 1810' b.r.
Oil on canvas, $40\frac{7}{16} \times 50\frac{11}{16}$ (102.8×128.6)
Bequeathed to the British Sporting Art Trust by Mrs F. Ambrose Clark from the collection of the late F. Ambrose Clark; presented to the Tate Gallery 1982

SIR DAVID WILKIE 1785–1841

T 03821
Four Preliminary Studies for Figures in 'The Village Holiday' 1809–10
Black crayon, drawn on the back of a letter dated 29 November 1809 from the Secretary of the Royal Academy to Wilkie, $7\frac{1}{4} \times 11$ (18.4×27.8)
Purchased from Mr R. Easson (Grant-in-Aid) 1984

RICHARD WILSON 1713 or '14–1782

T 03366
Meleager and Atalanta *c.*1760–70
Oil on canvas, $41\frac{1}{8} \times 51$ (104.5×129.5)
Purchased from Thomas Agnew & Sons Ltd (Grant-in-Aid) 1982

T 03665
Westminster Bridge under Construction 1744
Inscribed 'R Wilson 1744' on cartouche on wall b.l.c.
Oil on canvas, $28\frac{1}{2} \times 57\frac{1}{2}$ (72.5×146)
Purchased from Spink & Son Ltd (Grant-in-Aid and the Miss M. Deakin Bequest) with assistance from the National Heritage Memorial Fund 1983

The Modern Collection

IVOR ABRAHAMS b.1935

T 03369
Lady in Niche 1973
Not inscribed
Green flock, polystyrene, fibreglass, household paint and plywood, 82½ × 62 × 30 (209.5 × 157.5 × 76.2)
Purchased from the Mayor Gallery (Grant-in-Aid) 1982

ROGER ACKLING b.1947

T 03562
Five Sunsets in One Hour 1978
Inscribed 'Five Sunsets in One Hour/ Five One Minute Sun Lines' centre towards t., and 'A Country Sketch/ Chillerton Down Isle of Wight England/ June 24 1978' centre towards b.
Burnt lines and transfer letters on card, 22 × 14½ (55.8 × 36.7)
Presented by the Contemporary Art Society 1983

EILEEN AGAR b.1904

T 03809
Angel of Anarchy 1936–40
Inscribed 'AGAR/ANGEL OF ANARCHY' on back of neck
Fabric over plaster and mixed media, 20½ × 12½ × 13¼ (52 × 31.7 × 33.6)
Presented by the Friends of the Tate Gallery 1983

BORIS ANREP 1883–1969

T 03538
Nude among Ruins 1944
Not inscribed
Gouache on board, 23¾ × 14⅝ (60.4 × 37)
Bequeathed by Mrs M.J.A. Russell 1982

ARMAN b.1928

T 03380
Venus of the Shaving Brushes 1969
Not inscribed
Shaving brushes embedded in polyester, 32⅞ × 11⅜ × 12½ (83.5 × 29 × 32) on plinth 39½ × 15¼ × 13½ (105 × 38.7 × 34.4)
Purchased from the Galerie Reckermann (Grant-in-Aid) 1982

T 03381
Condition of Woman I 1960
Not inscribed
Bathroom rubbish in glass case on decorated wooden plinth, 75½ × 18¼ × 12⅝ (192 × 46.2 × 32)
Purchased from the Galerie Tarica (Grant-in-Aid) 1982

KENNETH ARMITAGE b.1916

T 03708
Seated Woman 1955–7
Inscribed 'Susse Fondeur Paris' and 'CIRC. 182–1960' at back of base
Bronze, 23⅝ × 9⅞ × 12¼ (60 × 25 × 31)
Transferred from the Victoria and Albert Museum 1983

ART AND LANGUAGE
(Michael Baldwin b.1945 and Mel Ramsden b.1944)

T 03453
Courbet's Burial at Ornans . . . 1981
comprising
a) The left-hand third of Courbet's 'Burial at Ornans' Expressing a Sensuous Affection . . .
b) The centre third of Courbet's 'Burial at Ornans' Expressing a Vibrant Erotic Vision . . .
c) The right-hand third of Courbet's 'Burial at Ornans' Expressing States of Mind that are Obsessive and Compelling . . .

Not inscribed
Black ink, wash and wax crayon on paper, mounted on canvas; three panels each 127⅝ × 91¾ (324 × 233)
Purchased from the Galerie Eric Fabre (Grant-in-Aid) 1982

T 03800
Index: The Studio at 3 Wesley Place, in the Dark (VI), showing the Position of 'Embarrassments' in (IV) 1982
Not inscribed
Photograph, black ink, wax crayon and metallic pencil on sandwich of paper and plastic foam, 31½ × 66¼ (79.7 × 168)
Presented by Art & Language and the Lisson Gallery 1983

T 03801
Index: The Studio at 3 Wesley Place, in the Dark (IV), and illuminated by an Explosion nearby (VI) 1982
Not inscribed
Photograph, pencil, watercolour and acrylic on tracing paper mounted on paper mounted on sandwich of paper and plastic foam, 30⅞ × 64⅛ (78.4 × 162.7)
Presented by Art & Language and the Lisson Gallery 1983

T 03802
Index: The Studio at 3 Wesley Place, executed by Mouth (II) 1982
Not inscribed
Pencil and carbon paper tracings on paper mounted on sandwich of paper and plastic foam, 38⅜ × 82¾ (97.5 × 210)
Presented by Art & Language and the Lisson Gallery 1983

T 03803
Index: The Studio at 3 Wesley Place (VI), illuminated by an Explosion nearby 1982
Not inscribed
Pencil on paper mounted on sandwich of paper and plastic foam, 42 × 63⅛ (106.7 × 160.3)
Presented by Art & Language and the Lisson Gallery 1983

T 03804
Index: The Studio at 3 Wesley Place 1981–2
Not inscribed
Photograph, pencil, pen and ink, watercolour, black washes and collage on paper mounted on sandwich of paper and plastic foam, 30 × 64 (76.2 × 162.3)
Purchased from the Lisson Gallery (Grant-in-Aid) 1983

RICHARD ARTSCHWAGER b.1923

T 03793
Table and Chair 1963–4
Not inscribed
Melamine laminate over wood: table, 29¾ × 52 × 37½ (75.5 × 132 × 95.2); chair, 45 × 17¼ × 21 (114.3 × 43.8 × 53.3)
Purchased from the Leo Castelli Gallery (Grant-in-Aid) 1983

LAWRENCE ATKINSON 1873–1931

T 03692
Composition No. 10 1914–15
Inscribed 'L∧' b.l. and r., on reverse 'Comp 10' and on original mount 'L. Atkinson, Composition No. 10 1914/15'
Pencil, crayons and gouache on paper, $19\frac{1}{2} \times 13$ (49.7 × 33)
Purchased from Anthony d'Offay Ltd (Grant-in-Aid) 1983

GILLIAN AYRES b.1930

T 03458
Antony and Cleopatra 1982
Inscribed 'Gillian/Ayres' b.r.
Oil on canvas, $114\frac{1}{4} \times 113\frac{5}{16}$ (289.3 × 287.2)
Purchased from the Knoedler Gallery (Grant-in-Aid) 1982

MICHAEL AYRTON 1921–1975

T 03611
The Temptation of St. Anthony 1942–3
Inscribed 'Michael Ayrton. J. / 1942–1943' t.r.
Oil on panel, $22\frac{7}{8} \times 29\frac{5}{8}$ (58.1 × 75.2)
Purchased from Christopher Hull (Gytha Trust) 1983

GEORG BASELITZ b.1938

T 03442
Rebel 1965
Inscribed 'G. Baselitz/65/Rebell' on back of canvas
Oil on canvas, $64\frac{1}{16} \times 51\frac{1}{4}$ (162.7 × 130.2)
Purchased from the Galerie Michael Werner (Grant-in-Aid) 1982

T 03672
Adieu 1982
Inscribed '17.III.82 G. Baselitz' b. centre
Oil on canvas, $98\frac{1}{2} \times 118\frac{1}{4}$ (205.2 × 300.4)
Purchased from Xavier Fourcade Inc. (Grant-in-Aid) 1983

JOSEPH BEUYS b.1921

T 03594
Four Blackboards 1972
Not signed: numerous expository inscriptions on blackboard
Chalk on four blackboards, each $47\frac{7}{8} \times 36 \times \frac{3}{4}$ (121.6 × 91.4 × 18)
Transferred from the Archive 1983

T 03825
Untitled (Vitrine) 1983
Not inscribed
Mixed media in glass, plywood and wood cabinet on steel framework, $81\frac{1}{8} \times 86\frac{5}{8} \times 19\frac{3}{4}$ (206 × 220 × 50)
Purchased from Anthony d'Offay Ltd (Grant-in-Aid) 1984

T 03826
Untitled (Vitrine) 1983
Not inscribed
Mixed media in glass, plywood and wood cabinet on steel framework, $81\frac{1}{8} \times 86\frac{5}{8} \times 19\frac{3}{4}$ (206 × 220 × 50)
Purchased from Anthony d'Offay Ltd (Grant-in-Aid) 1984

PETER BLAKE b.1932

T 03419
The First Real Target 1961
Inscribed 'THE FIRST REAL TARGET?' across the top, and 'PETER BLAKE, "THE FIRST REAL TARGET"/JUNE 1961.' on stretcher
Household gloss enamel on canvas and collage on hardboard, $21\frac{1}{8} \times 19\frac{7}{16}$ (53.7 × 49.3)
Purchased from the Waddington Galleries (Grant-in-Aid) 1982

T 03790
'The Meeting' or 'Have a Nice Day, Mr Hockney' 1981–3
Not inscribed
Oil on canvas, 39 × 49 (99.2 × 124.4)
Presented by the Friends of the Tate Gallery (purchased out of funds bequeathed by Miss Helen Arbuthnot) 1983

C.H. BLAYMIRES

T 03709
Inscription 'To be afraid'
Inscribed 'To be afraid and behave as if you/weren't afraid – *That is courage*/To be ashamed and behave as if you/weren't ashamed – *Is that courage!*/The Testament of Dominic Burleigh'
Portland stone, $15 \times 26\frac{3}{8} \times 3\frac{1}{2}$ (38 × 67 × 9)
Transferred from the Victoria and Albert Museum 1983

DAVID BOMBERG 1890–1957 and RICHARD MICHELMORE b.1928

T 03600
Recto: **Reclining Nude** 1953
Inscribed, b.l., 'Bomberg 53' and 'Michelmore'
Oil on board, $24 \times 36\frac{3}{8}$ (71.5 × 108)
Verso: **Reclining Nude** 1953
Inscribed, b.l., 'Bomberg 53' and 'Michelmore'
Oil on board, $24 \times 36\frac{3}{8}$ (71.5 × 108)
Presented by Richard Michelmore 1983

JAMES BOSWELL 1906–1971

T 03459
Le Sphinx 1939
Not inscribed
Black ink on paper, $12\frac{5}{8} \times 18\frac{1}{8}$ (32 × 46)
Presented by Ruth Boswell 1982

T 03460
Le Sphinx 1939
Not inscribed
Black ink on paper, $13\frac{1}{2} \times 19\frac{7}{8}$ (34.2 × 50.6)
Presented by Ruth Boswell 1982

T 03461
Recto: **Le Sphinx 4 a.m.** 1939
Inscribed 'Le Sphinx 4AM' b.r.
Black ink on paper, $13\frac{1}{2} \times 19\frac{7}{8}$ (34.1 × 50.5)
Verso: **Three figure studies** 1939
Not inscribed
Black ink with black and pink ink wash on paper, $19\frac{7}{8} \times 13\frac{1}{2}$ (50.5 × 34.1)
Presented by Ruth Boswell 1982

T 03462
Punch and Judy 1945
Not inscribed
Inks and gouache on paper, $6\frac{3}{4} \times 10\frac{15}{16}$ (17 × 27.7)
Presented by Ruth Boswell 1982

T 03463
Café, Kentish Town *c.*1947
Not inscribed
Inks and gouache on paper, $15\frac{1}{8} \times 20\frac{7}{8}$ (39.6 × 53)
Presented by Ruth Boswell 1982

ANDRE BRETON 1896–1966

T 03807
I saluted at six paces Commander Lefebvre des Noëttes 1942
Inscribed 'J'AI SALUÉ À SIX PAS/LE COMMANDANT LEFEBVRE DES NOËTTES' t.r., 'ET CACHÉ' near centre, 'BRAVAIT LE

HIBOU/TOUJOURS CLOUÉ' lower l., 'LA VIE' lower r., and 'ET SE REPARFUMAIT À LA TABLE MAGIQUE' across bottom
Collage with postcard, sewn thread, metal discs and pen and ink on paper, 13⅜ × 10½ (34 × 26.7)
Purchased from John Armbruster (Grant-in-Aid) 1983

A. BRIDGEWATER

T 03710
Inscription 'Remember Jane Snowfield'
Inscribed 'REMEMBER/JANE SNOWFIELD/ 1854 ÷ 1927'
Portland stone, 10⅝ × 21¼ × 2¾ (27 × 54 × 7)
Transferred from the Victoria and Albert Museum 1983

MARCEL BROODTHAERS 1924–1976

T 03696
Painting 1973
Not inscribed
Oil on nine unstretched canvases, each 31½ × 39½ (80 × 100.3)
Purchased from the Galerie Michael Werner (Grant-in-Aid) 1983

GÜNTER BRUS b.1938

T 03695
Run-through of an Action 1966
Seventeen pages of drawing, diagram and text, most inscribed 'Brus' or 'Brus 66' b.r.
Pencil and blue ball-point pen on paper, each 7⅞ × 8¼ (20 × 20.9) or 8¼ × 7⅞ (20.9 × 20)
Purchased from the Galerie Heike Curtze (Grant-in-Aid) 1983

REG BUTLER 1931–1981

T 03392
Maquette for 'Woman' 1949
Not inscribed
Forged and welded iron, 12½ × 4¼ × 4⅛ (31.7 × 10.9 × 10.7) including brick base
Purchased from Maxwell Davidson (Grant-in-Aid) 1982

T 03703
Musée Imaginaire 1963
Thirty-nine figures of various heights, each stamped 'RB' and '2/9'
Bronze, in wooden display cabinet, 31½ × 48½ × 4¾ (80 × 123.1 × 120)
Purchased from the Galería Freites (Grant-in-Aid) 1983

T 03711
Crouching Woman I 1948
Not inscribed
Forged and welded iron, 7½ × 4 × 2 (19 × 10 × 5)
Transferred from the Victoria and Albert Museum 1983

RICHARD CARLINE 1896–1980

T 03597
The Jetty, Seaford 1920
Inscribed 'Richard Carline 1920.' b.r. and 'sea shore/Richard Carline/14A Downshire Hill/Hampstead' on top turnover of canvas
Oil on canvas, 37 × 22⅛ (102 × 63)
Presented by Mrs Nancy Carline 1983

ANTHONY CARO b.1924

T 03455
Emma Dipper 1977
Not inscribed
Steel, rusted and painted grey, 84 × 67 × 126 (213.4 × 170.2 × 320)
Presented by the artist 1982

T 03457
Tundra 1975
Not inscribed
Steel, 105 × 228 × 52 (272 × 579 × 132)
Purchased from T. M. and P. M. Caro (Grant-in-Aid) 1982

EUGENE CARRIERE 1849–1906

T 03638
Head of a Child
Inscribed 'EUGENE CARRIERE' b. centre
Oil on board, 9¾ × 6¾ (24.7 × 17.1)
Presented anonymously in memory of Terence Rattigan 1983

JESSE DALE CAST 1900–1976

T 03598
The Windmill 1934
Inscribed 'J. Dale Cast' b.r. and on reverse 'Jesse Dale Cast, 73B Southside, Clapham Common SW4' and '"The Windmill" £300.'
Oil on canvas, 17 × 21½ (43.2 × 54.6)
Presented by David Cast, the artist's son, 1983

T 03599
Self Portrait 1934
Inscribed 'JDC 34' b.r.
Pastel on paper, 15¾ × 11½ (40.2 × 29)
Presented by David Cast, the artist's son, 1983

LYNN CHADWICK b.1914

T 03712
Conjunction
Inscribed 'CIRC 37-1954' underneath
Wrought iron and composition, 16½ × 11¾ × 7⅞ (42 × 30 × 20)
Transferred from the Victoria and Albert Museum 1983

MARC CAMILLE CHAIMOWICZ b.1947

T 03384
Le Désert, Chapter for Café du Rêve 1981
Inscribed 'Marc C.C.81' on each panel and 'Marc C.C. Spring 81' b.r. on last panel
Photographs, silkscreen, Xerox, acetate, watercolour and type on card, 13 framed panels, first panel 14⅜ × 11⅜ (36.5 × 29); remaining panels 37$\frac{9}{16}$ × 21 (37 × 53.3)
Purchased from Nigel Greenwood Inc. Ltd (Grant-in-Aid) 1982

WILLIAM CHAPPELL b.1907

T 03654
Young Man Playing a Guitar 1926
Inscribed 'chappell./1926' b.r.
Oil on papier maché, 11¼ × 8½ × ¾ (28.5 × 21.5 × 1.8)
Presented anonymously in memory of Terence Rattigan 1983

SANDRO CHIA b.1946

T 03469
Water Bearer 1981
Inscribed on back of canvas 'Sandro CHIA 1981' with an outline of a fish
Oil on pastel on canvas, 81½ × 67 (206.5 × 170)
Purchased from Anthony d'Offay Ltd (Grant-in-Aid) 1982

GEOFFREY CLARKE b.1924

T 03713
Head 1952
Not inscribed
Forged iron on stone base, 7⅛ × 3½ × 4⅜ (18.1 × 8.9 × 11.2)
Transferred from the Victoria and Albert Museum 1983

ROBERT CLATWORTHY b.1928

T 03714
Bull 1956
Inscribed 'CIRC 179–157' inside
Bronze, 7⅛ × 14⅞ × 5⅞ (18 × 38 × 15)
Transferred from the Victoria and Albert Museum 1983

FRANCESCO CLEMENTE b.1952

T 03551
The Midnight Sun II 1982
Not inscribed
Oil on canvas, 79 × 98¾ (201 × 250.7)
Purchased from Anthony d'Offay Ltd (Grant-in-Aid) 1983

PRUNELLA CLOUGH b.1919

T 03450
Yellow Mesh 1981
Inscribed '↑ Clough' on reverse
Oil on canvas, 48 × 75¼ (121.7 × 191.2)
Purchased from the New Art Centre (Knapping Fund) 1982

T 03451
Wire and Demolition 1982
Inscribed '↑ Clough' on reverse
Oil on canvas, 60 × 65¾ (152 × 167)
Purchased from the artist (Grant-in-Aid) 1982

T 03810
The White Root 1948
Inscribed 'Clough' and illegible date b.r. and on reverse '↑ ' and 'Mr Bowas . . . .' (illegible)
Oil on board, 19 × 15½ (50.5 × 39.5)
Purchased from Fischer Fine Art Ltd (Grant-in-Aid) 1983

SIR WILLIAM COLDSTREAM b.1908

T 03704
Seated Nude 1951–2
Inscribed 'William Coldstream. / Painted for Adrian Stokes.' on top turnover of canvas
Oil on canvas, 42 × 27⅞ (106.7 × 70.7)
Purchased from Mrs Ann Stokes Angus (Grant-in-Aid) 1983

CONSTANT b.1920

T 03705
Après Nous la Liberté 1949
Inscribed 'Constant/1949' centre and 'Constant 57 rue Pigalle IX' on stretcher
Oil on canvas, 55 × 42 (139.5 × 106.6)
Purchased from the Galerie van de Loo (Grant-in-Aid) 1983

JAMES COWIE 1886–1956

T 03549
An Outdoor School of Painting 1938–41
Inscribed 'J.Cowie' b.r.
Oil on canvas, 34 × 65 (86.4 × 165.1)
Purchased from Dr Barbara Cowie (Grant-in-Aid) 1983

STEPHEN COX b.1946

T 03794
Gethsemane 1982
Not inscribed
15 carved pieces of peperino stone, overall size 118 × 236 × 3½ (229.7 × 599.4 × 9)
Purchased from Nigel Greenwood Inc. Ltd (Grant-in-Aid) 1983

TONY CRAGG b.1949

T 03791
Axe Head 1982
Not inscribed
Wood and mixed media, 48 elements, overall dimensions approximately 43 × 154¾ × 193 (109.2 × 393.1 × 490.2)
Purchased from the Lisson Gallery (Grant-in-Aid) 1983

JOHN CRAXTON b.1922

T 03836
Dreamer in a Landscape 1942
Inscribed ' – Craxton 42 –' lower edge near centre
Ink and white chalk on paper laid on board, 21 13/16 × 29⅞ (55.4 × 75.9)
Purchased from Christopher Hull (Grant-in-Aid) 1984

T 03837
Dark Landscape 1944–5
Inscribed 'Craxton '44' b.r.
Oil on board, 21½ × 27¾ (54.6 × 70.5)
Purchased from Christopher Hull (Grant-in-Aid) 1984

T 03838
Pastoral for P.W. 1948
Inscribed '(to-P-W.) Craxton 48' b.l.
Oil on canvas, 78½ × 103⅜ (204.5 × 262.6)
Purchased from Christopher Hull (Grant-in-Aid) 1984

CARLOS CRUZ-DIEZ b.1923

T 03715
Physichromie 1964
Not inscribed
Construction of perspex, paper and board, painted, 15¾ × 9⅛ × 1⅝ (40 × 23 × 4)
Transferred from the Victoria and Albert Museum 1983

HUBERT DALWOOD 1924–1976

T 03474
Maquette for 'Arbor' 1971
Not inscribed
Painted plaster on wood, 14 × 19 × 18 (35.5 × 48.5 × 45.7)
Purchased from the New Art Centre (Gytha Trust) 1982

T 03475
O.A.S. Assassin 1962
Inscribed 'RF' on both sides of crest, one in reverse
Painted aluminium and ribbon, 30⅛ × 20 × 13⅜ (76.5 × 51 × 34)
Purchased from Gimpel Fils (Knapping Fund) 1982

T 03716
Lucca 1958
Inscribed 'XX 243–60 LUCCA V&A 1960' under wooden base
Painted aluminium, 26 × 24⅜ × 9½ (66 × 62 × 24)
Transferred from the Victoria and Albert Museum 1983

HANNE DARBOVEN b.1941

T 03410
Construction 19 × 42/60 Part 2 1975
Inscribed on centre of index panel
'hanne darboven, 1975.'
Writing and offset printing ink on paper,
mounted on board; 10 framed panels and
framed index, each panel 74 × 87
(188 × 221), index 37 × 86 (94 × 218.5)
Purchased from Sperone Westwater
Fischer Inc. (Grant-in-Aid) 1982

HONORE DAUMIER 1808–1879

T 03593
The Serenade c.1858
Not inscribed
Oil on panel, 12 × 15$\frac{9}{16}$ (30.5 × 39.5)
Bequeathed by Mrs A. F. Kessler 1983

ALAN DAVIE b.1920

T 03815
Village Myths No.36 1983
Inscribed on back of canvas 'Alan Davie/
June 83' and 'Village Myths No.36/
84″ × 68″/Opus 01019 June 83'
Oil on canvas, 84 × 68 (213.3 × 172.7)
Purchased from Gimpel Fils (Grant-in-
Aid) 1983

EDGAR DEGAS 1834–1917

T 03563
Woman in a Tub c.1885
Inscribed 'Degas' t.r.
Pastel on paper, 27$\frac{1}{2}$ × 27$\frac{1}{2}$ (70 × 70)
Bequeathed by Mrs A. F. Kessler 1983

PAUL DELVAUX b.1897

T 03361
Leda 1948
Inscribed 'P. DELVAUX/I-48' b.l.
Oil on blockboard, 60$\frac{1}{8}$ × 37$\frac{3}{8}$ (152.7 × 95)
Purchased from the executors of Sir
Robert Adeane through the Mayor
Gallery (Grant-in-Aid) 1982

GUNTHER DEMNIG b.1947

T 03521
Blood Trail (Kassel/London) 1981
a) Machine, 31$\frac{1}{2}$ × 19$\frac{1}{4}$ × 86 (80 × 50
× 218.5)
Not inscribed
b) Canvas, 223 × 24 (562 × 60)
Inscribed 'Blutspur Demnig 81 Kassel-
London Tate Gallery AM 23.9.81
Gunther Demnig'
Presented by the artist 1982

ANDRE DERAIN 1880–1954

T 03368
**Portrait of Madame Derain in a
White Shawl** c.1919–20
Not inscribed
Oil on canvas, 76$\frac{3}{4}$ × 38$\frac{3}{8}$ (195.5 × 97.5)
Purchased from the artist's son André
Derain through Stoppenbach and
Delestre Ltd (Grant-in-Aid) 1982

FRANÇOIS DESNOYER
1894–1972

T 03406
The Grand Port at Sète 1950
Inscribed 'DESNOYER' b.r.
Oil on canvas, 44$\frac{7}{8}$ × 63$\frac{3}{4}$ (114 × 162)
Presented by Mme Souza Desnoyer 1982

MICHAEL DILLON

T 03717
Op Structure 1967
Not inscribed
Construction of coloured, opalescent
and transparent perspex, 36 × 14$\frac{1}{8}$ × 5$\frac{3}{8}$
(91 × 36 × 13.6)
Transferred from the Victoria and
Albert Museum 1983

T 03718
Op Structure 1967
Not inscribed
Construction of coloured, opalescent
and transparent perspex, 26$\frac{3}{4}$ × 28$\frac{3}{4}$ × 18$\frac{1}{8}$
(68 × 73 × 46)
Transferred from the Victoria and
Albert Museum 1983

BRACO DIMITRIJEVIC b.1948

T 03684
**The Casual Passer-By I met at
11.28 A.M. London, October** 1972
Inscribed (text) 'The Casual Passer-By I
met at 11.28 A.M. [and then 'P.M.'
deleted]/London, Oct. 1972/Braco D./
Braco Dimitrijevic 1969'
3 photographs and one text mounted on
board, overall size 16$\frac{1}{8}$ × 40 (40.9 × 101.6)
Purchased from the Waddington
Galleries (Grant-in-Aid) 1983

T 03685
**Louvre ('J.M.W. Turner' 'Edward
Rampton')** 1975–9
'J.M.W Turner' inscribed 'JMW/TURNER'
on front of base, and 'Edward Rampton'
inscribed 'EDWARD/RAMPTON' on front of
base

Bronze on green marble base,
'J.M.W. Turner' 75$\frac{5}{8}$ × 13 × 13$\frac{3}{4}$
(187 × 33 × 35) and 'Edward Rampton'
73$\frac{1}{8}$ × 13 × 13$\frac{3}{4}$ (186 × 33 × 35)
Purchased from the Waddington
Galleries (Grant-in-Aid) 1983

T 03686
**Louvre ('Leonardo da Vinci' 'Albert
Evans')** 1975–9
'Leonardo da Vinci' inscribed 'LEONARDO/
DA/VINCI' on front of base, and
'Albert Evans' inscribed 'ALBERT EVANS'
on front of base
Bronze on green marble base, 'Leonardo
da Vinci' 72$\frac{1}{2}$ × 13 × 13$\frac{3}{4}$ (184.1 × 33 × 35)
and 'Albert Evans' 72 × 13 × 13$\frac{3}{4}$
(183 × 33 × 35)
Purchased from the Waddington
Galleries (Grant-in-Aid) 1983

T 03687
**Triptychos Post Historicus:
Entrance to the Palace of Light** 1982
Inscribed (engraved) on brass plate
centre b. 'BRACO DIMITRIJEVIC/
TRIPTYCHOS POST HISTORICUS/OR
ENTRANCE TO THE PALACE OF LIGHT/
TATE GALLERY 1982 / PART ONE:
ST BENEDETTO, LOOKING TOWARDS FUSINA
J.M.W. TURNER 1843/PART TWO: LIGHT
BULB INSTALLED BY PETER LOCKWOOD
1981 / PART THREE: PINEAPPLE'
Coloured photograph and brass title plate
mounted on card, overall size 44$\frac{3}{4}$ × 56$\frac{3}{4}$
(113.7 × 144.1)
Purchased from the Waddington
Galleries (Grant-in-Aid) 1983

T 03688
**Triptychos Post Historicus: Portrait
of Barry** 1982
Inscribed (engraved) on brass plate
centre b. 'BRACO DIMITRIJEVIC/
TRIPTYCHOS POST HISTORICUS/PORTRAIT
OF BARRY OR ARTISTS' HATS ARE HIGH
ABOVE THE RAINBOW/TATE GALLERY 1982/
PART ONE: "HENRI MATISSE" ANDRE
DERAIN 1905/ PART TWO: BARRY
FLANAGAN'S COAT AND HAT c.1970/PART
THREE: CUCUMBER AND APPLES'
Coloured photograph and brass title
plate mounted on card, overall size
45 × 56$\frac{1}{2}$ (114 × 143.5)
Purchased from the Waddington
Galleries (Grant-in-Aid) 1983

FRANK DOBSON 1888–1963

T 03719
Charnaux Venus 1933
Inscribed 'Charnaux' twice and 'A 24-1934' on base
Composition and plywood, in two pieces, painted, 67 × $19\frac{3}{4}$ × $15\frac{3}{4}$ (170 × 50 × 40)
Transferred from the Victoria and Albert Museum 1983
(Gift of Charnaux Patent Corset Co. Ltd 1934)

T 03720
Kneeling Figure 1935
Inscribed 'Dobson' on base and 'CIRC 320-1938' inside
Terracotta, $8\frac{1}{4}$ × $5\frac{1}{4}$ × $5\frac{3}{4}$ (21 × 13 × 15)
Transferred from the Victoria and Albert Museum 1983

T 03721
Crouching Woman 1923
Not inscribed
Bronze, $4\frac{3}{8}$ × $5\frac{3}{4}$ × $3\frac{1}{2}$ (11 × 14.6 × 8.9)
Transferred from the Victoria and Albert Museum 1983 (Gift of Dr Neville Goodman 1971)

THEO VAN DOESBURG 1883–1931

T 03374
Counter-Composition VI 1925
Inscribed 'THEO VAN DOESBURG/1925' on back of canvas
Oil on canvas, $19\frac{11}{16}$ × $19\frac{11}{16}$ (50 × 50)
Purchased from the Juda Rowan Gallery (Grant-in-Aid) 1982

JOHN DOUBLEDAY b.1947

T 03722
Maquette for 'Building Blocks' 1967
Inscribed 'Doubleday 1967' at back of base
Bronze, $10\frac{5}{8}$ × $5\frac{1}{8}$ × $2\frac{3}{4}$ (27 × 13 × 7) on stained wooden base, $1\frac{1}{8}$ × 5 × $2\frac{3}{4}$ (2.7 × 12.7 × 7)
Transferred from the Victoria and Albert Museum 1983 (Gift of William Gates 1979)

JEAN DUBUFFET b.1901

T 03679
The Ups and Downs 1977
Inscribed 'J.D.77' b.r. and 'n.42/Les vicissitudes' on back of canvas
Acrylic on paper mounted on canvas, $82\frac{3}{4}$ × $133\frac{1}{2}$ (210 × 339)
Purchased from the Pace Gallery (Grant-in-Aid) 1983

RAOUL DUFY 1877–1953

T 03564
Cornfield 1929
Inscribed 'Raoul Dufy' b. centre and again 'Raoul Dufy' b.r.
Oil on canvas, $51\frac{3}{16}$ × $63\frac{3}{4}$ (130 × 162)
Bequeathed by Mrs A. F. Kessler 1983

T 03565
Open Window at Saint-Jeannet *c.*1926–7
Inscribed 'Raoul Dufy' b.r.
Gouache on paper, $25\frac{3}{4}$ × 20 (65.6 × 50.7)
Bequeathed by Mrs A. F. Kessler 1983

T 03566
The Kessler Family on Horseback 1931
Not inscribed
Gouache on paper, $19\frac{5}{8}$ × $26\frac{3}{8}$ (50 × 66.9)
Bequeathed by Mrs A. F. Kessler 1983

T 03567
Landscape Study for 'The Kessler Family on Horseback' 1931
Not inscribed
Gouache on paper, $19\frac{3}{4}$ × 26 (50.3 × 66)
Bequeathed by Mrs A. F. Kessler 1983

SIR JACOB EPSTEIN 1880–1959

T 03358
Totem *c.*1913
Inscribed 'Epstein' b.r.
Pencil and watercolour on paper, $22\frac{7}{8}$ × $16\frac{3}{8}$ (58 × 41.5)
Purchased from Anthony d'Offay Ltd (Grant-in-Aid) 1982

JOHN ERNEST b.1922

T 03723
Triangulated Relief I 1965
Not inscribed
Construction of wood and formica, painted, $20\frac{7}{8}$ × $27\frac{1}{2}$ × $2\frac{1}{8}$ (53 × 70 × 6)
Transferred from the Victoria and Albert Museum 1983

MAX ERNST 1891–1976

T 03707
Dadaville *c.*1924
Not inscribed
Painted plaster and cork mounted on canvas, $26\frac{3}{4}$ × 22 × $2\frac{1}{2}$ (68 × 56 × 6.3)
Purchased from the Trustees of Sir Roland Penrose's Voluntary Settlement (Grant-in-Aid) 1983

FREDERICK ETCHELLS 1886–1973

T 03724
Inscription 'Let us now praise famous men' 1925
Inscribed 'LET US NOW PRAISE/FAMOUS MEN & OUR FATHERS/THAT BEGAT US + THE LORD/HATH WROUGHT GREAT GLORY/THROUGH THEM BY HIS GREAT/POWER FROM THE BEGINNING'
Stone, the letters painted, $20\frac{1}{8}$ × $35\frac{7}{8}$ × 1 (15 × 91 × 2.5)
Transferred from the Victoria and Albert Museum 1983

JOEL FISHER b.1947

T 03445
Wax Sculpture No. VIII 1982
Not inscribed
Three wax sculptures and three pencil drawings on hand-made paper mounted on board, dimensions of sculptures, $5\frac{1}{8}$ × 3 × $3\frac{1}{2}$ (13 × 7.5 × 9), $2\frac{1}{8}$ × 2 × $8\frac{3}{8}$ (5.3 × 5.1 × 21.3), $5\frac{1}{2}$ × $3\frac{1}{2}$ × $2\frac{3}{8}$ (14 × 9 × 6), dimension of mounted drawings, $17\frac{1}{8}$ × $30\frac{1}{2}$ (43.5 × 77.5)
Purchased from Nigel Greenwood Inc. Ltd (Grant-in-Aid) 1982

BARRY FLANAGAN b.1941

T 03608
Carving No. 13 1981
Not inscribed
Marble, 14 × $55\frac{1}{2}$ × 23 (35.5 × 141 × 58.5)
Purchased from the Waddington Galleries (Grant-in-Aid) 1983

T 03609
Carving No. 2 1981
Not inscribed
Five pieces of marble, overall size $24\frac{1}{2}$ × 24 × 24 (62.2 × 60.9 × 60.9)
Purchased from the Waddington Galleries (Grant-in-Aid) 1983

T 03725
Sand Muslin 2 1966
Not inscribed
Two muslin bags, sand, width about 12 (30.5)
Transferred from the Victoria and Albert Museum 1983

LUCIO FONTANA 1899–1968

T 03588
Natura 13 1959–60
Not inscribed
Bronze, 24 × 28¾ diameter (61 × 73)
Purchased from the Galerie Karsten Greve (Grant-in-Aid) 1983

EDWARD REGINALD FRAMPTON 1872–1923

T 03414
Brittany: 1914 *c.*1920
Inscribed 'E Reginald Frampton' b.r.
Oil on canvas, 30¼ × 36½ (76.8 × 92.6)
Purchased from a private collector through Roy Miles Fine Paintings Ltd (Grant-in-Aid) 1982

MEREDITH FRAMPTON b.1894

T 03415
Marguerite Kelsey 1928
Inscribed '19/MF/ 28', t.r., and 'MEREDITH FRAMPTON/90 CARLTON HILL. NW8. / LONDON / TITLE: WOMAN RECLINING' on horizontal cross-bar of stretcher. Reverse of canvas bears miscellaneous practical inscriptions
Oil on canvas, 47½ × 55⅝ (120.8 × 141.2)
Presented by the Friends of the Tate Gallery 1982

DAME ELISABETH FRINK b.1930

T 03416
In Memoriam I 1981
Inscribed 'Frink 3/6' on l. shoulder
Bronze, 50¼ × 43¼ × 26¾ (127.5 × 110 × 68)
Purchased from the Waddington Galleries (Grant-in-Aid) 1982

T 03417
In Memoriam II 1981
Inscribed 'Frink 3/6' on l. shoulder
Bronze, 49 × 46 × 26¾ (124.5 × 117 × 68)
Purchased from the Waddington Galleries (Grant-in-Aid) 1982

HENRI GAUDIER-BRZESKA 1891–1915

T 03726
The Dancer 1913
Inscribed 'H. Gaudier-Brzeska 1913' r. side of base
Painted plaster and metal, 31 × 7¼ × 7¼ (78.7 × 18.4 × 18.4)
Transferred from the Victoria and Albert Museum 1983
(Gift of Miss Sophie Brzeska 1918)

T 03727
Fallen Workman 1912
Inscribed 'A.88–1921' at back of base
Bronze, 12⅝ × 14½ × 15 (32 × 37 × 38)
Transferred from the Victoria and Albert Museum 1983
(Gift of A. E. Anderson 1921)

T 03728
Sleeping Fawn *c.*1913–14
Inscribed 'A 25–1939' underneath
Painted plaster, 4½ × 10 × 8½ (11.4 × 25.4 × 21.6)
Transferred from the Victoria and Albert Museum 1983
(Gift of the Leicester Galleries 1939)

T 03729
Crouching Fawn *c.*1913–14
Inscribed 'A.26–1939' underneath
Painted plaster, 10 × 12 × 5 (25.4 × 30.5 × 12.7)
Transferred from the Victoria and Albert Museum 1983
(Gift of the Leicester Galleries 1939)

T 03730
Head of an Idiot *c.*1912
Inscribed 'CIRC 47–1951' inside
Painted plaster, 7⅛ × 5½ × 6½ (18 × 14 × 16.5)
Transferred from the Victoria and Albert Museum 1983
(Gift of A. Zwemmer 1951)

T 03731
Torso of a Girl 1913
Not inscribed
Marble, 14 × 4⅛ × 3 (35.6 × 10.5 × 7.6)
Transferred from the Victoria and Albert Museum 1983
(Gift of Miss Sophie Brzeska 1915)

T 03732
Figure *c.*1912–13
Not inscribed
Bronze, 4½ × 2 × 1⅞ (11.4 × 5 × 4.8)
Transferred from the Victoria and Albert Museum 1983
(Gift of Dr Neville Goodman 1971)

ARTHUR GIARDELLI b.1911

T 03799
The Sea is all about us 1982
Inscribed on back '30 April 17 July 1982' and 'The Sea is all about us, Arthur Giardelli'
Acrylic, watercolour and paper construction on plywood, 32 × 32 (81.3 × 81.3)
Presented by Mr and Mrs Eric Estorick 1983

STEPHEN GILBERT b.1910

T 03698
Untitled 1948
Inscribed 'Stephen Gilbert 1948' on back of canvas
Oil on canvas, 21 × 28¼ (53.3 × 71.7)
Purchased from the artist (Knapping Fund) 1983

GILBERT AND GEORGE b.1943, b.1942

T 03452
The Nature of our Looking 1970
Each sheet of paper inscribed 'Art for All 1970 The Sculptors Gilbert and George' at bottom
Graphite on five separate sheets of paper:
(1) 'The Nature of our Looking' (1) 103 × 46 (263 × 118)
(2) 'The Nature of our Looking' (2) 103 × 35 (263 × 90)
(3) 'Here in the Country's Heart where the Grass is Green we stand very Still and Quiet' 152 × 106 (385 × 270)
(4) 'Forever we will search and give our Thoughts to the Picture we have in our Mind. We are walking round now as sad as can be' 137 × 93 (348 × 236)
(5) 'We believe that Love is the Path for a Better World of Art in which Good & Bad give way for Gilbert and George to be' 110 × 143 (278.5 × 362)
Purchased from Anthony d'Offay Ltd (Grant-in-Aid) 1982

ERIC GILL 1882–1940

T 03449
Christ 1922
Inscribed on base, not by the artist, 'Original carving made by Eric Gill to decorate a baby's crib'
Painted wood, outline drawing on reverse in red ink, $5\frac{1}{2} \times 13\frac{1}{2} \times \frac{1}{2}$ ($14 \times 34.1 \times 1.2$), excluding base
Purchased from Anthony d'Offay Ltd (Grant-in-Aid) 1982

T 03477
Ecstasy 1910–11
Inscribed with eye on hand monogram on r. edge
Portland stone, $54 \times 18 \times 9$ ($137.2 \times 45.7 \times 22.8$)
Purchased from Mrs D. Webber (Grant-in-Aid) 1982

T 03733
Alphabet and Numerals 1909
Inscribed 'ABCDEFGHIJ/KLMNOPQR/STUVWXY&Z/123/456/789 TAX AD/A.E.R. GILL Lettercutter Pub. by JOHN HOGG Paternoster Row, London C. SMITH & SONS Moulders, Kentish Town, London'
Hoptonwood stone, $13 \times 24\frac{3}{8} \times 2\frac{3}{8}$ ($32.9 \times 61.8 \times 6$)
Transferred from the Victoria and Albert Museum 1983

T 03734
Two Alphabets and Numerals 1909
Inscribed 'Aabcdefghijklmno/pqqrstuvw xyz & */abcdefghijklmnopqrst/uvwxyz* 1234567890/A.E.R. GILL Letter-cutter Pub. by JOHN HOGG Paternoster Row, London. C. SMITH & SONS, Moulders, Kentish Town, London'
Hoptonwood stone, the letters painted, $13 \times 18\frac{1}{4} \times 2\frac{1}{2}$ ($33 \times 46.3 \times 6.4$)
Transferred from the Victoria and Albert Museum 1983

T 03735
Alphabet 1909
Inscribed 'ABCDEFGH/IJKLMNOP/QRSTUVW/XYZ/A.E.R. GILL/Letter-cutter Pub. by JOHN HOGG Paternoster Row, London/ C. SMITH & SONS Moulders/ Kentish Town, London'
Hoptonwood stone, the letters painted, $12\frac{3}{8} \times 17 \times 3\frac{1}{8}$ ($32 \times 43.2 \times 7.9$)
Transferred from the Victoria and Albert Museum 1983

T 03736
Crucifix 1910–14
Inscribed 'O.E. FELICEM' at foot of cross
Hoptonwood stone, $17\frac{3}{4} \times 6\frac{3}{4} \times 1\frac{1}{2}$ ($45.5 \times 17.5 \times 3.8$)
Transferred from the Victoria and Albert Museum 1983

T 03737
The North Wind 1928
Inscribed 'A. 10 19 . .' (illegible) on top edge
Portland stone, $10 \times 27\frac{1}{2} \times 4$ ($25.4 \times 69.8 \times 10.1$)
Transferred from the Victoria and Albert Museum 1983

T 03738
Inscription 'Ex Divina Pulchritudine' 1926
Inscribed 'EX DIVINA/PVLCHRITVDINE/ESSE OMNIVM/DERIVATVR'
Hoptonwood stone, the letters painted, $14\frac{1}{8} \times 20\frac{1}{8} \times 3\frac{1}{8}$ ($35.8 \times 51.1 \times 7.9$)
Transferred from the Victoria and Albert Museum 1983

T 03739
Alphabet 1927
Inscribed 'ABCDEF/GHIJKLM/NOPQRST/UVWXYZ'
Hoptonwood stone, $21\frac{1}{8} \times 20\frac{1}{2} \times 2$ ($53.2 \times 52 \times 5$)
Transferred from the Victoria and Albert Museum 1983

T 03740
Alphabet 1927
Inscribed 'ABC/DEFGHIJKL/MNOPQRST/UVWXY&Z/SG 27'
Hoptonwood stone, $20\frac{1}{8} \times 21\frac{1}{2} \times 2$ ($51.2 \times 54.6 \times 5$)
Transferred from the Victoria and Albert Museum 1983

T 03741
Inscription 'Homines Divites' 1922
Inscribed 'HOMINES . DIVITES . IN . VIRTUTE/PULCHRITUDINIS . STUDIUM . HABENTES/PACIFICANTES . IN DOMIBUS . SUIS' and on top edge 'MISC 1–1947'
Portland stone, $9\frac{1}{2} \times 35\frac{1}{4} \times 1$ ($23.7 \times 89.7 \times 3.5$)
Transferred from the Victoria and Albert Museum 1983
(Gift of Lady Carmichael 1947)

T 03742
Inscription 'In Terra Pax' 1922
Inscribed 'IN TERRA PAX HOMINIBUS/BONÆ VOLUNTATIS' and on reverse 'Misc 2–1947'
Slate, $6 \times 32\frac{3}{4} \times 1$ ($15.4 \times 83.2 \times 2.7$)
Transferred from the Victoria and Albert Museum 1983
(Gift of Lady Carmichael 1947)

T 03743
Inscription 'Gloria in Altissimis Deo' 1922
Inscribed 'GLORIA/IN ALTISSIMIS/DEO' and on reverse 'Misc 3–1947'
Slate, $10 \times 21 \times 1$ ($25.3 \times 53.2 \times 2.5$)
Transferred from the Victoria and Albert Museum 1983
(Gift of Lady Carmichael 1947)

T 03744
Sundial 1924
Inscribed 'PENSA . CHE . QUESTO . DI/MAI . NON . RAGGIORNA/VI/VII/VIII/IX/X XI XII I/II/III/IV' and on reverse a monogram and 'MISC 4–1947'
Slate, with metal gnomon, $18\frac{1}{8} \times 15 \times 8\frac{3}{4}$ ($46 \times 38.1 \times 22.2$)
Transferred from the Victoria and Albert Museum 1983
(Gift of Lady Carmichael 1947)

T 03745
St. Sebastian 1919–20
Inscribed 'A. 10–1934' at back of base
Portland stone, $41 \times 8 \times 10$ ($104 \times 20.2 \times 25.4$)
Transferred from the Victoria and Albert Museum 1983

CHARLES GINNER 1878–1952

T 03841
Victoria Embankment Gardens 1912
Inscribed 'C. Ginner' b.r.
Oil on canvas, $26\frac{1}{8} \times 18\frac{3}{16}$ (66.4×46.1)
Purchased from Anthony d'Offay Ltd (Grant-in-Aid) 1984

DORA GORDINE b.1906

T 03746
Guadaloupe Head
Inscribed 'Dora Gordine 8/8' on back of head and 'C. VALSUANI CIRE PERDUE BRONZE' and 'CIRC. 80 1952' on back of neck
Bronze, $14\frac{1}{4} \times 9\frac{1}{8} \times 9\frac{1}{8}$ ($36 \times 23 \times 23$)
Transferred from the Victoria and Albert Museum 1983
(Bequest of Mrs A. O. Patullo 1952)

SPENCER GORE 1878–1914

T 03561
The Artist's Wife 1913
Not inscribed, but bears studio stamp
S.F.GORE, b.r.
Oil on canvas, $30\frac{1}{8} \times 25\frac{1}{16}$ (76.5 × 63.6)
Presented by Frederick Gore, R.A., 1983

ANTHONY GORMLEY b.1950

T 03681
Natural Selection 1981
Not inscribed
Twenty-three objects encased in lead, dimensions variable; total length when displayed approx. 432 (1097.3)
Presented by the Contemporary Art Society 1983

ALAN GREEN b.1932

T 03443
One to Four 1982
Inscribed 'ALAN GREEN/1982/ONE TO FOUR/1 OF 3 (LEFT PANEL)/←CENTRE' on back of left canvas, 'TOP/ALAN GREEN 1982/ONE TO FOUR (2 OF 3)/←(CENTRE PANEL)→' on back of centre canvas, 'ALAN GREEN 1982/ONE TO FOUR/3 OF 3/(RIGHT PANEL)/CENTRE→' on back of right canvas
Oil on canvas, three panels,
each $67\frac{1}{8} \times 67\frac{1}{8}$ (170.6 × 170.6)
Purchased from the Juda Rowan Gallery (Grant-in-Aid) 1982

T 03835
Check 1973
Inscribed 'ALAN GREEN 73/CHECK' on back of canvas
Acrylic on cotton canvas,
84 × 108 (213.4 × 274.3)
Purchased from the Juda Rowan Gallery (Grant-in-Aid) 1984

PHILIP GUSTON 1913–1980

T 03364
Black Sea 1977
Inscribed 'Philip Guston' b.r.
Oil on canvas, $68\frac{1}{8} \times 117$ (173 × 297)
Purchased from the David McKee Gallery (Grant-in-Aid) 1982

MAGGI HAMBLING b.1945

T 03542
Max Wall and his Image 1981
Inscribed 'Hambling/1981' on back of canvas
Oil on cotton duck canvas,
66 × 48 (167.7 × 121.9)
Presented by the Trustees of the Chantrey Bequest 1983

STANLEY WILLIAM HAYTER b.1901

T 03407
Teatro Olimpico 1980
Inscribed 'Hayter 80' b.r. and 'June 17 80 Teatro Olimpico' on reverse
Acrylic on canvas, $44\frac{3}{4} \times 57\frac{3}{8}$ (113.7 × 145.8)
Presented by the artist 1982

T 03408
Ophelia 1936
Inscribed 'Hayter 36' t.l. and 'Ophelia 36' and 'No. 11' on reverse, and 'No. 1 S.W. Hayter' on stretcher
Oil, casein tempera and gesso on canvas,
$39\frac{3}{8} \times 56\frac{7}{8}$ (100 × 144.5)
Purchased from the artist (Grant-in-Aid) 1982

DAME BARBARA HEPWORTH 1903–1975

T 03399
Ball, Plane and Hole 1936
Not inscribed
Teak, 8 × 24 × 12 (20.4 × 61.1 × 30.5)
Purchased from the Waddington Galleries (Grant-in-Aid) 1982

T 03749
Involute II 1956
Inscribed 'CIRC 249–1960' on side of base
Bronze, in two parts,
$16\frac{1}{4} \times 16\frac{1}{2} \times 14\frac{1}{4}$ (41 × 42 × 36)
Transferred from the Victoria and Albert Museum 1983

PATRICK HERON b.1920

T 03660
Cadmium with Violet, Scarlet, Emerald, Lemon and Venetian: 1969 1969
Inscribed 'Patrick Heron/1969' on back of canvas and 'Cadmium with Violet, Scarlet, Emerald, Lemon and Venetian: 1969' on stretcher
Oil on canvas, $78\frac{1}{4} \times 156\frac{1}{2}$ (198.5 × 379)
Presented by Lord McAlpine 1983

ANTHONY HILL b.1930

T 03750
Low Relief 1963
Inscribed on reverse '↑ANTHONY HILL 1963 24 CHARLOTTE STREET Ⓦ B 17 AH 63'
Construction, perspex and metal,
$13 \times 7\frac{1}{4} \times 12\frac{5}{8}$ (33 × 18.4 × 32)
Transferred from the Victoria and Albert Museum 1983

JOHN HOSKIN b.1921

T 03752
Black Beetle 1957
Inscribed 'HEAD→' and 'CIRC 188–1957' underneath
Welded iron wire,
$6\frac{3}{4} \times 6\frac{3}{4} \times 13\frac{3}{8}$ (17.2 × 17.2 × 31.4)
Transferred from the Victoria and Albert Museum 1983

JOHN HOYLAND b.1934

T 03701
April 1961 1961
Inscribed on canvas overlap 'HOYLAND APRIL 61'
Oil on canvas, $60 \times 60\frac{1}{8}$ (152.5 × 152.7)
Presented by E. J. Power 1983

JOHN HUBBARD b.1931

T 03371
Light Structure 1966
Inscribed on back of canvas ' "Light Structure"/68″ × 80″ 1966 / John Hubbard'
Oil on canvas, $67\frac{7}{8} \times 80$ (172.7 × 203.2)
Purchased from Fischer Fine Art (Grant-in-Aid) 1982

T 03372
Haytor Quarry 1981
Inscribed on back of canvas 'Haytor Quarry/1981 80″ × 76″' and 'John Hubbard'
Oil on canvas, 80 × 76 (203.2 × 193)
Purchased from Fischer Fine Art (Grant-in-Aid) 1982

MALCOLM HUGHES b.1920

T 03753
Maquette for 'Square Relief' 1968
Not inscribed
Construction, card on plywood, painted,
$13 \times 12\frac{1}{4}$ (33 × 31)
Transferred from the Victoria and Albert Museum 1983

T 03754
Square Relief 1968
Inscribed on reverse 'MALCOLM HUGHES
19 OXFORD RD: ↑ TOP LONDON SW15 * USE
PERSPEX ANTI-STATIC POLISH'
Construction, painted wood,
24 × 24 (61 × 61)
Transferred from the Victoria and
Albert Museum 1983

LOUISE HUTCHINSON
c.1897–1983

T 03751
Three-fold Head
Inscribed 'CIRC 74–1964' inside
Terracotta, 13 × 12⅝ × 7¼ (33 × 32 × 18)
Transferred from the Victoria and
Albert Museum 1983
(Gift of the Contemporary Art Society
1964)

PAUL HUXLEY b.1938

T 03589
Fable 1982
Inscribed on canvas turnover 'Paul
Huxley ↑ 77 × 77'
Acrylic on canvas, 77 × 77 (195.6 × 195.6)
Purchased from the Juda Rowan Gallery
(Grant-in-Aid) 1983

ALBERT IRVIN b.1922

T 03590
Empress 1982
Inscribed 'Irvin '82' on top turnover of
canvas
Acrylic on canvas, 84⅛ × 120 (213.5 × 304.7)
Purchased from Gimpel Fils (Knapping
Fund) 1983

**SIR WILLIAM GOSCOMBE
JOHN** 1860–1952

T 03747
Pan
Inscribed 'Goscombe John To Frank
Short' on r. of base
Bronze, 26¾ × 8¼ × 4¾ (68 × 21 × 12)
Transferred from the Victoria and
Albert Museum 1983
(Bequest of Miss Dorothea Short 1973)

WILLIAM JOHNSTONE
1897–1981

T 03659
Large Brush Drawing c.1975–6
Inscribed 'W Johnstone' b.l.
Black ink on paper, 36 × 51⅞ (91.6 × 131.8)
Presented anonymously in memory of
Terence Rattigan 1983

ALLEN JONES b.1937

T 03379
Wet Seal 1966
Inscribed 'Allen Jones Wet Seal 1966/
36″ × 36″' on stretcher and 'Allen Jones
1966' on back of canvas
Oil on canvas and wood with attached
melamine 36¾ × 36 × 4 (93.4 × 91.5 × 10)
Purchased from the Waddington
Galleries (Grant-in-Aid) 1982

DAVID JONES 1895–1974

T 03677
Sanctus Christus de Capel-y-ffin
1925
Inscribed 'DMJ 25' b.l. and 'SANCTVS
CHRISTVS DE CAPEL-Y-FFIN' in sky beside
body of Christ
Gouache and pencil on paper,
7⅝ × 5¼ (19.3 × 13.3)
Presented by the Friends of the Tate
Gallery 1983

KARIN JONZEN b.1914

T 03755
Head of a Youth
Inscribed 'KJ' on back of neck and
'CIRC 95–1964' on side of neck
Painted plaster, 6¼ × 4 × 5½ (16 × 10 × 14)
Transferred from the Victoria and
Albert Museum 1983
(Gift of the Contemporary Art Society
1964)

PETER JOSEPH b.1929

T 03467
**No.55: Green with Dark Blue
Surround** 1981
Inscribed 'Peter Joseph Oct '81' on top
overlap and 'Green with Dark Blue
Surround 55 65″ × 74″', on stretcher
Acrylic on canvas,
64¹⁵⁄₁₆ × 73½ (165 × 187.8)
Purchased from Gillespie-Laage-Salomon
(Grant-in-Aid) 1982

ANISH KAPOOR b.1954

T 03675
**As if to celebrate, I discovered a
mountain blooming with red flowers**
1981
Wood, cement, polystyrene and pigment,
3 elements, 38¼ (at highest point) × 30
(at widest point) × 63 (97 × 76.2 × 160);
13 × 28 × 32 (33 × 71.1 × 81.3);
8¼ × 6 × 18½ (21 × 15.3 × 47)
Purchased from the artist through the
Lisson Gallery (Grant-in-Aid) 1983

ALEX KATZ b.1927

T 03805
Hiroshi and Marsha 1981
Not inscribed
Oil on canvas, 72 × 96 (182.8 × 243.7)
Presented by Paul Schupf 1983

SIR GERALD KELLY 1879–1972

T 03650
Boulevard Montparnasse 1904
Inscribed 'Kelly' b. centre and on
reverse 'Boulevard Montparnasse
'04'
Oil on panel, 7 × 4⅝ (18 × 12)
Presented anonymously in memory of
Terence Rattigan 1983

T 03651
**Alex and Demary dancing in a
Music Hall at Algiers** 1906
Inscribed 'Kelly' b.l. and on reverse
'Alex and Demary dancing in a
Music Hall/at Alger at Alg/1st March
1906'
Oil on panel, 5⅞ × 7 (14.8 × 18)
Presented anonymously in memory of
Terence Rattigan 1983

T 03652
Terrace at Monte Carlo 1908
Inscribed on reverse 'Terrace at Monte
Carlo/Febry. 1908/Gerald Kelly'
Oil on panel, 5⅞ × 7⅛ (14.9 × 18)
Presented anonymously in memory of
Terence Rattigan 1983

T 03653
Beach at Etretat 1908
Inscribed on reverse 'Etretat Gr. Kelly
29 July 08'
Oil on panel, 8½ × 10⅝ (21.5 × 27)
Presented anonymously in memory of
Terence Rattigan 1983

ZOLTAN KEMENY 1907–1965

T 03595
Moonlight 1948
Inscribed ' "CLAIR DE LUNE"/KEMENY/ NO 344' on back of board
Oil on incised strawboard, $47\frac{3}{4} \times 29\frac{7}{8}$ (122.7 × 76.2)
Presented by Mme Madeleine Kemeny 1983

T 03596
Cat Mask 1947
Inscribed with studio stamp b.r. and 'KEMENY 314' on back of board
Painted relief-collage in plaster, canvas and lace, $16\frac{3}{4} \times 23\frac{5}{8} \times 3\frac{1}{8}$ (42.4 × 60 × 8)
Presented by Mme Madeleine Kemeny 1983

ANSELM KIEFER b.1945

T 03403
Parsifal I 1973
Inscribed 'Herzeleide' above centre right
Oil on paper laid down on canvas, $127\frac{7}{8} \times 86\frac{1}{2}$ (324.7 × 219.8)
Purchased from the Galerie Paul Maenz (Grant-in-Aid) 1982

T 03404
Parsifal II 1973
Inscribed 'Parsifal' above centre right and 'ither' above centre left
Oil and blood on paper laid down on canvas, $126\frac{5}{8} \times 86\frac{1}{8}$ (321.7 × 218.8)
Purchased from the Galerie Paul Maenz (Grant-in-Aid) 1982

T 03405
Parsifal III 1973
Inscribed 'Gamuret' and 'Fal parsi' centre top, 'Amfortas' and 'Titurel' centre right, 'Kundry' bottom right, 'Klingsor' bottom left, and 'Oh, wunden-wundervoller heiliger Speer!' along bottom edge
Oil and blood on paper laid down on canvas, $118\frac{3}{8} \times 171\frac{1}{16}$ (300.7 × 434.5)
Purchased from the Galerie Paul Maenz (Grant-in-Aid) 1982

KEN KIFF b.1935

T 03612
Person Cutting an Image 1965–71
Inscribed 'Ken Kiff' on reverse
Tempera and pastel on hardboard, 24 × 24 (61 × 61)
Purchased from the Nicola Jacobs Gallery (Grant-in-Aid) 1983

PETER KINLEY b.1926

T 03476
Fire 1982
Inscribed 'Fire 66 × 84 1982 P. Kinley' on stretcher
Oil on canvas, 66 × 84 (167.6 × 213.4)
Purchased from the Knoedler Gallery (Grant-in-Aid) 1982

OSKAR KOKOSCHKA 1886–1980

T 03829
Study for 'Ambassador Ivan Maisky' 1942
Not inscribed
Coloured pencil on paper, $14 \times 9\frac{15}{16}$ (35.5 × 25.3)
Presented by Mrs Olda Kokoschka 1984

T 03830
Study for 'Ambassador Ivan Maisky' 1942
Not inscribed
Coloured pencil on paper, $14 \times 9\frac{15}{16}$ (35.5 × 25.3)
Presented by Mrs Olda Kokoschka 1984

T 03834
The Crab 1939–40
Inscribed 'O.K.' b.l.
Oil on canvas, 25 × 30 (63.4 × 76.2)
Purchased from Marlborough Fine Art (Grant-in-Aid) with the aid of the NACF 1984

STANISLAV KOLÍBAL b.1925

T 03806
Identity 1982
Inscribed 'Kolíbal' on back of wood panel
Plaster, string, iron rod, nails, oil and crayon on wood, $57\frac{1}{2} \times 62\frac{3}{4} \times 10$ (146 × 159.5 × 25)
Presented anonymously 1983

HEINZ KOPPEL 1919–1980

T 03798
Snow, Sunshine, Rain 1957
Inscribed 'Snow. Sunshine. Rain' at lower edge
Oil on canvas, 48 × 86 (122 × 219)
Presented anonymously 1983

LEON KOSSOFF b.1926

T 03680
Two Seated Figures No.2 1980
Not inscribed
Oil on hardboard, 96 × 72 (243.8 × 182.8)
Purchased from Fischer Fine Art (Grant-in-Aid) 1983

JANNIS KOUNELLIS b.1936

T 03796
Untitled 1979
Not inscribed
Wall drawing, two impaled stuffed birds and five charcoal drawings on paper; height of birds 25 (63) and 17 (43), dimensions of drawings each $27\frac{3}{4} \times 39\frac{3}{8}$ (70.3 × 100); overall dimensions variable
Purchased from the Galleria Christian Stein (Grant-in-Aid) 1983

GERALD LAING b.1936

T 03842
Sky Diver VI 1964
Inscribed 'Skydiver 6 1964/Gerald Laing' on back of canvas
Oil and pencil on canvas mounted on two stretchers attached to one another, top one $22 \times 57\frac{3}{4}$ (55.9 × 146.7), lower one $58 \times 47\frac{5}{8}$ (147.3 × 121); overall dimensions $80 \times 57\frac{3}{4}$ (232 × 146.7)
Purchased from the artist (Grant-in-Aid) 1984

MAURICE LAMBERT 1901–1964

T 03756
Man with a Bird 1929
Inscribed 'ML' r. of base and 'A.35–1930' on stand
Serravezza marble, $35 \times 8 \times 7\frac{1}{2}$ (89 × 20.3 × 19)
Transferred from the Victoria and Albert Museum 1983
(Gift of H. Daniel Conner 1930)

PETER LANYON 1918–1964

T 03693
The Wreck 1963
Inscribed 'Wreck/Lanyon Dec. 63' on back of canvas
Oil on canvas, $48\frac{1}{8} \times 72\frac{1}{8}$ (122 × 183)
Presented by the Friends of the Tate Gallery 1983

JOHN LATHAM b.1921

T 03706
Observer IV 1960
Not inscribed
Mixed media, plaster, books, metal etc.,
96 × 72 × 15 (244 × 183 × 38)
Purchased from the artist (Grant-in-Aid)
1983

CHRISTOPHER LeBRUN b.1951

T 03454
Dream, Think, Speak 1981–2
Inscribed on reverse with a number of
titles crossed out, but the following
untouched: '19.12.81→13.1.82 /
Christopher LeBrun / Dream, Think,
Speak', and on overlap between right
outer side of canvas and right-hand
canvas turnover '19.12.81', a further
illegible date and a date crossed out
Oil on canvas, 96 × 90 (244 × 228.5)
Purchased from Nigel Greenwood Inc.
Ltd (Grant-in-Aid) 1982

JULIO LE PARC b.1928

T 03774
Construction 1965
Inscribed 'CIRC 30 1966' on reverse
Construction, wood and aluminium,
14¾ × 23¾ × 14½ (37 × 60 × 37), with
four double-sided printed cards,
each 14 × 14 (35.5 × 35.5)
Transferred from the Victoria and
Albert Museum 1983

JACQUES LIPCHITZ 1891–1973

T 03397
Half Standing Figure 1915
Inscribed 'J. Lipchitz/15' on back of base
Stone, 38½ × 11 × 7½ (98 × 28 × 18)
Purchased from Marlborough Fine Art
(Grant-in-Aid) with the help of the
Friends of the Tate Gallery, the
Rayne Foundation and Mrs Jack
Steinberg

T 03479 – 03535 presented by the
Jacques and Yulla Lipchitz Foundation
1982

T 03479
Gertrude Stein 1938
Inscribed 'J. Lipchitz' at back of neck
Terracotta, 12 × 10 × 8 (30.5 × 25.9 × 20.3)

T 03480
**Sketch for 'Bellerophon Taming
Pegasus'** 1964
Not inscribed
Plaster, 20¾ × 16 × 5 (52.2 × 40.7 × 12.7)

T 03481
**Sketch for 'Government of the
People'** 1967–8
Not inscribed
Plaster, 34 × 10¼ × 10¼ (86.4 × 26 × 26)

T 03482
Pregnant Woman 1912
Inscribed '13' under base
Plaster, 25¼ × 5¾ × 5 (64.2 × 14.6 × 12.2)

T 03483
The Rape of Europa 1938
Not inscribed
Painted plaster,
16 × 23½ × 13¼ (40.7 × 59.7 × 33.7)

T 03484
The Joy of Orpheus 1945
Not inscribed
Plaster, 20½ × 13½ × 10 (52.1 × 34.2 × 25.4)

T 03485
Spanish Servant Girl 1915
Inscribed 'Lipchitz' incised into base at
rear, with thumbprint
Plaster, 35 × 9 × 5½ (88.9 × 22.8 × 13.9)

T 03486
Bather III 1917
Not inscribed
Plaster, 29 × 10 × 10½ (73.7 × 25.4 × 26.7)

T 03487
Toreador 1914–15
Not inscribed
Plaster, 33¼ × 10½ × 10 (84.5 × 26.7 × 25.4)

T 03488
Seated Man with Clarinet I 1920
Inscribed 'JL-V-20' incised on base at rear,
and '96' in pencil on base at front
Plaster, 30½ × 11½ × 11 (77.5 × 59.7 × 58.4)

T 03489
Song of Songs 1944–6
Not inscribed
Painted plaster,
5½ × 8½ × 3½ (13.9 × 21.6 × 8.9)

T 03490
Picador c.1932
Not inscribed
Terracotta and plaster,
20 × 25½ × 4 (50.8 × 64.7 × 10.2)

T 03491
Sketch for 'Our Tree of Life' c.1962
Not inscribed
Plaster, 32½ × 10 × 10½ (82.5 × 25.4 × 26.7)

T 03492
Sculpture (Seated Woman) 1916
Not inscribed
Plaster, 46 × 14½ × 13½ (116 × 36.8 × 34.2)

T 03493
Sketch for 'Enterprise' c.1953
Inscribed '#' incised into top of base and
'396' and '40#' under base
Painted plaster,
11¾ × 13 × 6 (21.8 × 33 × 15.2)

T 03494
Head of Géricault 1933
Inscribed '131' inside neck
Terracotta, 9½ × 7 × 8 (24.1 × 17.7 × 20.2)

T 03495
David and Goliath 1933
Not inscribed
Plaster, 11 × 11 × 6 (27.9 × 27.9 × 15.2)

T 03496
Head and Hands 1932
Inscribed 'L' incised under base and
'427' inside
Terracotta, 7¾ × 6¼ × 3¾ (19.7 × 15.8 × 9.5)

T 03497
Study for 'Prometheus' 1936
Inscribed 'J. Lipchitz' incised under
base and '4' and '421' under base
Terracotta, 10⅜ × 9 × 4½ (26 × 22.7 × 11.4)

T 03498
Head, Bust and Arms 1932
Inscribed '979 6 off' under base
Terracotta, 7⅜ × 6½ × 3¾ (18.7 × 16.5 × 9.5)

T 03499
Seated Bather 1916
Inscribed '742' incised on base and '17'
(partly illegible) under base
Painted plaster,
29 × 9¾ × 10 (73.6 × 24.7 × 25.4)

T 03500
Study for 'Prometheus' 1936
Not inscribed
Painted plaster,
7½ × 9 × 3½ (19 × 22.8 × 8.9)

T 03501
Figure 1915
Not inscribed
Plaster, 19¾ × 5⅜ × 4 (50.2 × 13.6 × 10.1)

T 03502
First Study for 'Pastoral' 1934
Inscribed '104' under base
Terracotta, $4\frac{3}{4} \times 5 \times 3\frac{1}{4}$ (12 × 12.7 × 8.2)

T 03503
Reclining Figure 1929
Not inscribed
Terracotta, $6 \times 10 \times 4\frac{3}{4}$ (15.2 × 25.4 × 12)

T 03504
Bust of a Woman 1932
Not inscribed
Terracotta, $7\frac{1}{2} \times 4\frac{1}{4} \times 4\frac{1}{4}$ (19 × 10.8 × 10.8)

T 03505
Sketch for a Figure (Study for Ploumanach) 1926
Inscribed 'L' incised under base
Terracotta, $8\frac{1}{2} \times 4\frac{1}{4} \times 1\frac{1}{2}$ (21.6 × 10.8 × 3.8)

T 03506
The Snuffer 1930
Inscribed illegibly underneath and inside
Painted plaster,
$7 \times 6 \times 6$ (17.7 × 15.2 × 15.2)

T 03507
Head 1932
Not inscribed
Painted plaster,
$9 \times 5\frac{3}{4} \times 5\frac{1}{2}$ (22.8 × 14.6 × 13.9)

T 03508
Head of a Woman 1912
Inscribed '491' on back of head
Plaster, $6\frac{1}{4} \times 2\frac{1}{2} \times 2\frac{1}{4}$ (15.8 × 6.3 × 5.4)

T 03509
Musical Instruments – Bas Relief 1923
Not inscribed
Terracotta, $6\frac{1}{4} \times 8 \times 1$ (15.8 × 20.3 × 2.5)

T 03510
Meditation 1931
Inscribed '14' (twice) under base of arms
Plaster, $7\frac{3}{4} \times 7 \times 5\frac{3}{4}$ (19.7 × 17.8 × 14.6)

T 03511
Woman with Hair 1932
Not inscribed
Plaster, $5 \times 3\frac{1}{2} \times 2\frac{1}{2}$ (12.7 × 8.9 × 6.3)

T 03512
First study for 'Toward a New World' 1934
Not inscribed
Plaster, $4\frac{1}{4} \times 3\frac{1}{2} \times 2$ (10.8 × 8.9 × 5.1)

T 03513
Bull and Condor 1932
Inscribed 'J. Lipchitz' incised on base and '52' under base
Plaster, $8\frac{1}{4} \times 12\frac{1}{2} \times 6\frac{1}{4}$ (20.9 × 31.7 × 15.8)

T 03514
Study for a Monument 1934
Not inscribed
Plaster, partly painted,
$12\frac{1}{2} \times 3\frac{1}{2} \times 3\frac{1}{2}$ (31.7 × 8.9 × 8.9)

T 03515
David and Goliath 1933
Not inscribed
Plaster, $11 \times 11 \times 6$ (27.9 × 27.9 × 15.2)

T 03516
Jacob and the Angel 1931
Inscribed 'J. Lipchitz' incised under base and '53'
Plaster, $9\frac{3}{4} \times 13\frac{3}{4} \times 7\frac{1}{4}$ (24.7 × 34.9 × 18.4)

T 03517
First Study for 'Prometheus' 1931
Inscribed '67' under base
Plaster, $4\frac{3}{4} \times 11 \times 5\frac{1}{2}$ (12 × 27.9 × 14)

T 03518
Musical Instruments – Bas Relief 1923
Not inscribed
Plaster, $9\frac{3}{4} \times 8 \times 2\frac{1}{4}$ (24.8 × 20.3 × 5.7)

T 03519
Hagar 1948
Not inscribed
Painted plaster,
$6 \times 7\frac{1}{4} \times 4\frac{1}{4}$ (15.2 × 18.4 × 10.8)

T 03520
Reclining Woman 1921
Inscribed with an illegible number under base
Plaster, $3 \times 4\frac{1}{4} \times 1\frac{1}{2}$ (7.6 × 10.8 × 3.8)

T 03521
Woman Leaning on a Column 1929
Inscribed '32' under base
Painted plaster,
$10 \times 5\frac{1}{4} \times 3\frac{1}{2}$ (25.4 × 13.3 × 8.9)

T 03522
Dancer with Veil 1928
Inscribed '143 3 off' under base
Terracotta, $6\frac{3}{4} \times 3\frac{1}{4} \times 2\frac{3}{4}$ (17.4 × 7.9 × 7)

T 03523
Study for a Garden Statue 1921
Inscribed '144' under base
Plaster, $5\frac{1}{2} \times 1\frac{3}{8} \times 1\frac{1}{2}$ (14 × 3.5 × 3.8)

T 03524
Head of a Woman c.1920
Inscribed 'J. Lipchitz' incised at back of neck and '77' (twice) under base
Terracotta, $12 \times 8 \times 8\frac{1}{4}$ (33.5 × 20.3 × 20.9)

T 03525
Sketch for 'Our Tree of Life' c.1960
Not inscribed
Plaster, $22 \times 7 \times 9$ (55.8 × 17.7 × 22.8)

T 03526
Musical Instruments – Bas Relief 1919
Inscribed 'LI' and 'L' on reverse and '554' and 'B 3 OFF' at edge
Plaster, $15\frac{1}{4} \times 19 \times 3\frac{3}{4}$ (38.8 × 48.2 × 9.5)

T 03527
Variation on Theme of Hagar 1948
Inscribed 'JL' incised in monogram under base and '2 off' and '2' (partly illegible)
Plaster, $6 \times 9 \times 4$ (15.2 × 22.8 × 10.2)

T 03528
Sketch for Duluth Monument c.1963-5
Not inscribed
Plaster, $21 \times 5 \times 5$ (53.3 × 12.7 × 12.7)

T 03529
Guitar Player in Armchair 1922
Inscribed '1922 J. Lipchitz' incised on back and 'w' and '3 off GUITAR PLAYER IN ARMCHAIR 1922 251' under base
Plaster, $15\frac{1}{2} \times 11\frac{1}{2} \times 12$ (39.4 × 29.2 × 30.4)

T 03530
Mother and Child c.1949
Not inscribed
Plaster, $19 \times 11\frac{1}{4} \times 10$ (48.3 × 28.5 × 25.4)

T 03531
The Dance 1929
Not inscribed
Plaster, partly painted,
$3\frac{1}{4} \times 2\frac{1}{2} \times 2$ (8.2 × 6.3 × 5.1)

T 03532
Song of Songs 1945-8
Inscribed 'Lipchitz' under base
Plaster, $10\frac{3}{4} \times 38 \times 18\frac{1}{2}$ (27.3 × 96.6 × 47)

T 03533
Study for a Statue c.1936
Not inscribed
Plaster, $20\frac{1}{4} \times 10 \times 8\frac{3}{4}$ (51.4 × 25.4 × 22.2)

T 03534
Study for Hagar 1948
Inscribed 'JL / 10' at rear
Painted plaster,
$9\frac{1}{2} \times 8\frac{3}{4} \times 8$ (24.1 × 22.2 × 20.3)

T 03535
The Dance 1929
Inscribed 'JL' incised under base and
'150'
Terracotta, $3\frac{1}{4} \times 2\frac{1}{2} \times 2$ (8.2 × 6.3 × 5.1)

RICHARD LONG b.1945

T 03808
A Sculpture in Bristol 1965
Inscribed 'A Sculpture in Bristol/1965'
on card with text
I card with text and 7 black and white
photographs, each $11\frac{1}{8} \times 11\frac{1}{8}$ (27.6 × 27.6)
Purchased from Anthony d'Offay Ltd
(Grant-in-Aid) 1983

ROBERT LONGO b.1953

T 03782
Sword of the Pig 1983
Not inscribed
Left section: paint on melamine
laminate on wood relief,
$82\frac{1}{4} \times 87\frac{1}{8} \times 20\frac{1}{8}$ (209 × 221 × 51)
Centre section: charcoal and acrylic on
paper, $97\frac{5}{8} \times 49\frac{5}{8}$ (248 × 126)
Right section: silkscreen on aluminium,
$48\frac{5}{8} \times 96\frac{1}{2}$ (123.5 × 243.5)
Overall dimensions
$97\frac{5}{8} \times 231\frac{1}{8} \times 20\frac{1}{8}$ (248 × 588 × 51)
Presented by the Patrons of New Art
through the Friends of the Tate Gallery
1983

LEONARD McCOMB b.1930

T 03601
**Zarrin Kashi overlooking
Whitechapel High Street** 1981
Inscribed 'Leonard / McComb / 1981'
b.l., and 'My name is Zarrin   I am my
fathers daughter and my father loves me'
just above lower edge
Watercolour on paper laid on cotton
duck, $72\frac{1}{8} \times 74\frac{1}{4}$ (184 × 188)
Presented by the Trustees of the
Chantrey Bequest 1983

HEINZ MACK b.1931

T 03748
Relief 1964
Not inscribed
Aluminium relief over hardboard,
$14\frac{3}{8} \times 16\frac{3}{8} \times 1\frac{5}{8}$ (36.5 × 41.5 × 4)
Transferred from the Victoria and
Albert Museum 1983

STEPHEN McKENNA b.1939

T 03540
An English Oak Tree 1981
Inscribed 'SMcK' b.r., and 'Stephen
McKenna/ 1981 / OIL ON OIL' on reverse
Oil on canvas, $78\frac{3}{4} \times 59$ (200 × 150)
Purchased from the artist (Grant-in-Aid)
1982

T 03541
Venus and Adonis 1981
Inscribed 'SMcK' b.r., and 'Stephen
McKenna/ 1981 / OIL ON CANVAS/OIL
GROUND' on reverse
Oil on canvas, $59 \times 78\frac{3}{4}$ (150 × 200)
Purchased from the artist (Grant-in-Aid)
1982

BRUCE McLEAN b.1945

T 03411
**Study for 'Possibly a Nude by a Coal
Bunker'** 1980
Not inscribed
Black oil pastel and acrylic on
photographic paper, five panels,
each $157\frac{1}{2} \times 54\frac{5}{8}$ (400 × 138.7)
Purchased from Anthony d'Offay Ltd
(Grant-in-Aid) 1982

F.E. McWILLIAM b.1909

T 03758
Mother and Daugher 1952
Inscribed 'CIRC. 2 1953' under base
Plastic wood, $12\frac{5}{8} \times 15 \times 5\frac{1}{4}$ (32 × 38 × 12)
Transferred from the Victoria and
Albert Museum 1983

ARISTIDE MAILLOL 1861–1964

T 03757
Figure of a Woman
Inscribed 'AM' in monogram on base
Bronze, $10\frac{3}{8} \times 4\frac{3}{8} \times 4\frac{3}{8}$ (26.4 × 11.2 × 11.2)
Transferred from the Victoria and
Albert Museum 1983
(Gift of A. E. Anderson 1928)

PAUL MAITLAND 1863–1909

T 03622
Hyacinth in a Ginger Jar
Inscribed 'P Maitland' b.l.
Oil on canvas, $12 \times 9\frac{7}{8}$ (30.5 × 25)
Presented anonymously in memory of
Terence Rattigan 1983

T 03623
Factories Bordering the River
Inscribed 'P Maitland' b.l. and on
reverse 'No.12'
Oil on canvas, $10\frac{1}{8} \times 14\frac{1}{2}$ (25.7 × 37)
Presented anonymously in memory of
Terence Rattigan 1983

T 03624
The Sun Pier, Chatham
Inscribed 'P Maitland' b.l.
Oil on panel, $9\frac{5}{8} \times 10\frac{3}{4}$ (24.6 × 27.2)
Presented anonymously in memory of
Terence Rattigan 1983

T 03625
A Morning in Spring
Inscribed on reverse 'A morning in
spring by Paul Maitland' (not by the
artist)
Oil on panel, $11 \times 10\frac{1}{2}$ (28 × 26.5)
Presented anonymously in memory of
Terence Rattigan 1983

T 03626
Surrey Side of the River – Grey Day
Inscribed 'P Maitland' b.l. and on
reverse 'Surreyside of the river – grey
day by Paul Maitland' (not by the artist)
Oil on panel (cigar box lid),
$4\frac{1}{4} \times 8\frac{1}{4}$ (10.7 × 20.8)
Presented anonymously in memory of
Terence Rattigan 1983

T 03627
Warehouses across the River
Inscribed 'P Maitland' b.l.
Oil on panel, $5\frac{3}{8} \times 9\frac{1}{4}$ (13.7 × 23.5)
Presented anonymously in memory of
Terence Rattigan 1983

T 03628
Warehouses across the River
Inscribed 'Paul Maitland' b.r.
Oil on panel, $4\frac{1}{4} \times 6$ (11 × 15.2)
Presented anonymously in memory of
Terence Rattigan 1983

T 03629
Warehouses across the River
Inscribed 'P Maitland' b.l.
Oil on panel, $6\frac{1}{2} \times 5\frac{1}{8}$ (16.5 × 13)
Presented anonymously in memory of
Terence Rattigan 1983

T 03630
London Garden with Three Trees
Inscribed 'P.M.' b.l.
Oil on panel (cigar box lid),
$3\frac{7}{8} \times 7\frac{1}{8}$ (9.9 × 18)
Presented anonymously in memory of
Terence Rattigan 1983

T 03631
Fall of Leaves – Kensington Gardens
Inscribed 'PM' b.l.
Oil on panel (cigar box lid),
$5\frac{3}{8} \times 8\frac{1}{8}$ (13.6 × 20.6)
Presented anonymously in memory of
Terence Rattigan 1983

T 03632
Autumn – Kensington Gardens
Inscribed 'PM' b.l.
Oil on panel, $4\frac{1}{4} \times 6\frac{3}{4}$ (10.2 × 17.3)
Presented anonymously in memory of
Terence Rattigan 1983

T 03633
**The Flower Walk – Kensington
Gardens**
Inscribed 'PM' b.r.
Oil on panel, 5×7 (12.8 × 17.8)
Presented anonymously in memory of
Terence Rattigan 1983

T 03634
Kensington Gardens, Morning
Inscribed 'P Maitland' b.l.
Oil on panel, $4\frac{1}{4} \times 6\frac{7}{8}$ (10.8 × 17.5)
Presented anonymously in memory of
Terence Rattigan 1983

T 03635
The Embankment after a Shower
Inscribed 'P Maitland' b.l.
Oil on panel, $5\frac{3}{8} \times 8\frac{5}{8}$ (13.7 × 21.9)
Presented anonymously in memory of
Terence Rattigan 1983

T 03636
Buckinghamshire Fields, Autumn
Inscribed 'P Maitland' b.l.
Oil on panel, $5\frac{3}{4} \times 9\frac{1}{2}$ (14.6 × 24)
Presented anonymously in memory of
Terence Rattigan 1983

T 03637
A Yacht off Sheerness
Inscribed 'PM' b.l.
Oil on panel, $9\frac{1}{4} \times 5\frac{3}{8}$ (23.5 × 13.7)
Presented anonymously in memory of
Terence Rattigan 1983

RAYMOND MASON b.1922

T 03678
Barcelona Tram 1953
Inscribed on lower front edge 'A.BRUNI
FUSE. ROMA. Barcelona Raymond Mason
1953'
Bronze, $30\frac{3}{4} \times 49\frac{1}{4} \times 9\frac{3}{4}$ (78 × 125 × 250)
Purchased from the Pierre Matisse Gallery
(Grant-in-Aid) 1983

T 03797
**St. Mark's Place, East Village, New
York City** 1972
Inscribed 'Raymond Mason/1973 5/6' on
upper face of horizontal board at bottom
front of interior of box, and 'ST. MARK'S
PLACE EAST VILLAGE N.Y.C. as seen
through the window of the Village
East Coffee Shop. 1972', along front
edge of base-board of whole work
Acrylic on epoxy resin in glazed and
painted wood box,
$27 \times 49\frac{1}{16} \times 19\frac{3}{8}$ (68.5 × 124.9 × 49.1)
Presented by Mme Andrée Stassart 1983

HENRI MATISSE 1869-1954

T 03568
Cap d'Antibes 1922
Inscribed 'Henri-Matisse' b.r.
Oil on canvas, $19\frac{7}{8} \times 24\frac{1}{16}$ (50.6 × 61.2)
Bequeathed by Mrs A. F. Kessler 1983

BERNARD MEADOWS b.1915

T 03409
Black Crab 1952
Inscribed '(M) / $\frac{4}{4}$' on underside of larger
oval form
Bronze: $16\frac{3}{4} \times 13\frac{3}{8} \times 9\frac{1}{2}$ (42.5 × 34 × 24.2)
Purchased from the Whitechapel Art
Gallery (Grant-in-Aid) 1982

T 03759
Crab 1953
Inscribed 'CIRC 4-1953' underneath
Bronze, partly painted,
$5\frac{1}{8} \times 3\frac{1}{2} \times 4\frac{3}{8}$ (15.5 × 9 × 11)
Transferred from the Victoria and
Albert Museum 1983

T 03811
Lovers 1980
Not inscribed
Bronze on stone base,
$55\frac{1}{2} \times 22 \times 25\frac{1}{2}$ (141 × 55.8 × 64.7)
Presented by the Friends of the Tate
Gallery 1983

ELSE MEIDNER b.1901

T 03694
Death and the Maiden c.1940-50
Not inscribed
Charcoal on paper,
$21\frac{5}{8} \times 19\frac{3}{4}$ (55 × 49.7)
Presented by Dr J. P. Hodin 1983

MARIO MERZ b.1925

T 03673
Fibonacci Tables 1970
Not inscribed
Charcoal, acrylic and metallic paint with
neon on cotton canvas,
$105 \times 150\frac{1}{2}$ (266.7 × 382.2)
Purchased from Anthony d'Offay Ltd
(Grant-in-Aid) 1983

T 03674
Cone 1966
Not inscribed
Willow basket work,
$87 \times 51 \times 51$ (221 × 129.5 × 129.5)
Purchased from Anthony d'Offay Ltd
(Grant-in-Aid) 1983

JOAN MIRÓ 1893-1983

T 03401
Woman 1949
Inscribed 'Miró $\frac{1}{4}$' and stamped with
foundry mark inside cast
Bronze, $7\frac{3}{8} \times 10\frac{3}{8} \times 8\frac{3}{4}$ (18.6 × 26.4 × 22.4)
Purchased from the Waddington
Galleries (Grant-in-Aid) 1982

T 03402
The Tightrope Walker 1970
Inscribed 'Miró 2/2' and stamped with
foundry mark on back
Bronze and steel on wooden base,
$22 \times 11 \times 5\frac{7}{8}$ (56 × 28 × 15)
Purchased from the Waddington
Galleries (Grant-in-Aid) 1982

T 03690
**A Star caresses the Breast of a
Negress (Painting-Poem)** 1938
Inscribed 'miró' b.l. and 'une étoile/
caresse le sein d'une/négresse' t.l.; also
'JOAN MIRÓ./peinture-poème./IV-938.' on
back of canvas
Oil on canvas, $51 \times 76\frac{1}{2}$ (129.5 × 194.3)
Purchased from the Pierre Matisse
Gallery (Grant-in-Aid) 1983

T 03691
Message from a Friend 1964
Inscribed on back of canvas 'MIRÓ.
"MESSAGE/D'AMI" ' and '12/4/64'
Oil on canvas, $103\frac{1}{4} \times 108\frac{1}{2}$ (262 × 275.5)
Purchased from the Galerie Maeght
(Grant-in-Aid) with a substantial
contribution from funds bequeathed by
Miss H. M. Arbuthnot through the
Friends of the Tate Gallery 1983

AMEDEO MODIGLIANI
1884–1920

T 03569
Madame Zborowska 1918
Inscribed 'modigliani' b.r.
Oil on canvas, 25⅜ × 18⅛ (64.5 × 46)
Bequeathed by Mrs A. F. Kessler 1983

T 03570
Caryatid with a Vase 1914
Inscribed 'modigliani' b.r.
Watercolour and crayon on paper, 25 × 19 (63.3 × 48.1)
Bequeathed by Mrs A. F. Kessler 1983

T 03760
Head *c.*1911–12
Inscribed 'MODI/GLIANI' on back of base
Euville stone, 25 × 5 × 13⅞ (63.5 × 12.5 × 35)
Transferred from the Victoria and Albert Museum 1983

SIR THOMAS MONNINGTON
1902–1976

T 03832
Trees and Rocks 1952
Not inscribed
Pencil on paper, 19¾ × 25 (50.3 × 63.5)
Purchased from Lady Monnington (Grant-in-Aid) 1984

T 03833
Trees *c.*1938
Not inscribed
Oil on canvas, 14 × 17⅞ (35 × 45.2)
Purchased from Lady Monnington (Grant-in-Aid) 1984

HENRY MOORE O.M. b.1898

T 03761
Reclining Figure 1939
Inscribed 'CIRC 17–1940' underneath
Lead, 5⅞ × 11 × 4 (15 × 28 × 10)
Transferred from the Victoria and Albert Museum 1983

T 03762
Head 1928
Inscribed 'CIRC 11–1950' at r. side
Cast concrete, 7⅞ × 7⅛ × 5⅛ (20 × 18 × 13)
Transferred from the Victoria and Albert Museum 1983
(Gift of H. Bergen 1950)

T 03763
Three Motifs against a Wall No.1
1958
Inscribed 'CIRC 234–1961' on reverse
Bronze, 19⅞ × 42½ × 17⅞ (50.5 × 108 × 44)
Transferred from the Victoria and Albert Museum 1983

SIR CEDRIC MORRIS, Bt
1889–1982

T 03592
Patisseries and a Croissant *c.*1922
Inscribed 'C.MORRIS' and indecipherable date, b.r.
Oil on canvas, 14⅛ × 12⅞ (35.9 × 32.7)
Presented by Miss Nancy Morris 1983

T 03831
Frances Hodgkins *c.*1917
Not inscribed
Gouache on paper, 9½ × 6⅜ (24.2 × 16.2)
Presented by the Executor of Frances Hodgkins 1984

DAVID NASH b.1945

T 03470
Standing Frame 1982
Not inscribed
Beech wood, ht. 108 (274)
Purchased from the artist (Grant-in-Aid) 1982

T 03471
Rostrum with Bonks 1971
Not inscribed
Pine, chestnut, ash and birch woods, 68½ × 24¾ × 24¾ (174 × 63 × 63)
Purchased from the artist (Grant-in-Aid) 1982

T 03472
Wood Quarry, Otterlo 1982
Inscribed 'Wood Quarry – Beech, Otterlo, May 1982 David Nash' centre top and with numerous titles
Charcoal and earth on paper, 48⅛ × 95½ (122.4 × 242.6)
Purchased from the artist (Grant-in-Aid) 1982

T 03473
Family Tree 1967–1982 1982
Inscribed 'FAMILY TREE 1970–'82. David Nash '82' b.l. and with numerous titles and dates
Charcoal, chalk and pastel on paper, 38⅛ × 74¼ (96.9 × 188.4)
Purchased from the artist (Grant-in-Aid) 1982

PAUL NASH 1889–1946

T 03820
The Colne 1925
Inscribed 'Paul Nash/1925' b.r.
Watercolour and gouache on paper, 15½ × 22¾ (39.2 × 57.2)
Bequeathed by Mrs Ernestine Carter 1984

C.R.W. NEVINSON 1889–1946

T 03676
A Bursting Shell 1915
Not inscribed
Oil on canvas, 36 × 22½ (76.2 × 55.8)
Purchased from the MacLean Gallery (Grant-in-Aid) 1983

SIR WILLIAM NICHOLSON
1872–1949

T 03792
Harbour in Snow, La Rochelle 1938
Inscribed '.N.' b.l. and on reverse '(No. 3) HARBOUR in Snow (La Rochelle)', '1938' and, not by artist, 'LB no: cat 481'
Oil on canvas over board, 13¾ × 17¾ (35 × 45)
Presented by the Friends of the Tate Gallery 1983

HERMANN NITSCH b.1938

T 03412
Blood Picture 1962
Inscribed 'hermann nitsch 1962' on stretcher
Blood on three linen or cotton squares laid down on coarse canvas, 41⅞ × 31⅝ (106.2 × 80.4)
Purchased from the Galerie Heike Curtze (Grant-in-Aid) 1982

SIR SIDNEY NOLAN O.M.
b.1917

T 03553
Desert Storm *c.*1953
Not inscribed
Ripolin on hardboard, 36 × 48 (91.4 × 121.9)
Presented by Lord McAlpine 1983

T 03554
Head 1964
Inscribed 'G/New/Frame/ADELAIDE' on back of board
Oil on hardboard, 48 × 48 (121.9 × 121.9)
Presented by Lord McAlpine 1983

T 03555
Carcase in Swamp 1955
Inscribed 'N.' b.r. and, on back of board, 'Not for/Sale', 'CARCASE IN SWAMP./1955', 'Nolan', 'ABANDONED MINE' and 'DUR'
Ripolin on hardboard,
36 × 48 (91.4 × 121.9)
Presented by Lord McAlpine 1983

T 03556
Helmet 1956
Inscribed 'N.' b.r. and, on back of board, 'HELMET./1956/Nolan', 'NOV. 16th. 1956.', 'NOLAN/NOVEMBER 16th/1956' and 'TOP [with an arrow]'
Ripolin on hardboard,
48 × 36 (121.9 × 91.4)
Presented by Lord McAlpine 1983

T 03557
In the Cave 1957
Inscribed 'N.' b. centre and, on back of board, 'MRS FRASER/1957', '1957/CAVE/ (Mrs FRASER/Series)', 'NO 53', 'FOR/ BRITISH/COUNCIL' and '2'
Polyvinyl acetate on hardboard,
48 × 60 (121.9 × 152.4)
Presented by Lord McAlpine 1983

T 03558
Antarctica 1964
Inscribed '30. Aug 1964/nolan' b.r.
Oil on hardboard, 48 × 48 (121.9 × 121.9)
Presented by Lord McAlpine 1983

T 03559
Camel and Figure 1966
Inscribed 'nolan/1966' b.r., '20 Sept/ 1966/nolan' on back of board, and 'CAMEL/AND/FIGURE/1966' on backing board
Oil on hardboard,
47⅝ × 48 (121 × 121.9)
Presented by Lord McAlpine 1983

T 03560
Grimes's Apprentice 1977
Inscribed 'Aldeburgh/Britten' and 'Grimes's Apprentice/Nolan/27 March 77' on back of board
Oil on hardboard, 36 × 48 (91.4 × 121.9)
Presented by Lord McAlpine 1983

JULIAN OPIE b.1958

T 03783
Making It 1983
Inscribed on back 'Julian Opie 83' and 'Julian Opie'
Painted steel construction,
102¾ × 46½ × 75¾ (261 × 118 × 192.5)
Presented by the Patrons of New Art through the Friends of the Tate Gallery 1983

DENNIS OPPENHEIM b.1938

T 03468
Life Support System for a Premature By-Product 1981
Inscribed 'LIFE SUPPORT SYSTEM FOR A PREMATURE BY-PRODUCT/(FROM A LONG DISTANCE) 1981/SONNABEND GALLERY NEW YORK, THE CONTEMPORARY ARTS CENTER CINCINNATI OHIO. THE LOWE ART MUSEUM/ MIAMI FLORIDA. DIMENSIONS 15′ × 40′ × 80′′ on right panel and 'Dennis Oppenheim 1981' b.r.
Dry powdered pigment in metallic silver with bronzing liquid and pencil on paper, 2 panels framed as one,
38¼ × 100¼ (97.1 × 254.6)
Purchased from the artist through the Lewis Johnstone Gallery (Grant-in-Aid) 1982

WILLIAM EVELYN OSBORN
*c.*1863–1906

T 03647
Three Public Houses
Not inscribed
Oil on canvas, 30 × 27¾ (76 × 70.5)
Presented anonymously in memory of Terence Rattigan 1983

T 03648
Royal Avenue, Chelsea
Not inscribed
Oil on canvas, 19⅞ × 24 (50.5 × 61)
Presented anonymously in memory of Terence Rattigan 1983

T 03649
Beach at Dusk, St. Ives Harbour
Inscribed 'Will. Osborn' b.l.
Oil on canvas, 24 × 20⅛ (61 × 51)
Presented anonymously in memory of Terence Rattigan 1983

EDUARDO PAOLOZZI b.1924

T 03764
Mr Cruickshank 1950
Inscribed 'E. Paolozzi 1950' and 'MORRIS SINGER FOUNDER LONDON' behind r. shoulder, and 'CIRC 682–1971' under base
Polished bronze,
11⅜ × 11⅜ × 7⅞ (29 × 29 × 20)
Transferred from the Victoria and Albert Museum 1983
(Gift of the artist 1971)

T 03765
Plaster for 'Mr Cruickshank' 1950
Inscribed 'CIRC 683–1971' underneath and, on smaller piece, 'CIRC 683A–1971'
Plaster and pencil, varnished, in two pieces, 11⅜ × 11⅜ × 7⅞ (29 × 29 × 20)
Transferred from the Victoria and Albert Museum 1983
(Gift of the artist 1971)

GIUSEPPE PENONE b.1947

T 03420
Breath 1978
Not inscribed
Terracotta, 61 × 32¾ × 33 (154 × 83 × 84)
Purchased from the Galerie Durand-Dessert (Grant-in-Aid) 1982

SIR ROLAND PENROSE
1900–1984

T 03377
Last Voyage of Captain Cook 1936–7
Inscribed 'Roland Penrose 1936–7' on base b.r.
Oil on wood, plaster and steel,
27¼ × 26 × 33½ (69.2 × 66 × 82.5)
Presented by Mrs Gabrielle Keiller through the Friends of the Tate Gallery 1982

T 03400
Portrait 1939
Inscribed 'R Penrose '39' t.l.; there are also numerous inscriptions integrated into the composition
Oil on canvas, 30 × 25 (76.2 × 63.7)
Purchased from the Mayor Gallery (Grant-in-Aid) 1982

T 03819
House the Light-house 1983
Inscribed 'Roland Penrose 1983' b.r. and on verso 'House the Light-house 1983'
Pencil, gouache, ink and collage on paper, 23½ × 33⅛ (59.4 × 84)
Presented anonymously 1984

PABLO PICASSO 1881–1973

T 03571
Circus Artist and Child 1905
Not inscribed
Indian ink and watercolour on paper, 6⅝ × 4⅛ (16.8 × 10.5)
Bequeathed by Mrs A. F. Kessler 1983

T 03572
Dish of Pears 1936
Inscribed '15D.XXXVI.' b.l. and 'Picasso' b.r.
Oil on canvas, 14 15/16 × 24 (38 × 61)
Bequeathed by Mrs A. F. Kessler 1983

T 03670
Reclining Nude with Necklace 1968
Inscribed 'Picasso' t.l. and '8.10 / 68. / I' on reverse
Oil and oil/alkyd on canvas, 44 11/16 × 63⅝ (113.5 × 161.7)
Purchased from the Galerie Louise Leiris (Grant-in-Aid) 1983

JOHN PIPER b.1903

T 03818
Covehithe Church 1983
Inscribed 'John Piper' b.r. and 'Covehithe Church (Suffolk) 1983' on back of canvas
Oil on canvas, 34 × 44 (86.3 × 111.8)
Presented by the artist 1984

VIVIAN PITCHFORTH 1895–1982

T 03661
Seated Model
Not inscribed
Brown ink and pastel on paper, 12¾ × 10 (32.5 × 25.4)
Bequeathed by the artist 1983

T 03662
Model seen from the back
Not inscribed
Brown ink and pastel on paper, 10 × 13⅛ (25.4 × 33.4)
Bequeathed by the artist 1983

T 03663
View of a Harbour
Not inscribed
Watercolour on paper, 19¼ × 29⅛ (48.9 × 74)
Bequeathed by the artist 1983

T 03664
Wet Windscreen, Ramsgate Harbour
Inscribed on verso 'West Windscreen/ Ramsgate Harbour'
Watercolour on paper, 18¾ × 24⅝ (47.7 × 62.5)
Bequeathed by the artist 1983

NICHOLAS POPE b.1949

T 03536
Big Hoos 1982
Not inscribed
Silver birch wood, 91¾ × 68 × 35 (233 × 174 × 89)
Purchased from the Waddington Galleries (Grant-in-Aid) 1982

MABEL PRYDE 1871–1918

T 03464
The Harlequin *c.*1910
Inscribed on stretcher 'The Harlequin by Mabel Nicholson' and 'B. Nicholson, 97 King's Road, Chelsea'
Oil on canvas, 40 × 25¼ (101.8 × 64.3)
Presented by Timothy Nicholson 1982

ARNULF RAINER b.1929

T 03385
Untitled (Death Mask) 1978
Inscribed 'R.' b.r.
Oil pastel on black and white photograph, 23⅜ × 16¾ (59.4 × 42.5)
Purchased from the Galerie Heike Curtze (Grant-in-Aid) 1982

T 03387
Untitled (Death Mask) 1978
Inscribed 'A Rainer' b.r.
Oil pastel on black and white photograph, 24 × 19⅞ (60.9 × 50.5)
Purchased from the Galerie Heike Curtze (Grant-in-Aid) 1982

T 03388
Untitled (Body Language) *c.*1973
Inscribed 'A. Rainer' b.r.
Oil on black and white photograph, 23⅞ × 19¾ (59.5 × 50.1)
Purchased from the Galerie Heike Curtze (Grant-in-Aid) 1982

T 03389
Two Flames (Body Language) 1973
Inscribed '2 Flammen/A Rainer' t.l.
Oil on black and white photograph, 19⅞ × 23⅞ (50.5 × 60.7)
Purchased from the Galerie Heike Curtze (Grant-in-Aid) 1982

T 03390
Untitled (Face Farce) *c.*1971
Inscribed 'A Rainer' b.r.
Oil and oil pastel on black and white photograph, 24 × 20 (61 × 50.7)
Purchased from the Galerie Heike Curtze (Grant-in-Aid) 1982

T 03391
A Nose Adjustment (Face Farce) 1971
Inscribed 'A.R.71/eine nasen korrektur' b.l.
Oil on black and white photograph, 24 × 20 (60.8 × 50.7)
Purchased from the Galerie Heike Curtze (Grant-in-Aid) 1982

T 03671
Wine Crucifix 1957/78
Inscribed 'A.R.57/78' b.r. and 'Dunkel-/ Rotes KREUZ A. Rainer 57/1972 . . . [illegible] und/neu aufgezogen/dabei restaur . . . [illegible]/A Rainer' on back of lining canvas
Oil on canvas, 66¼ × 40¾ (168 × 103)
Purchased from Galerie ak (Grant-in-Aid) 1983

WILLIAM RATCLIFFE 1870–1955

T 03359
Clarence Gardens 1912
Inscribed 'W. Ratcliffe 1912' b.l.
Oil on canvas, 20 × 30 (50.8 × 76.2)
Purchased from Anthony d'Offay Ltd (Grant-in-Aid) 1982

ROBERT RAUSCHENBERG b.1925

T 03376
Revenue (Spread) 1980
Inscribed on back: left panel '80.50 REVENUE (SPREAD)/PANEL A 1 OF 2/ RAUSCHENBERG 80'; centre panel 'IRONING BOARD IS NEVER TO BE REMOVED'; right panel '80.50 REVENUE (SPREAD)/Panel B 2 OF 2 RAUSCHENBERG 80'
Mixed media on wooden support with collaged elements, 96 × 104 × 26⅜ (243.5 × 264 × 67)
Purchased from the Sonnabend Gallery (Grant-in-Aid) 1982

MARTIAL RAYSSE b.1936

T 03383
Necropolis I 1960
Inscribed 'MARTIAL RAYSSE 60' on top
Plastic assemblage,
23½ × 5 × 5 (59.7 × 12.5 × 12.5)
Purchased from the Galerie Bonnier (Grant-in-Aid) 1982

PAULA REGO b.1935

T 03839
Nanny, Small Bears and Bogeyman 1982
Inscribed on verso 'Nanny/Paula Rego 1982' and '7'
Acrylic on paper, 47¼ × 59⅞ (120 × 152)
Presented by the Patrons of New Art through the Friends of the Tate Gallery 1984

SIR NORMAN REID b.1915

T 03478
Mr Pencil at Anneston 1960–80
Inscribed 'Sir Norman Reid/50 Brabourne Rise/Beckenham/Kent/"Mr Pencil at Anneston"' on back of board
Oil on fabric mounted on board,
17 15/16 × 20¾ (45.2 × 51.8)
Presented anonymously 1982

AUGUSTE RENOIR 1841–1919

T 03573
Nude on a Couch 1914–15
Inscribed 'Renoir.' b.l.
Oil on canvas, 21⅜ × 25⅜ (51.8 × 65.2)
Bequeathed by Mrs A. F. Kessler 1983

T 03574
Peaches and Almonds 1901
Inscribed 'Renoir.' b.l.
Oil on canvas, 12¼ × 16¼ (31.2 × 41.3)
Bequeathed by Mrs A. F. Kessler 1983

BRIDGET RILEY b.1931

T 03375
To a Summer's Day 2 1980
Inscribed 'RILEY '80' on edge of canvas t.l.; also on back of canvas 'RILEY/TO A SUMMER'S/DAY 2', '1980/ACRYLIC/ ON LINEN', 'TOP [with an arrow]' and '45⅝ × 110⅝ INS'; along centre bar of stretcher 'RILEY TO A SUMMER'S DAY 2 1980 ACRYLIC ON LINEN'; and on vertical bar of stretcher 'TOP [with an arrow]'
Acrylic on canvas, 45½ × 110⅝ (115.5 × 281)
Purchased from the artist through the Juda Rowan Gallery (Grant-in-Aid) 1982

T 03816
Achaian 1981
Inscribed 'Riley/'81' on edge of canvas b.l.; along centre bar of stretcher 'ACHAIAN Riley 1981 Oil on linen'; on back of canvas 'ACHAIAN/Riley 1981/ Oil on linen, 94 ins. × 79⅝ ins.', 'This painting looks/best in natural/ daylight', and 'TOP' twice, with arrows
Oil on canvas, 94⅛ × 79⅝ (239 × 202.3)
Purchased from the artist through the Juda Rowan Gallery (Grant-in-Aid) 1983

DIETER ROTH b.1930

T 03610
Harmonica Curse 1981
74 audio cassettes inscribed 'Dieter Roth' and numbered 1 to 74 t.r.
76 Polaroid photographs each
4¼ × 3½ (10.9 × 9); each inscribed 'Harmonica Curse Dieter Roth' and numbered b.r., also dated variously from 14 February 1981 to 8 August 1981 and number of edition noted
Edition of 5
Purchased from Audio Arts (Grant-in-Aid) 1983

SIR WILLIAM ROTHENSTEIN 1872–1945

T 03682
Study of the Attendant for 'The Princess Badroulbadour' *c.*1908
Not inscribed
Red chalk on paper,
15¼ × 11 (38.7 × 28.1)
Presented by Sir John Rothenstein through the Friends of the Tate Gallery 1983

PIERRE ROY 1880–1950

T 03537
Boris Anrep in his Studio 1949
Inscribed 'P. Roy/1949' b.r. and 'BORIS ANREP/IN HIS STUDIO/ 65 BOULEVARD ARAGO/1949' on back of canvas
Oil on canvas, 25¾ × 19⅝ (63.3 × 50.1)
Bequeathed by Mrs M. J. A. Russell 1982

ROBERT RYMAN b.1930

T 03550
Ledger 1982
Inscribed on back 'RYMAN 82 "LEDGER"'
Enamelac on fibreglass with aluminium support, 30 1/16 × 28 × 1⅝ (76.3 × 71.1 × 3.6)
Purchased from the Mayor Gallery (Grant-in-Aid) 1983

NIKI DE SAINT PHALLE b.1930

T 03824
Shooting Picture 1961
Not inscribed
Paint on plaster relief,
56⅜ × 30¾ × 3⅛ (143 × 78 × 81)
Purchased from Jean Tinguely (Grant-in-Aid) 1984

DAVID SALLE b.1952

T 03444
Walking the Dog 1982
Not inscribed
Two panels – left: acrylic, oil and charcoal on cotton, 86⅛ × 56⅛ (218.8 × 142.5)
right: acrylic and oil on linen,
86⅛ × 56⅛ (218.8 × 142.5)
Purchased from Anthony d'Offay Ltd (Grant-in-Aid) 1982

JULIAN SCHNABEL b.1951

T 03441
Humanity Asleep 1982
Inscribed 'HUMANITY ASLEEP' centre r.
Mixed media on wooden support,
108¼ × 144 × 11 (274.3 × 365.6 × 28)
Purchased from the Mary Boone Gallery (Grant-in-Aid) 1982

EMILE SCHUFFENECKER 1851–1934

T 03639
Spring-like Morning *c.*1896
Inscribed with studio stamp b.r.
Pastel on paper, 13 × 17¾ (33 × 45.2)
Presented anonymously in memory of Terence Rattigan 1983

T 03640
Seascape (Cliffs) *c.*1895
Inscribed with studio stamp b.l.
Pastel on paper, 5¼ × 8¼ (13.5 × 20.9)
Presented anonymously in memory of Terence Rattigan 1983

T 03641
Cliffs and the Sea *c.*1895
Inscribed with studio stamp b.r.
Pastel on paper, 5½ × 8¼ (14 × 21)
Presented anonymously in memory of
Terence Rattigan 1983

T 03642
Cliff, Grey Day *c.*1895
Inscribed with studio stamp b.l.
Pastel on paper, 8¾ × 10⅞ (22.2 × 27.5)
Presented anonymously in memory of
Terence Rattigan 1983

KURT SCHWITTERS 1887-1948

T 03766
The Autumn Crocus 1926-8
Inscribed 'DIE HERBSTZEITLOSE' on side of
base
Plaster, 32 × 11½ × 11½ (81 × 29.3 × 29.3)
Transferred from the Victoria and
Albert Museum 1983

TERRY SETCH b.1936

T 03591
**Once upon a Time There was Oil III,
panel I** 1981-2
Not inscribed
Oil, wax, scrim and paper on canvas,
102½ × 171½ (260 × 436), irregular
Purchased from Nigel Greenwood Inc.
Ltd (Grant-in-Aid) 1983

JOEL SHAPIRO b.1941

T 03697
Untitled 1978
Stamped '78¼' and inscribed 'SHAPIRO'
on underside
Bronze, 13¼ × 21¾ × 6¼ (33.7 × 55.3 × 15.7)
Purchased from the Paula Cooper
Gallery (Grant-in-Aid) 1983

WALTER RICHARD SICKERT
1860-1942

T 03360
Miss Earhart's Arrival 1932
Not inscribed
Oil on canvas, 28¼ × 72¼ (71.7 × 183.2)
Purchased from C. G. C. Hyslop
(Grant-in-Aid) 1982

T 03548
La Hollandaise *c.*1906
Inscribed 'Sickert' b.r.
Oil on canvas, 20⅛ × 16 (51.1 × 40.8)
Purchased from a private collector
through Browse and Darby (Grant-in-
Aid) 1983

JOHN SKEAPING 1901-1980

T 03767
Buffalo 1930
Inscribed 'JRS' and 'A.20-1941'
underneath
Lapis lazuli,
3⅛ × 7⅛ × 4⅜ (8 × 18 × 11) on marble base
⅞ × 7 × 3⅛ (2 × 17.5 × 8)
Transferred from the Victoria and
Albert Museum 1983
(Bequest of Mrs A. A. Creswell 1941)

T 03768
Burmese Dancer 1928
Inscribed 'J. SKEAPING 28' on side, and
'CIRC 79-1964' and '336' under base
Alabaster, 18½ × 6¾ × 5½ (47 × 17 × 14)
Transferred from the Victoria and
Albert Museum 1983
(Gift of the Contemporary Art Society
1964)

JACK SMITH b.1928

T 03812
Written Activity No.7 1967
Inscribed on back of canvas 'WRITTEN
ACTIVITY NO:7' and 'Jack Smith/1969'
Oil on canvas, 60 × 60 (152.4 × 152.4)
Purchased from Kenneth Powell
(Knapping Fund) 1983

T 03813
Activities, Major and Minor 1972
Inscribed on back of plywood 'Jack Smith
1972' and 'ACTIVITIES. MAJOR + MINOR'
Oil on plywood, 48⅛ × 48 (122.2 × 122.1)
Purchased from the artist through
Fischer Fine Art (Grant-in-Aid) 1983

T 03814
Inside, Outside 3 1980
Inscribed on back of hardboard 'INSIDE
OUTSIDE ③' and 'Jack Smith/1980'
Oil on hardboard, 36⅛ × 36⅛ (91.8 × 91.8)
Purchased from the artist through
Fischer Fine Art (Grant-in-Aid) 1983

JESUS-RAPHAEL SOTO b.1923

T 03769
Twelve Black and Four Silver 1965
Inscribed on backboard 'HAUT Soto
1965' and 'CIRC 38 1966'
Construction of wood and painted metal
sheets, 41¾ × 41¾ × 6⅜ (106 × 106 × 16.2)
Transferred from the Victoria and
Albert Museum 1983

T 03770
Spiral Relief 1965
Inscribed on reverse 'CIRC 140-1966'
Construction of wood and nylon, ink on
paper, 18½ × 11¾ × 5⅛ (47 × 29.8 × 13.1)
Transferred from the Victoria and
Albert Museum 1983

JOSEPH EDWARD
SOUTHALL 1861-1944

T 03699
Belgium supported by Hope 1918
Inscribed 'EJS 1918' b.r., on canvas
turnover 'COLOUR BEGUN VIII 1918' and
on reverse 'Marian E. Longford /
Christmas 1918/HGL [in monogram]
With Love'
Tempera on canvas, 12½ × 16¼ (31.8 × 41)
Purchased from the Fine Art Society
(Grant-in-Aid) 1983

DANIEL SPOERRI b.1930

T 03382
Prose Poems 1960
Inscribed 'Tableau Piège:/"Poèmes en
Prose/sur Fond Vasarely"/Daniel
Spoerri/Nov.60' on back of board
Assemblage of objects on wooden
board, 27⅛ × 21⅜ × 14¼ (69 × 54.2 × 36.1)
Purchased from the Galerie Bonnier
(Grant-in-Aid) 1982

THEOPHILE-ALEXANDRE
STEINLEN 1859-1923

T 03771
A Cat
Inscribed 'Steinlen' l. of base
Bronze, 5 × 2 × 2½ (12.8 × 5 × 6.5)
Transferred from the Victoria and
Albert Museum 1983

ADRIAN STOKES 1902-1972

T 03579
Still Life: Last Eleven 1972
Not inscribed
Oil on canvas marouflaged onto board,
12⅞ × 16⅛ (32.8 × 41)
Purchased from Mrs Ann Stokes Angus
(Grant-in-Aid) 1983

T 03580
Still Life: Last Eleven (3 November)
1972
Inscribed on top canvas turnover
'ADS '72'

Oil on canvas, 14 × 18 (35.6 × 45.7)
Purchased from Mrs Ann Stokes Angus
(Grant-in-Aid) 1983

T 03581
**Still Life: Last Eleven
(10–13 December) 1972**
Not inscribed
Oil on canvas, 14 × 18 (35.6 × 45.7)
Purchased from Mrs Ann Stokes Angus
(Grant-in-Aid) 1983

T 03582
Still Life: Last Eleven 1972
Inscribed on top canvas turnover
'ADS '72'
Oil on canvas, 14 × 18 (35.6 × 45.7)
Purchased from Mrs Ann Stokes Angus
(Grant-in-Aid) 1983

T 03583
Still Life: Last Eleven 1972
Inscribed on top canvas turnover
'ADS '72'
Oil on canvas, 20 × 16 (50.8 × 40.7)
Purchased from Mrs Ann Stokes Angus
(Grant-in-Aid) 1983

T 03584
Still Life: Last Eleven (No. 7) 1972
Inscribed on top canvas turnover
'ADS '72'
Oil on canvas, 14 × 18 (35.6 × 45.7)
Purchased from Mrs Ann Stokes Angus
(Grant-in-Aid) 1983

T 03585
**Still Life: Last Eleven (9 December)
1972**
Inscribed on top canvas turnover
'9/12 ADS '72'
Oil on canvas, 22 × $29\frac{7}{8}$ (55.9 × 75.9)
Purchased from Mrs Ann Stokes Angus
(Grant-in-Aid) 1983

T 03586
Still Life: Last Eleven 1972
Inscribed on top canvas turnover
'ADS '72'
Oil on canvas, 20 × 21 (50.8 × 53.4)
Purchased from Mrs Ann Stokes Angus
(Grant-in-Aid) 1983

T 03587
Still Life: Last Eleven (No. 4) 1972
Not inscribed
Oil on canvas, 20 × 24 (50.8 × 61)
Purchased from Mrs Ann Stokes Angus
(Grant-in-Aid) 1983

ARTHUR STUDD 1863–1919

T 03644
The Artist's Wife
Not inscribed
Oil on panel, $8\frac{1}{8}$ × $6\frac{1}{4}$ (22 × 15.7)
Presented anonymously in memory of
Terence Rattigan 1983

T 03645
Venetian Lyric (San Giorgio)
Inscribed 'Studd' b.l.
Oil on panel, 5 × $8\frac{1}{2}$ (12.7 × 21.7)
Presented anonymously in memory of
Terence Rattigan 1983

T 03646
**Venetian Lyric (Santa Maria della
Salute)**
Inscribed 'Studd' b.r.
Oil on panel, 5 × $8\frac{1}{2}$ (12.7 × 21.7)
Presented anonymously in memory of
Terence Rattigan 1983

PATRICK SYMONS b.1925

T 03552
**Oak Arch Grey (Wimbledon
Common) 1977–81**
Inscribed 'Symons '77–'81' b.r., and
various mathematical calculations on
right-hand canvas turnover
Oil on canvas, $35\frac{1}{8}$ × $31\frac{1}{4}$ (89.2 × 79.5)
Purchased from Browse and Darby
(Grant-in-Aid) 1983

RUFINO TAMAYO b.1899

T 03370
Man and Woman 1981
Inscribed 'tamayo/o-81' b.r. and
'HOMBRE Y MUJER/180 × 125/OLEO' on
back on canvas
Oil on canvas, $49\frac{1}{8}$ × $70\frac{7}{8}$ (124.7 × 180)
Purchased from Marlborough Fine Art
(Grant-in-Aid) 1982

GEOFFREY TIBBLE 1909–1952

T 03655
Three Women 1930
Inscribed on reverse 'G.TIBBLE /
"THREE WOMEN" / 1930'
Oil on canvas, 12 × 16 (30.5 × 40.6)
Presented anonymously in memory of
Terence Rattigan 1983

T 03656
The Mug 1948
Inscribed 'Tibble' b.l. and 'Tibble / Oct.
48' on reverse
Oil on canvas, $14\frac{1}{8}$ × $17\frac{1}{2}$ (37 × 44.5)

Presented anonymously in memory of
Vivien Leigh 1983

T 03657
**Interior with Self-Portrait and
Woman** c.1944
Not inscribed
Conté crayon on paper,
$16\frac{1}{4}$ × $12\frac{1}{2}$ (42.5 × 32)
Presented anonymously in memory of
Terence Rattigan 1983

T 03658
Dressing 1944
Inscribed 'Tibble' b.l. and 'Tibble' on
reverse
Oil on canvas, 30 × 39 (76.2 × 99)
Presented anonymously in memory of
Terence Rattigan 1983

JOE TILSON b.1928

T 03772
Ziglical Column 1966
Inscribed '8' under base
Screenprint on enamelled and stainless
steel, $32\frac{1}{4}$ × 12 × $6\frac{1}{8}$ (82 × 30.5 × 15.5)
Transferred from the Victoria and
Albert Museum 1983

JEAN TINGUELY b.1925

T 03822
Débricollage 1970
Inscribed in relief 'TINGuely' on metal
bar on top
Assemblage of household tools and
welded metal,
20 × 30 × $25\frac{1}{2}$ (50.8 × 76.2 × 64.8)
Purchased from the artist (Grant-in-Aid)
with the help of the Friends of the Tate
Gallery 1984

T 03823
**Metamechanical Sculpture with
Tripod 1954**
Not inscribed
Wire, painted cardboard and welded
metal, 93 × 32 × 36 (236 × 81.5 × 91.5)
Purchased from the artist (Grant-in-Aid)
1984

HENRI DE TOULOUSE-
LAUTREC 1864–1901

T 03575
Horsewoman 1899
Inscribed 'HT Lautrec' (monogram) b.r.
Oil and gouache on board,
$21\frac{7}{8}$ × $16\frac{3}{4}$ (55.5 × 42.5)
Bequeathed by Mrs A. F. Kessler 1983

DAVID TREMLETT b.1945

T 03689
The Cards 1972
Each card inscribed by the artist with the name of a county in Great Britain
Felt tip pen on commercial postcards, 81 cards, framed in sets of 3, each card $3\frac{1}{2} \times 5\frac{1}{2}$ (8.8 × 14)
Purchased from John Dunbar and J. E. Matthews (Grant-in-Aid) 1983

WILLIAM TURNBULL b.1922

T 03773
Mask I 1953
Inscribed 'CIRC 194-1964' on back
Bronze, $9\frac{1}{8} \times 8\frac{1}{8} \times 2\frac{3}{4}$ (23 × 20.5 × 7)
Transferred from the Victoria and Albert Museum 1983

EUAN UGLOW b.1932

T 03418
Zagi 1981–2
Inscribed on top canvas turnover '41.5 × 58.7 Varnish Rowneys No 800/ "Wax Matt Euan Uglow 1981–82 /\ / oil on canvas.'
Oil on canvas, $59\frac{1}{8} \times 42\frac{1}{8}$ (150 × 107)
Purchased from Browse and Darby (Grant-in-Aid) 1982

LEON UNDERWOOD 1890–1975

T 03775
Herald of a New Day 1934
Not inscribed
Plaster, $25\frac{1}{2} \times 11\frac{1}{2} \times 12\frac{1}{2}$ (64.7 × 29.2 × 31.7)
Transferred from the Victoria and Albert Museum 1983
(Gift of the artist 1934)

KEITH VAUGHAN 1912–1977

T 03700
Ninth Assembly of Figures (Eldorado Banal) 1976
Inscribed on back of canvas 'ELDORADO BANAL/(9th ASSEMBLY OF FIGURES 1976) / 45 × 60/Keith Vaughan/"Quelle est cette île triste et noire – c'est Cythère/Nous dit-on un pays fameux dans les chansons/ Eldorado banal de tous les vieux garçons/ Regarde, après tout, c'est une pauvre terre"'
Oil on canvas, $45\frac{1}{4} \times 60\frac{1}{4}$ (115 × 153)
Purchased from Professor John N. Ball and Dr Gordon Hargreaves (Grant-in-Aid) 1983

EDWARD WADSWORTH 1889–1949

T 03398
Regatta 1928
Inscribed 'EDWARD WADSWORTH / 1928' on painting of a label, towards b.r.
Tempera, with oil border, on canvas, laid on plywood, $30 \times 36\frac{1}{8}$ (76.3 × 91.7)
Purchased from the Mayor Gallery (Grant-in-aid) with the help of the Friends of the Tate Gallery 1982

EDWARD ARTHUR WALTON 1860–1922

T 03447
Berwickshire Field-workers 1884
Inscribed 'E·A·Walton·84·' b.r.
Oil on canvas, $35\frac{7}{8} \times 24\frac{1}{16}$ (91.4 × 60.9)
Purchased from the Fine Art Society (Grant-in-Aid) 1982

STEPHEN WILLATS b.1943

T 03795
Are you good enough for the Cha Cha Cha? 1982
Inscribed 'DO YOU THINK' t.l., 'YOU ARE GOOD ENOUGH' b. towards r. and 'FOR THE CHA CHA CHA' t. towards r.; also with numerous further inscriptions as part of the work
Collage on paper, three panels, each $58 \times 32 \times 32\frac{3}{4}$ (147.3 × 81.3 × 7); overall dimensions when displayed $100 \times 185 \times 2\frac{3}{4}$ (254 × 470 × 7)
Purchased from the Lisson Gallery (Grant-in-Aid) 1983

GILLIAN WISE-CIOBOTARU b.1936

T 03776
Relief Constructed from Unicursal Curve No.2 1967
Not inscribed
Construction, aluminium and perspex on wood, $32 \times 32 \times 1\frac{5}{8}$ (81.3 × 81.3 × 4)
Transferred from the Victoria and Albert Museum 1983

FRANCIS DERWENT WOOD 1871–1926

T 03777
Torso of a Girl 1903
Inscribed 'F. Derwent Wood' r. of base
Plaster, $42\frac{1}{2} \times 8\frac{1}{2} \times 12\frac{1}{4}$ (108 × 21.6 × 31.2)
Transferred from the Victoria and Albert Museum 1983
(Gift of Mrs Derwent Wood 1927)

BRYAN WYNTER 1915–1975

T 03362
Saja 1969
Inscribed on back of canvas 'Bryan Wynter/"Saja" 1969/ 84″ × 84″'
Oil and acrylic on canvas, $83\frac{7}{8} \times 66\frac{3}{8}$ (213 × 168.5)
Purchased from the New Art Centre (Grant-in-Aid) 1982

T 03363
Green Confluence 1974
Inscribed on back of canvas 'Green Confluence/(June)/72″ × 48″'
Oil on canvas, $71\frac{3}{4} \times 47\frac{3}{4}$ (182.5 × 121.5)
Purchased from the New Art Centre (Grant-in-Aid) 1982

The Print Collection

VITO ACCONCI b.1941

P 07639
3 Flags for 1 Space and 6 Regions
1979–81
Inscribed 'VA 79–81' b.r. and '3 Flags for 1 Space and 6 Regions' and '2/25'
Six-part etching with aquatint, printed and published by Crown Point Press, California,
overall size 95⅝ × 73¼ (243 × 186)
Purchased from Crown Point Press (Grant-in-Aid) 1982

NORMAN ACKROYD b.1938

P 08210
The Avenue at Avington 1982
From 'Itchen Water: poems by Jeremy Hooker and etchings by Norman Ackroyd'
Inscribed 'Norman Ackroyd 1982' b.r. and 'The Avenue at Avington' and '59/90'
Aquatint, printed and published by Winchester School of Art Press,
3¾ × 4½ (9.5 × 11.4)
Transferred from Library 1983

JOHN BALDESSARI b.1931

P 07808–16, 07853
Black Dice 1982
P 07808–16 inscribed 'BALDESSARI' b.r. and '31/35'
P 07853 not inscribed
Nine etchings with photo-etching and aquatint, and one photograph, printed by Peter Kneubühler, Zürich, published by Peter Blum Editions, New York,
each approx. 6⅜ × 8 (16.2 × 20.3)
Purchased from Peter Blum Editions (Grant-in-Aid) 1983

GEORG BASELITZ b.1938

P 07737
Rebel 1965
Inscribed 'Baselitz 65' b.r. and '31/60'
Etching with drypoint and aquatint, printed and published by the artist,
12⅜ × 9¼ (31.4 × 23.5)
Purchased from Sabine Knust (Grant-in-Aid) 1982

P 07738
Untitled 1965
Inscribed 'Baselitz 65' b.r. and '13/20'
Etching with drypoint and open-bite, printed and published by the artist,
12¼ × 9½ (31 × 24.3)
Purchased from Sabine Knust (Grant-in-Aid) 1982

P 07739
Untitled (with Dog and Axe) 1967
Inscribed 'Baselitz 67' b.r. and '7/20'
Etching with drypoint, printed and published by the artist,
13⅛ × 9½ (33.3 × 24.3)
Purchased from Sabine Knust (Grant-in-Aid) 1982

P 07779
Eagle 1981
from 'Sixteen Red and Black Woodcuts' 1981/2
Inscribed 'Baselitz 82' b.r.
Woodcut, printed and published by the artist in an edition of 12,
25 × 19½ (63.5 × 49.5)
Purchased from Waddington Galleries (Grant-in-Aid) 1982

P 07780
Head 1982
from 'Sixteen Red and Black Woodcuts' 1981/2
Inscribed 'Baselitz 82' b.r.
Woodcut, printed and published by the artist in an edition of 15,
25 × 19½ (63.5 × 49.5)
Purchased from Waddington Galleries 1982

P 07998
Drummer 1982
Inscribed 'Baselitz' b.r. and '12. XII 82' and 'Nr. 9'
Linocut on canvas textured paper, printed and published by the artist in an edition of 10,
79⅛ × 59⅜ (201 × 150.8)
Purchased from Sabine Knust (Grant-in-Aid) 1984

JOHN BELLANY b.1942

P 07901
Death Knell for John Knox 1972–83
Inscribed 'John Bellany. 72' b.r. and 'Death Knell for John Knox' and '3/23'
Etching, printed by Jack Shirreff, Westbury, published by the artist,
18¾ × 19¾ (47.6 × 50.2)
Purchased from Monika Kinley (Grant-in-Aid) 1983

P 07902
Janus 1982
Inscribed 'Bellany '82' b.r. and 'A/P'
Screenprint, printed by Chris Betambeau, Advanced Graphics, published by the artist,
33¾ × 24½ (85.8 × 62.2)
Purchased from Monika Kinley (Grant-in-Aid) 1983

JONATHAN BOROFSKY b.1942

P 07817–29
2740475 1982
Thirteen prints, each inscribed 'Jonathan Borofsky' in various positions and '39/50'
P 07817, 19, 21, 23, 25, 27, 29: screenprints printed by H. M. Büchi, Basel
P 07818, 20, 22, 24, 26, 28: etchings, printed by Robert Aull and Leslie Sutcliffe, Los Angeles. All published by Peter Blum Editions,
in range 2¾ × 1½–30⅛ × 22⅛ (7 × 3.8–76.5 × 56.2)
Purchased from Peter Blum Editions (Grant-in-Aid) 1983

GÜNTER BRUS b.1938

P 07991–3
Great Fear of the Earth 1982
Each inscribed 'Günter Brus 1982' b.r. and
P 07991: '1/5 I'
P 07992: '1/15 II'
P 07993: '1/15 III'
Three etchings with drypoint and aquatint, printed and published by Crown Point Press, California,
23¾ × 35¾ (60.4 × 90.9)
Purchased from Crown Point Press (Grant-in-Aid) 1984

P 11081 8
Night Quartet 1982
Each inscribed 'G. Brus' b.r. and '19/30'
Eight etchings with drypoint, printed by
Manfred Maly, Vienna, published by
Galerie Heike Curtze and Edition
Sabine Knust, Munich
9¼ × 6⅜ (23.5 × 16.2)
Purchased from Galerie Heike Curtze
(Grant-in-Aid) 1984

STEPHEN BUCKLEY b.1942

P 07754
Les Flons Flons 1981-82
Inscribed 'Stephen Buckley 1981' b.r.
and '18/70'
Screenprint, printed at Kelpra Studio,
published by Waddington Graphics,
30⅜ × 40⅛ (77.2 × 101.8)
Purchased from Waddington Graphics
(Grant-in-Aid) 1982

JOHN CAGE b.1912

P 07903
Déreau No.33 1982
Inscribed 'John Cage 1982' b.c. and
'Dereau 33 two of two impressions'
and '33 2'
Etching, engraving, drypoint and
aquatint, printed and published
by Crown Point Press,
18¼ × 24¾ (46.3 × 62.9)
Purchased from Crown Point Press
(Grant-in-Aid) 1983

PATRICK CAULFIELD b.1936

P 07755
Brown Jug 1982
Inscribed 'Patrick Caulfield' b.r. and
'2/80'
Screenprint, printed at Kelpra Studio,
published by Waddington Graphics,
39⅜ × 30½ (100 × 77.6)
Purchased from Waddington Graphics
(Grant-in-Aid) 1982

SANDRO CHIA b.1946

P 07632-6
April Manual 1981
Each inscribed 'Sandro Chia 1981' b.r.
and '30/50'
Five etchings with drypoint, printed
by Sarah Feigenbaum at Aeropress,
New York, published by Peter Blum
Editions, New York,

each approx. 11⅝ × 12¼ (29.5 × 31.2)
Purchased from Anthony d'Offay
Gallery (Grant-in-Aid) 1982

P 07637
Man Running 1981
Inscribed 'Sandro Chia 1981' b.r. and
'prova d'artista'
Etching, printed by the artist. This
print was not yet editioned at the
time of acquisition.
25½ × 19¼ (65 × 49)
Purchased from Anthony d'Offay
Gallery (Grant-in-Aid) 1982

P 07638
Man with Apron 1981
Inscribed 'Sandro Chia 1981' b.r. and
'prova d'artista'
Etching, printed by the artist. This
print was not yet editioned at the
time of acquisition.
25⅜ × 19¼ (64.5 × 49)
Purchased from Anthony d'Offay
Gallery (Grant-in-Aid) 1982

CHRISTO b.1935

P 07640
Der Spiegel 1963
Inscribed 'Christo 63' b.r. and '96'
Magazine folded and wrapped in
transparent plastic and twine,
published by Hans Möller, Düsseldorf
in an edition of 130 (each one a
different issue of the magazine),
12 × 4½ (30.5 × 11.5)
Purchased at Sotheby's Los Angeles
(Grant-in-Aid) 1982

BRIAN CLARKE b.1953

P 11062-9
The Two Cultures 1981
Each inscribed 'Brian Clarke 1981' b.r.
and '7.75'
Eight screenprints, printed at Kelpra
Studio, published by Swellfame Ltd and
the Robert Fraser Gallery
in an edition of 75,
in range 29¾ × 19¾-44⅛ × 27
(75.5 × 50.4-112 × 68.5)
Presented by Mr Paul Beldock 1983

FRANCESCO CLEMENTE
b 1952

P 07830-8, 07848
High Fever 1982
Each inscribed 'Francesco Clemente'
b.r. and '5/35'
P 07848 not inscribed
Ten woodcuts, printed by François
Lanfranca, Locarno, published by
Peter Blum Editions, New York,
in range 14 × 14-17¼ × 20⅜
(35.6 × 35.6-43.8 × 51.8)
Purchased from Peter Blum Editions
(Grant-in-Aid) 1983

P 07904
Seascape 1981
Inscribed 'Francesco Clemente' on
reverse and '6/10'
Printed by Hidekatsu Takuda at Crown
Point Press and published by Crown
Point Press,
24½ × 18⅝ (62.2 × 47.3)
Purchased from Crown Point Press
(Grant-in-Aid) 1983

P 07905
Self Portrait No.6 (Stoplight) 1981
Inscribed 'Francesco Clemente' b.c. and
'1/10'
Printed and published by Crown Point
Press
9¼ × 13¼ (23.5 × 33.6)
Purchased from Crown Point Press
(Grant-in-Aid) 1983

PRUNELLA CLOUGH b.1919

P 07906
Geological Landscape 1949
Inscribed '1949' on reverse
Lithograph,
5⅞ × 7⅞ (14.9 × 20.1)
Purchased from the artist (Grant-in-Aid)
1983

P 07907
Can and Basket 1950
Inscribed '1950' on reverse
Lithograph,
6⅝ × 6⅜ (16.7 × 16.2)
Purchased from the artist (Grant-in-Aid)
1983

P 07908
Jellyfish 1950
Inscribed '1950' on reverse
Lithograph,
10 × 12⅞ (25.4 × 32.5)
Purchased from the artist (Grant-in-Aid)
1983

P 07909
Float 1950–5
Not inscribed
Lithograph,
6⅝ × 4½ (17 × 11.6)
Purchased from the artist (Grant-in-Aid) 1983

P 07910
Cranes 1952
Inscribed 'Clough' b.r. and '3/20'
Lithograph,
16⅞ × 14½ (43 × 36.8)
Purchased from the artist (Grant-in-Aid) 1983

P 07911
Kippers 1954
Inscribed '1954' on reverse
Etching,
3⅞ × 5⅞ (10 × 14.9)
Purchased from the artist (Grant-in-Aid) 1983

P 07912
Marsh Plants 1954–83
Not inscribed
Etching,
5⅞ × 3⅞ (15 × 10)
Purchased from the artist (Grant-in-Aid) 1983

P 07913
Pimentoes 1954
Inscribed '1954' on reverse
Etching,
3 × 4 (7.5 × 10.2)
Purchased from the artist (Grant-in-Aid) 1983

P 07914
Skull and Pomegranate 1954
Inscribed '1954' on reverse
Etching with aquatint,
3⅜ × 4⅞ (8.8 × 12.5)
Purchased from the artist (Grant-in-Aid) 1983

P 07915
Corrugated Fence 1955
Inscribed '1955' on reverse
Etching,
3⅜ × 4⅞ (8.7 × 12.3)
Purchased from the artist (Grant-in-Aid) 1983

P 07916
Off the Tracks 1977
Inscribed 'Clough' b.r.
Etching,
10 × 8⅝ (25.4 × 22)
Purchased from the artist (Grant-in-Aid) 1983

P 07917
Fence/Climbing Plant 1979
Inscribed '1978' on reverse
Lithograph with hand colouring,
9½ × 11½ (24.1 × 29.3)
Purchased from the artist (Grant-in-Aid) 1983

P 07918
Gate Detail 1980
Not inscribed
Screenprint with hand colouring,
19⅛ × 22½ (48.4 × 57.3)
Purchased from the artist (Grant-in-Aid) 1983

P 07919
Gate 1981
Not inscribed
Screenprint with hand colouring,
6⅝ × 7⅝ (17 × 19.2)
Purchased from the artist (Grant-in-Aid) 1983

P 07920
Untitled 1981
Not inscribed
Woodcut (monoprint),
10½ × 11¾ (26.8 × 30)
Purchased from the artist (Grant-in-Aid) 1983

BERNARD COHEN b.1933

P 07756
Imitations 1981
Inscribed 'Bernard Cohen 1981' b.r. and '6/60'
Printed at Kelpra Studio, published by Waddington Graphics,
27 × 21¼ (68.5 × 54)
Purchased from Waddington Graphics (Grant-in-Aid) 1982

ROBERT COTTINGHAM b.1935

P 07641–3
Carl's 1977
Black Girl 1980
Frankfurters 1980
from 'The Landfall Set'
P 07641 inscribed 'Cottingham 77' b.r. and '30/50' and 'Carl's'
P 07642 inscribed 'Cottingham 1980' b.r. and '30/50'
P 07643 inscribed 'Cottingham 1980' b.r. and '34/50'
P 07641 etching
P 07642–3 lithographs
Printed and published by the Landfall Press, Chicago,
each approx. 10 × 10¼ (25.5 × 26)
Purchased at Sotheby's Los Angeles (Grant-in-Aid) 1982

SIMON CUTTS b.1944

P 08181
Winter Fruit 1980
Inscribed '26/50' (on bottom of cover)
Letterpress, printed by the artist, published by Coracle Press,
2½ × 3⅝ (6 × 9)
Transferred from Library 1982

RICHARD DIEBENKORN b.1922

P 07644
No. 4 1978
from 'Five Aquatints with Drypoint'
Inscribed 'RD 78 ' b.r. and '20/35' and '#4'
Aquatint with drypoint and open bite, printed and published by Crown Point Press,
10⅞ × 7⅞ (27.7 × 20)
Purchased at Christie's New York (Grant-in-Aid) 1982

JIM DINE b.1935

P 07757
Two Hearts in a Forest 1981
Inscribed 'Jim Dine 1981' b.l. and '16/24'
Woodcut with hand colouring, printed by the artist with his son at his Putney, Vermont Studio, published by Pace Editions, New York,
36 × 60⅛ (91.5 × 152.7)
Purchased from Waddington Graphics (Grant-in-Aid) 1983

MARTIN DISLER b.1948

P 07839–46, 07990
Endless Modern Licking of Crashing Globe by Black Doggie-Time Bomb 1981
Each inscribed 'Martin Disler' b.r. and '49/49'
Eight etchings, printed at Aeropress Inc., New York by Paul Marcus, published by Peter Blum Editions, New York (the portfolio is accompanied by a cassette tape and a pen-knife mounted on board),
each approx. 20⅞ × 28¾ (53 × 73)
Purchased from Peter Blum Editions (Grant-in-Aid) 1983

JEAN DUBUFFET b.1901

P 07781
Man in a Cap 1953
Inscribed 'J. Dubuffet '53' b.r. and 'L'Homme à la Casquette' and '10/20'
Lithograph,
20 × 6 (50.8 × 15.2)
Purchased from Sotheby's (Grant-in-Aid) 1983

LUCIANO FABRO b.1936

P 07994-7
SS Redentore 1972
Not inscribed
Four-part screenprint (each part consists of 12 sheets), printed by Alfredo and Enrico Rossi, published by the artist with Alfredo and Enrico Rossi in an edition of 120,
each panel $97\frac{1}{4} \times 92\frac{7}{8}$ (247 × 235.9)
Purchased from Galleria Pieroni (Grant-in-Aid) 1983

STANISLAW FIJALKOWSKI b.1922

P 07921
October 18, 1971 1971
Inscribed 'S. Fijalkowski' b.r. and '14/35' and '18 × 71'
Linocut, printed and published by the artist,
$15\frac{3}{4} \times 12\frac{1}{8}$ (40 × 30.8)
Purchased from the artist (Grant-in-Aid) 1983

P 07922
Motorway XLV 1976
Inscribed 'S. Fijalkowski 76' b.r. and 'XLV Autostrodov' and '13/70'
Linocut, printed and published by the artist,
$20\frac{1}{2} \times 16\frac{1}{8}$ (52.1 × 41)
Purchased from the artist (Grant-in-Aid) 1983

IAN HAMILTON FINLAY b.1925

P 07646
At the Field's Edge 1978
Inscribed 'Ian Hamilton Finlay' on transparent central sheet and '89'
Screenprint, printed at Girdwood, Edinburgh, published by the Wild Hawthorn Press, Lanark in an edition of about 300,
$11\frac{5}{8} \times 23\frac{3}{4}$ (29.6 × 60.3)
Purchased from the artist (Grant-in-Aid) 1982

P 07645
Sailing Barge Red Wing 1975
Inscribed 'Ian Hamilton Finlay' on flyleaf and '129'
Screenprint, printed at Girdwood, Edinburgh, published by the Wild Hawthorn Press in an edition of about 300,
13 × 12 (33 × 30.5)
Purchased from the artist (Grant-in-Aid) 1982

P 07647
Homage to Agam 1978
Inscribed 'Ian Hamilton Finlay' on flyleaf and '66'
Screenprint, printed at Girdwood, Edinburgh, published by the Wild Hawthorn Press in an edition of 150,
$15 \times 10\frac{3}{8}$ (38 × 26.4)
Purchased from the artist (Grant-in-Aid) 1982

P 07932-3
Midway I and II 1977
Not inscribed
Two screenprints, printed at Girdwood, Edinburgh, published by the Wild Hawthorn Press in an edition of about 300,
each approx. $22\frac{1}{4} \times 27\frac{1}{4}$ (56.5 × 69.2)
Purchased from the artist (Grant-in-Aid) 1983

P 07927-30
The Arts Council Must be Utterly Destroyed

Death to the Arts Council

Let Perish the Money Tyrants

Peace to the Cottages War on the Arts Council 1982

Not inscribed
Four linocuts,
each 12 × 17 (30.5 × 43.2)
Purchased from the artist (Grant-in-Aid) 1983

P 07931
Apollo and Daphne 1975
Not inscribed
Screenprint, printed at Girdwood, Edinburgh, published by the Wild Hawthorn Press in an edition of about 300,
$19 \times 13\frac{5}{8}$ (48.2 × 34.6)
Purchased from the artist (Grant-in-Aid) 1983

P 07926
Propaganda for the Wood-Elves 1981
Not inscribed
Photograph (collaboration with Harvey Dwight),
$8\frac{1}{4} \times 5\frac{7}{8}$ (21 × 14.8)
Purchased from the artist (Grant-in-Aid) 1983

P 07934
Venus of the Hours 1975
Not inscribed
Screenprint, printed at Girdwood, Edinburgh, published by the Wild Hawthorn Press in an edition of about 300,
$29\frac{1}{2} \times 14\frac{1}{2}$ (74.9 × 36.8)
Purchased from the artist (Grant-in-Aid) 1983

P 07923-4
Two Trees 1982
Not inscribed
Two woodcuts (collaboration with Richard Healy), published by the Wild Hawthorn Press,
$3\frac{5}{8} \times 4\frac{3}{8}$ (9.2 × 11.3), $4\frac{5}{8} \times 5\frac{1}{2}$ (11.8 × 14)
Purchased from the artist (Grant-in-Aid) 1983

P 07925
Homage to Malevich 1978
Inscribed 'Ian Hamilton Finlay' b.l. on folder and '118'
Screenprint (collaboration with Michael Harvey), printed at Girdwood, published by the Wild Hawthorn Press, in an edition of about 300,
$9\frac{7}{8} \times 9\frac{7}{8}$ (25.1 × 25.1)
Purchased from the artist (Grant-in-Aid) 1983

JOEL FISHER b.1947

P 07718
Untitled 1981
Inscribed 'J Fisher 1981' on reverse and 'Unique screenprint and chine collé'
Screenprint with chine collé, printed by the artist,
$29\frac{7}{8} \times 22\frac{1}{2}$ (75.9 × 57.2)
Purchased from Nigel Greenwood Inc. Ltd (Grant-in-Aid) 1983

BARRY FLANAGAN b.1941

P 07935
Field Day 1983
Inscribed 'BF' b.r. and '47/75'
Etching, printed by the artist and
Colin Dyer, published by
Waddington Graphics,
$7\frac{1}{4} \times 9\frac{1}{2}$ (18.4 × 21.6)
Purchased from Waddington Graphics
(Grant-in-Aid) 1983

P 07936
Welsh Cob 1983
Inscribed 'BF' b.r. and '2/50'
Linocut, printed by the artist and
Colin Dyer, published by
Waddington Graphics,
$14\frac{1}{4} \times 10$ (35.8 × 25.4)
Purchased from Waddington Graphics
(Grant-in-Aid) 1983

SAM FRANCIS b.1923

P 11070
Untitled
Inscribed 'Sam Francis' b.r. and '25/75'
Lithograph,
$33\frac{1}{2} \times 24\frac{7}{8}$ (85.1 × 63.2)
Presented by J. G. Cluff, 1984

P 11071
Untitled
Inscribed 'Sam Francis' b.r. and '31/50'
Lithograph,
$33\frac{1}{4} \times 24\frac{7}{8}$ (84.4 × 63.2)
Presented by J. G. Cluff, 1984

LUCIAN FREUD b.1922

P 07782
Head of a Woman 1982
Inscribed 'L.F' b.r. and 'A/P IV/X'
Etching, printed at Palm Tree Editions
by Terry Willson, published by Thames
& Hudson in an edition of 25 (from a set
of 4 published with 'de luxe' copies of
Lucian Freud by Lawrence Gowing),
5×5 (12.7 × 12.7)
Purchased from Anthony d'Offay
Gallery (Grant-in-Aid) 1982

P 07783
The Painter's Mother 1982
Inscribed 'L.F.' b.r. and 'A.P. IX/X'
Etching, printed at Palm Tree Editions
by Terry Willson, published by Thames
& Hudson in an edition of 25,
7×6 (17.8 × 15.2)
Purchased from Anthony d'Offay Gallery
(Grant-in-Aid) 1982

TERRY FROST b.1915

P 07981
Blue Moon 1952
Inscribed 'Terry Frost 52' b.r.
Lithograph with linocut, printed at Bath
Academy of Art, Corsham (not editioned),
$14 \times 10\frac{7}{8}$ (35.5 × 27.5)
Purchased from the artist (Grant-in-Aid)
1983

P 07982
Boat Shapes 1952
Inscribed 'Terry Frost' b.r. and 'lino cut
printed in 52 but all different possibly
20 in all'
Linocut, not editioned,
$6\frac{1}{2} \times 6\frac{3}{8}$ (16.7 × 16.2)
Purchased from the artist (Grant-in-Aid)
1983

P 07983
Boat Shapes c.1954
Inscribed 'Terry Frost' b.r. and 'never
editioned'
Linocut, not editioned,
$5\frac{5}{8} \times 6\frac{3}{4}$ (14.2 × 17.3)
Purchased from the artist (Grant-in-Aid)
1983

P 07984
Boat Shapes 1954
Linocut, not editioned,
$8\frac{7}{8} \times 11$ (22.5 × 28)
Purchased from the artist (Grant-in-Aid)
1983

P 07985
Leeds 1956
Inscribed 'Terry Frost 56' b.r. and
'Leeds. Cottage Rd never editioned
possibly 4 printed'
Etching, not editioned,
$4\frac{7}{8} \times 6\frac{5}{8}$ (12.5 × 16.8)
Purchased from the artist (Grant-in-Aid)
1983

P 07986
Camping, Anduze 1979
Inscribed 'Terry Frost' b.r. and 'A/P.
Camping Anduze' and 'not editioned
possibly 6 printed 1967 or 68'
Etching, not editioned,
$10\frac{1}{4} \times 8\frac{1}{4}$ (26 × 21)
Purchased from the artist (Grant-in-Aid)
1983

P 07987
Umea, Sweden 1979
Inscribed 'Terry Frost 79' b.r. and
'Umea A/P'
Etching, not editioned,
$13\frac{3}{4} \times 10\frac{1}{4}$ (35 × 26)
Purchased from the artist (Grant-in-Aid)
1983

P 07988
Self Portrait 1980
Inscribed 'Terry Frost 80' b.r. and
'A/P'
Etching, not editioned,
$10\frac{7}{8} \times 7\frac{7}{8}$ (27.7 × 20)
Purchased from the artist (Grant-in-Aid)
1983

PHILIP GUSTON 1913-1980

Eight lithographs, printed and published
by Gemini G.E.L., Los Angeles,
presented by David and Renée McKee
through the American Federation of Arts
1984

P 11077
Car 1980
Inscribed 'Philip Guston 80' b.r. and
'Car' and '22/50'
$18\frac{1}{4} \times 30$ (46.3 × 76.2)

P 11079
Coat 1980
Inscribed 'Philip Guston 80' and 'Coat'
and '22/50'
$23\frac{3}{4} \times 37\frac{3}{4}$ (60.4 × 95.9)

P 11073
East Side 1980
Inscribed 'Philip Guston 80' b.r. and
'East Side 22/50'
$30 \times 39\frac{3}{4}$ (76.2 × 101)

P 11078
Elements 1980
Inscribed 'Philip Guston 80' b.c.
and 'Elements' and '22/50'
$26\frac{3}{4} \times 39$ (67.9 × 99)

P 11072
Room 1980
Inscribed 'Philip Guston 80' b.r. and
'Room' and '22/50'
$28\frac{3}{4} \times 40$ (73 × 101.6)

P 11074
Rug 1980
Inscribed 'Philip Guston 80' b.r. and
'Rug' and '22/50'
$19\frac{1}{2} \times 29$ (49.5 × 73.6)

P 11076
Sea 1980
Inscribed 'Philip Guston 80' b.r. and
'Sea' and '22/50'
58.4 × 99 (23 × 39)

P 11075
Summer 1980
Inscribed 'Philip Guston 80' b.c.
and 'Summer' and '22/50'
46.4 × 73 (18¼ × 28¾)

P 07999
Door 1980
Inscribed 'Philip Guston '80' b.r. and
'Door 42/50'
Lithograph, printed and published
by Gemini G.E.L.,
19½ × 29½ (49.5 × 74.9)
Purchased from Gemini G.E.L. (Grant-
in-Aid) 1984

P 77009
Painter 1980
Inscribed '34/50' b.l., stamped with an
estate stamp
Lithograph, printed, published and
numbered by Gemini G.E.L.,
32 × 42½ (81.3 × 107.9)
Purchased from Gemini G.E.L. (Grant-
in-Aid) 1984

RICHARD HAMILTON b.1922

P 07648-53
Reaper d, e, g, h, i and j 1949
Reaper d: etching and mezzotint,
inscribed '4/20'
Reaper e: etching and mezzotint,
inscribed 'RH' t.r. and '2/10'
Reaper g: etching, inscribed
'R Hamilton' b.r. and '3/25'
Reaper h: drypoint and mezzotint,
inscribed 'R Hamilton' b.r. and '8/20'
Reaper i: aquatint, inscribed
'R. Hamilton' b.r. and '5/25'
Reaper j: etching and mezzotint,
inscribed 'R Hamilton' b.r. and '1/20'
Printed by the artist at the Slade
School of Art, published by the artist,
in range 4 × 8⅞–8½ × 12¾
(10 × 22.5–22.5 × 32.5)
Purchased from the artist (Grant-in-Aid)
1982

P 07654
Plant Cycle 1950
Inscribed 'R. Hamilton' b.r. and '5/20'
Etching with drypoint and aquatint,
printed by the artist at the Slade
School of Art, published by the artist,

7 × 8¾ (17.7 × 22.5)
Purchased from the artist (Grant-in-Aid)
1982

P 07655
Structure 1950
Inscribed 'R Hamilton' b.r. and '6/20'
Etching with aquatint, printed by the
artist at the Slade School of Art,
published by the artist,
40 × 30.3 (15¾ × 11⅞)
Purchased from the artist (Grant-in-Aid)
1982

P 07658
Still-Life? 1955
Inscribed 'R. Hamilton' b.r. and 'proof'
Etching, printed by the artist, not
editioned,
9⅝ × 6⅞ (24.5 × 17.5)
Purchased from the artist (Grant-in-Aid)
1982

P 07657
Self Portrait 1951
Inscribed 'Richard Hamilton' b.l. and
'Self portrait'
Etching with aquatint and mezzotint,
printed by the artist, not editioned,
11¾ × 7⅞ (30 × 20)
Purchased from the artist (Grant-in-Aid)
1982

P 07656
Heteromorphism 1951
Inscribed 'R. Hamilton' b.r. and '8/20'
Etching with aquatint, printed by the
artist at the Slade School of Art,
published by the artist,
10 × 7⅞ (25.5 × 20)
Purchased from the artist (Grant-in-Aid)
1982

P 07659
Picasso's Meninas 1973
from 'Homage to Picasso'
Inscribed 'Richard Hamilton' b.r. and
'Picasso's Meninas' and 'EA /15'
Etching with aquatint, printed at Studio
Crommelynck, Paris, published by
Propylaen Verlag, Berlin, in an edition
of 90,
22½ × 19¼ (57 × 49)
Purchased from Desmond Page
(Grant-in-Aid) 1982

P 07937
Fashion Plate 1969-70
Inscribed 'Tony's Proof from Richard' b.r.
Lithography, screenprint with collage,
pochoir and cosmetics, lithographed by
Sergio and Fausta Tosi, Milan,

screenprinted by Kelpra Studio,
published by Petersburg Press
in an edition of 70,
29¼ × 23¾ (74.3 × 60.4)
Purchased at Sotheby's (Grant-in-Aid)
1983

HARRY HOLLAND b.1941

P 07805
Door 1982
Inscribed 'W H Holland' b.r. and '4/30'
Lithograph, printed by Nick Hunter,
published by Garton and Cooke,
7⅝ × 5⅛ (19.2 × 13)
Purchased from Robin Garton Gallery
(Grant-in-Aid) 1983

P 07806
Lovers 1982
Inscribed 'W.H. Holland' b.r. and '6/30'
Lithograph, printed by Nick Hunter,
published by Garton and Cooke,
5⅜ × 4½ (13.6 × 11.5)
Purchased from Robin Garton Gallery
(Grant-in-Aid) 1983

P 07807
TV 1982
Inscribed 'W H Holland' b.r. and '1/30'
Lithograph, printed by Nick Hunter,
published by Garton and Cooke,
5⅞ × 6⅛ (14.9 × 15.5)
Purchased from Robin Garton Gallery
(Grant-in-Aid) 1983

JENNY HOLZER b.1950

P 07847 (i)–(xxix)
Essays 1979-82
One inscribed 'Jenny Holzer' on reverse
29 offset lithographs, printed at Milner
Bros., New York, published by the
artist in an unlimited edition,
43.2 × 43.2 (17 × 17)
Purchased from the Lisson Gallery
(Grant-in-Aid) 1983

BILL JACKLIN b.1943

P 02559-65
Anemones 1977
Each inscribed 'Jacklin 77' b.r. and
'19/40' and 'Anemones I' to 'Anemones
VII' respectively
Seven etchings with aquatint, printed by
Michael Rand, published by the artist,
each 11¾ × 7⅞ (30 × 20)
Presented by the artist 1982

JASPER JOHNS b.1930

P 07736
Savarin 1982
Inscribed 'J Johns 82' b.r. and '4/4'
Monotype: lithograph with painting and
hand colouring, printed at Universal
Limited Art Editions by Thomas Cox,
James V. Smith and Bill Goldston
in an edition of 4 (varying),
$39\frac{3}{4} \times 29\frac{7}{8}$ (101 × 76)
Purchased from Universal Limited Art
Editions (Grant-in-Aid) 1983

ALLEN JONES b.1937

P 07449
Box 1980
Inscribed 'Allen Jones 80' b.r. and '46/70'
Lithograph on 4 sheets, printed by
Ian Lawson, published by
Waddington Graphics,
$41\frac{3}{4} \times 59\frac{7}{8}$ (106 × 152) overall
Purchased from Waddington Graphics
(Grant-in-Aid) 1982

P 07759
Take it from the Top 1982
Inscribed 'Allen Jones 82' b.r. and '25/50'
Lithograph, printed at Solo Press,
New York, published by
Waddington Graphics,
$28\frac{5}{8} \times 37$ (72.7 × 94)
Purchased from Waddington Graphics
(Grant-in-Aid) 1983

PETER LANYON 1918–1964

P 07741
The Returned Seaman 1949
Inscribed 'Peter Lanyon/49' b.l. and
'The Returned Seaman'
Linocut with watercolour, printed by the
artist,
21 × 29 (53.2 × 73.6)
Purchased from the New Art Centre
(Grant-in-Aid) 1983

SOL LEWITT b.1928

P 07660–5
Location of Six Geometric Figures
1975
Each inscribed 'LeWitt' b.r. and '2/25'
and 'I/VI' – 'VI/VI'
Six etchings, printed at Crown Point
Press, published by Parasol Press,
New York,
each $15\frac{3}{4} \times 16$ (40 × 40.6)
Purchased from the Lisson Gallery
(Grant-in-Aid) 1982

RICHARD PAUL LOHSE b.1902

P 07666–71
Untitled 1981
Each inscribed 'Lohse' b.r. and
'a 47/90', 'b 47/90', 'c 47/90', 'd 47/90',
'e 47/90' and 'f 47/90' respectively
Six screenprints, printed and published
by Editions Média, Neuchâtel,
each 26 × 26 (66 × 66)
Purchased from Editions Média
(Grant-in-Aid) 1982

ROBERT LONGO b.1953

P 07899
Jules, Gretchen, Mark, State II
1982–83
Inscribed 'Robert Longo 83' b.r. and
'19/30'
Lithograph and embossing, printed at
Derrière l'Etoile Studios Ltd.,
New York, published by Brooke
Alexander Gallery, New York,
30 × $52\frac{3}{4}$ (76.2 × 134)
Purchased from Brooke Alexander
Gallery (Grant-in-Aid) 1983

BRICE MARDEN b.1938

P 07849–52
Tiles 1979
Each inscribed 'B. Marden 79' b.r. and
'15/50'
Four etchings, P 07851 with aquatint,
printed at Crown Point Press, California,
published by Parasol Press, New York,
each 8 × 8 (20.3 × 20.3)
Purchased from Parasol Press (Grant-
in-Aid) 1983

KENNETH MARTIN b.1905

P 07743
Pier and Ocean 1980
Inscribed 'Kenneth Martin 80' b.r.
and '57/70'
Screenprint on two sheets, printed at
Editions Média, Neuchâtel,
published by Waddington Graphics,
17 × $26\frac{5}{8}$ (43 × 67.5)
Purchased from Waddington Graphics
(Grant-in-Aid) 1982

P 07742
Venice 1980
Inscribed 'Kenneth Martin 80' b.r.
and '57/70'
Screenprint on two sheets, printed at
Editions Média, Neuchâtel,
published by Waddington Graphics,

$17\frac{3}{4} \times 27\frac{3}{4}$ (45 × 70.5)
Purchased from Waddington Graphics
(Grant-in-Aid) 1982

JOAN MIRÓ 1893–1984

P 07900
Series II 1952
Inscribed 'Miro 1952' b.r. and '4/13'
Etching, printed at Lacourière
Imprimeur, published by Maeght Editeur,
Paris,
$14\frac{7}{8} \times 17\frac{7}{8}$ (37.7 × 45.5)
Purchased from the Isselbacher Gallery,
New York (Grant-in-Aid) 1983

NICHOLAS MONRO b.1936

P 07672
Estuary 1982
Inscribed 'Nicholas Monro 82' b.r. and
'8/70'
Screenprint, printed at Kelpra Studio,
published by Helen Chetwynd,
$27\frac{3}{4} \times 38\frac{3}{8}$ (70.5 × 97.5)
Purchased from Helen Chetwynd
(Grant-in-Aid) 1982

HENRY MOORE O.M., C.H. b.1898

P 02566–2637
P 02640–2722

Group of 157 lithographs and etchings
made between 1973–81. This is the latest
part of Henry Moore's ongoing gift to
the Print Collection of one copy of every
impression he makes.

All are dedicated proofs apart from
P 02576, 02577–80, 02585, 02594–5,
02599–601, 02603, 02604, 02610, 02612,
02649–52, 02676, 02691, 02701–3,
02707–12

BRUCE NAUMAN b.1941

P 07938
NO (Black State) 1981
Inscribed 'B Nauman 81' b.r. and '9/25'
Lithograph, printed and published
by Gemini G.E.L.,
$27\frac{1}{2} \times 40\frac{7}{8}$ (69.8 × 103.8)
Purchased from Castelli Graphics
(Grant-in-Aid) 1983

DENNIS OPPENHEIM b 1938

P 07939
The Diamond Cutter's Wedding
1979–80
Inscribed 'Dennis Oppenheim' b.c. and
'1980' and 'AP 17/46'
Screenprint, published by ARC, Paris,
38⅛ × 49⅞ (96.8 × 126.7)
Purchased from Galerie Malacorda
(Grant-in-Aid) 1983

MIMMO PALADINO b.1948

P 07631
Peter's Stone 1980
Inscribed 'Mimmo Paladino 1980' b.r.
and '17/35'
Etching with drypoint and aquatint,
printed at Aeropress, New York,
published by Multiples Inc., New York,
15 × 14½ (38 × 37)
Purchased from Waddington Graphics
(Grant-in-Aid) 1982

P 07630
Pool Water
Inscribed 'Mimmo Paladino 1980' b.r.
and '10/35'
Etching with aquatint, printed at
Aeropress, New York, published
by Multiples Inc., New York,
22½ × 35¼ (57.2 × 89.5)
Purchased from Waddington Graphics
(Grant-in-Aid) 1982

P 07854
Menacing Caves 1982
Inscribed 'Mimmo Paladino' b.r. and
'1/35'
Etching with linocut, printed at
Aeropress, New York, published by
Multiples Inc., New York,
15¾ × 9½ (40 × 24.2)
Purchased from Waddington Graphics
(Grant-in-Aid) 1983

GIULIO PAOLINI b.1940

P 07673-8
Collection 1974
Each inscribed 'Giulio Paolini 1974'
b.r. and '80/80' and:
P 07673 'Antologia'
P 07674 'Collezione'
P 07675 'Epidaurus'
P 07676 'Isfahan'
P 07677 'Monitor'
P 07678 'Rebus'
Six screenprints, printed at Multirevol,

Milan, published by Studio Marconi,
Milan,
each approx. 12½ × 12½ (31.7 × 31.7)
Purchased from the Lisson Gallery
(Grant-in-Aid) 1982

EDUARDO PAOLOZZI b.1924

P 07621
Nettleton
from 'Calcium Light Night' 1974–6
Inscribed 'Eduardo Paolozzi 1977' b.r.
and 'A/P 2/25'
Screenprint, printed at Advanced
Graphics, published by the artist in an
edition of 200,
31½ × 21½ (80 × 54.5)
Purchased from the artist (Grant-in-Aid)
1982

P 07679
Head 1977
Inscribed 'Eduardo Paolozzi 1977' b.r.
and 'A/P'
Etching (trial proof), printed by the
artist at the Royal College of Art,
11¼ × 8¼ (28.5 × 21)
Purchased from the artist (Grant-in-Aid)
1982

P 07680
Head 1979
Inscribed 'E Paolozzi 1979' b.r. and
'drypoint' and 'AP'
Drypoint etching, printed by the artist
at the Royal College of Art,
12¼ × 8⅛ (31 × 20.7)
Purchased from the artist (Grant-in-Aid)
1982

P 07681
Head 1980
Inscribed 'Eduardo Paolozzi 1980' b.r.
and 'A/P'
Transfer from etching (trial proof),
printed by the artist at the Royal
College of Art,
17⅝ × 11¾ (44.8 × 30)
Purchased from the artist (Grant-in-Aid)
1982

P 07682
Head 1980
Inscribed 'Eduardo Paolozzi 1980' b.r.
and 'A/P'
Etching (trial proof), printed by the artist
at the Royal College of Art,
17¾ × 12 (45 × 30.5)
Purchased from the artist (Grant-in-Aid)
1982

P 07683
After Antonio di Bioggio 1980
Not inscribed
Lithograph (trial proof), not editioned,
5⅞ × 9⅞ (15 × 25)
Purchased from the artist (Grant-in-Aid)
1982

P 07684
Parkplatz 1980
Inscribed 'Eduardo Paolozzi 1980' b.r.
and 'A/P'
Etching and engraving,
13½ × 19⅛ (34.3 × 48.5)
Purchased from the artist (Grant-in-Aid)
1982

TOM PHILLIPS b.1937

Dante's Inferno 1979–83
P 07685-8	Canto I
P 07761-4	Canto IV
P 07765-8	Canto VI
P 07689-92	Canto VIII
P 07769-72	Canto IX
P 07693-6	Canto X
P 07773-6	Canto XI
P 07784-7	Canto XIV
P 07788-91	Canto XVI
P 07792-5	Canto XVII
P 07697-700	Canto XVIII
P 07701-4	Canto XX
P 07705-8	Canto XXI
P 07796-9	Canto XXII
P 07800-3	Canto XXIII
P 07855-8	Canto XXIV
P 07883-6	Canto XXV
P 07859-62	Canto XXVI
P 07863-6	Canto XXVII
P 07867-70	Canto XXVIII
P 07871-4	Canto XXIX
P 07875-8	Canto XXX
P 07879-82	Canto XXXI
P 07887-90	Canto XXXII
P 07891-4	Canto XXXIII
P 07895-8	Canto XXXIV

All inscribed 'T.P.' b.r. and, on
colophon: 'of the edition proper
consisting of one hundred copies this is
no.77'
Each Canto contains four images;
etching, aquatint, lithography and
screenprinting were used. The complete
work (the other eight Cantos were
acquired in 1981) was printed and
published by the artist, various sizes
Purchased from the artist (Grant-in-Aid)
during 1982 and 1983

JOHN PIPER b.1903

P 02997-3304
Eightieth Anniversary Portfolio 1983
Each inscribed 'John Piper' b.r. and
'For the Tate Gallery'
Three etchings, one etching with
screenprinting and four
screenprints, printed at Kelpra Studio,
published by Orde Levinson in an
edition of 75,
each approx. $17\frac{1}{2} \times 25\frac{3}{8}$ (44.6 × 64.5)
Presented by Orde Levinson 1983

LUCIEN PISSARRO 1863-1944

P 08182-209
The Parish Priest c.1884
The Pastry Cook c.1884
Young Girl 1889
April 1890-1
Floreal 1890-1
Contentment and Tennis 1890-1
Ex Libris Isa Taylor c.1892
Portrait of Camille Pissarro 1893
Boy and Pine Tree 1894-1980
Illustration to 'A Simple Heart' 1900-1
Choice of Sonnets 1902
Geese c.1903
Boy Breaking a Stick c.1905
Consultation I-III c.1905
Love Chained Down c.1905
New Year Card 1905
Reading c.1905
Women in Roundel c.1908
New Year Card 1910 1909-10
The Shepherdess c.1912
Landscape: Blackpool, Devon 1914
Rye 1920
New Year Card 1924 1923-4
Christmas Card 1925 1925
New Year Card 1927 1925-7
Shepherdess 1929
28 woodcuts, printed by Iain Bain and
David Chambers in 1980, published by
the Ashmolean Museum, Oxford in
an edition of 175,
in range $1 \times 1\frac{1}{8}$ (2.5 × 2.9) - $3\frac{7}{8} \times 7\frac{1}{2}$
(9.8 × 19)
Transferred from Library 1982

ARNULF RAINER b.1929

P 07709-13
Five Reds 1972-79
Each inscribed 'A. Rainer' b.r. and '3/35'
Five etchings, printed by Karl Imhof,
Munich, published by Edition Galerie
Heiner Friedrich, Munich,
in range $9\frac{1}{2} \times 13\frac{1}{4}$ - $12\frac{3}{8} \times 17$

(24 × 33.5 - 31.4 × 43.2)
Purchased from Gallery Heike Curtze
(Grant-in-Aid) 1982

P 07714
Cross 1977-80
Inscribed 'A. Rainer' b.r. and '32/35'
Etching, printed by Karl Imhof, Munich,
published by Edition Galerie Heiner
Friedrich, Munich,
$45\frac{1}{4} \times 19\frac{1}{2}$ (115 × 49.5)
Purchased from Gallery Heike Curtze
(Grant-in-Aid) 1982

ROBERT RAUSCHENBERG
b.1925

P 07715
Preview 1974
from 'Hoarfrost Series'
Inscribed 'Rauschenberg 74' b.l. and
'AP II'
Lithograph, printed and published by
Gemini G.E.L., Los Angeles, in an edition
of 32,
$68\frac{7}{8} \times 80\frac{1}{2}$ (175 × 204.5) overall
Purchased from Delahunty Gallery
(Grant-in-Aid) 1982

P 77010
Yellow Body 1971
Inscribed 'RAUSCHENBERG 71' b.l. and '7/80'
Screenprint, printed at Styria Studio,
New York, published by Styria Studio
with Untitled Press, Captiva Island,
Florida,
$48\frac{5}{8} \times 62\frac{1}{2}$ (123.5 × 158.8)
Purchased at Christie's (Grant-in-
Aid) 1984

SUSAN ROTHENBERG b.1945

P 07740
Head and Bones 1980
Inscribed 'S. Rothenberg 80' b.r. and
'12/20'
Woodcut, printed at Aeropress,
New York, published by Multiples Inc.,
New York,
$13 \times 11\frac{1}{4}$ (33 × 28.5)
Purchased from Multiples Inc.
(Grant-in-Aid) 1983

FELIX ROZEN b.1938

P 11052-61
Uncertain Opus 1981
P 11052 inscribed 'Rozen' and 'III/XXXIII',
the other sheets not inscribed
Ten screenprints, printed at Atelier 55,

Paris, in an edition of 33,
each $13\frac{3}{8} \times 23\frac{3}{8}$ (34 × 59.5)
Presented by Mrs Leslie Oliver through
The Friends of the Tate Gallery 1983

EDWARD RUSCHA b.1937

P 07716
Hollywood 1969
Inscribed 'E. Ruscha 1969' b.r. and
'2/18'
Lithograph, printed by Tamarind
Lithography Workshop, Los Angeles,
published by the artist and
Tamarind Lithography Workshop,
$4\frac{1}{8} \times 17$ (10.5 × 43)
Purchased at Sotheby's Los Angeles
(Grant-in-Aid) 1982

P 07940
**Roughly 92% Angel, but about
8% Devil** 1982
Inscribed 'Ed Ruscha 82' b.r. and '6/25'
Softground etching, printed by Peter
Pettengill at Crown Point Press,
published by Crown Point Press,
$14\frac{1}{2} \times 15\frac{1}{4}$ (36.8 × 38.8)
Purchased from Crown Point Press
(Grant-in-Aid) 1983

ROBERT RYMAN b.1930

P 07717-23
Seven Aquatints 1972
Each inscribed 'Ryman 72' (various
places) and '23/50'
Seven aquatints, printed at Crown
Point Press, California, published by
Parasol Press, New York,
in range $11\frac{5}{8} \times 11\frac{3}{4}$ - 24 × 24
(29.7 × 30 - 61 × 61)
Purchased from the Lisson Gallery
(Grant-in-Aid) 1982

COLIN SELF b.1941

P 07747
Bomber No.1 1963
Inscribed 'Colin Self 1963' b.r. and
'(Bomber No.1)' and '1/1' and 'Edition of
5 or 6 varying prints, No 2'
Etching from cut and assembled plates
with embossing, transfers and drawing,
$12\frac{3}{4} \times 11\frac{5}{8}$ (32.5 × 29.6)
Purchased from the artist (Grant-in-Aid)
1982

P 07941
Margaret in a Chair. No.1 1963
Inscribed 'Colin Self. 1963.' and
'Margaret in a chair. No. 1.' and '1/5'
Etching,
$7\frac{1}{2} \times 5\frac{7}{8}$ (19.2 × 14.8)
Purchased from the artist (Grant-in-Aid)
1983

P 07942
Fifth Monument 1964
Inscribed 'Colin Self, 1964' b.l. and
'1/3 5th Monument'
Etching from cut and assembled
plates,
$27\frac{1}{2} \times 17$ (69.8 × 43.2)
Purchased from the artist (Grant-in-Aid)
1983

P 07943
Pluto *c*.1965
Not inscribed
Monoprint from paper with hand
colouring,
$16\frac{3}{4} \times 23\frac{3}{4}$ (42.7 × 60.5)
Purchased from the artist (Grant-in-Aid)
1983

P 07944
Out of Focus Object and Flowers
1968
Inscribed 'Colin Self 1968' b.r. and
'Out of focus object & flowers.' and
'Trial Proof 1/1 3'
Etching,
$10\frac{3}{4} \times 9\frac{3}{4}$ (27.3 × 24.8)
Purchased from the artist (Grant-in-Aid)
1983

P 07945
Picasso's 'Guernica' and the Nazis
1968
Inscribed 'c.s. 1968' and 'Lithotrial 2 1/3'
and 'Picasso's Guernica and the Nazis'
Lithograph with biro,
$7\frac{3}{8} \times 12\frac{3}{8}$ (18.8 × 31.5)
Purchased from the artist (Grant-in-Aid)
1983

P 07946
A Letter to Christopher Logue 1980
Inscribed 'Colin Self' and '1980' and
'4/14' and 'A letter to Christopher
Logue'
Xerox print with collage and ink,
$5\frac{7}{8} \times 9\frac{5}{8}$ (14.8 × 24.5)
Purchased from the artist (Grant-in-Aid)
1983

P 07746
Power and Beauty No.3 1968
from 'Power and Beauty'
Inscribed 'Colin Self' b.l. and
'Power and Beauty No. 3 72/75'
Screenprint with embossing, printed
and published by Editions Alecto,
$26\frac{5}{8} \times 40\frac{5}{8}$ (67.6 × 103.2)
Purchased from the artist (Grant-in-Aid)
1982

P 07745
Power and Beauty No.6 1968
from 'Power and Beauty'
Inscribed 'Colin Self' b.l. and
'Power and Beauty No.6 68/75'
Screenprint, printed and published by
Editions Alecto,
$27\frac{7}{8} \times 38\frac{3}{4}$ (70.7 × 98.5)
Purchased from the artist (Grant-in-Aid)
1982

P 07744
Power and Beauty No.7 1968
from 'Power and Beauty'
Inscribed 'Colin Self' b.c. and 'Power
and Beauty No 7 2/2'
Screenprint, printed by Editions Alecto
(but not editioned),
$28\frac{5}{8} \times 39\frac{1}{8}$ (72.8 × 99.3)
Purchased from the artist (Grant-in-Aid)
1982

P 07748
Lonewolf 1981
Inscribed 'Colin Self August 1981' b.c.
and 'The Lonewolf' and '3/4'
Blockprint, printed by the artist in an
edition of 4 (varying),
$2\frac{3}{4} \times 2\frac{7}{8}$ (7 × 7.3)
Purchased from the artist (Grant-in-Aid)
1982

CINDY SHERMAN b.1954

P 07804 (i)–(iv)
Untitled 1982
Four-part photograph (numbered 97, 98,
99, 100), in an edition of 10,
each 45 × 30 (114.3 × 76.2)
Purchased from Metro Pictures
(Grant-in-Aid) 1983

FRANK STELLA b.1936

P 07735
Estoril Five II 1982
from 'Circuits' series
Inscribed 'F. Stella 82' b.r. and '30/30'
Etching with relief on dyed, handmade
paper, printed and published by

Tyler Graphics, New York,
$66\frac{1}{4} \times 51\frac{1}{2}$ (168.2 × 130.8)
Purchased from Waddington Graphics
(Grant-in-Aid) 1982

WAYNE THIEBAUD b.1920

P 07724
Chocolate Cake 1971
Inscribed 'Thiebaud 1971' b.r. and '13/50'
Lithograph, printed by Michael Knigin,
published by Parasol Press, New York,
17 × 13 (44.5 × 33)
Purchased at Sotheby's Los Angeles
(Grant-in-Aid) 1982

VALERIE THORNTON b.1931

P 02638
Monterde 1980
Inscribed 'Valerie Thornton '80' b.r. and
'Monterde' and 'A.P'
Etching,
$19\frac{3}{8} \times 27\frac{1}{4}$ (49.2 × 69.2)
Presented by the artist 1983

P 02639
Sangüesa 1982
Inscribed 'Valerie Thornton 82' and
'Sangüesa' and '35/60'
Etching, printed and published by the
artist,
$25\frac{1}{2} \times 16\frac{3}{8}$ (64.8 × 41.6)
Presented by the artist 1983

JOHN WALKER b.1939

P 07749–53
Prahran 3, 5, 8, 12 and 17
from 'Prahran' portfolio 1981
Each inscribed 'Walker 81' b.r. and:
P 07749: '17/25' and 'Prahran 3'
P 07750: '14/25' and 'Prahran 5'
P 07751: '1/25' and 'Prahran 8'
P 07752: '1/25' and 'Prahran 12'
P 07753: '1/25' and 'Prahran 17'
Five etchings, printed by the artist at the
Prahran School of Art, Victoria,
published by the artist,
in range $4\frac{3}{4} \times 4\frac{3}{4} - 17\frac{1}{2} \times 23\frac{5}{8}$
(12 × 12 - 44.5 × 60)
Purchased from Nigel Greenwood Inc.
Ltd (Grant-in-Aid) 1982

P 11051
Pacifica 1982
Inscribed 'Walker 82' b.r. and '15/35'
and 'Pacifica'
Screenprint, printed at Advanced
Graphics, published by the artist,
61 × 46⅞ (115 × 119)
Presented by the Contemporary Art
Society 1982 to commemorate Nancy
Balfour's retirement as Chairman

ANDY WARHOL b.1928

P 07725-34
Electric Chairs 1971
Each inscribed 'Andy Warhol 71' b.l.
Ten screenprints, printed by Factory
Additions, New York, published by the
artist in an edition of 250,
each 35⅜ × 47⅞ (90 × 121.6)
Purchased at Sotheby's Los Angeles
(Grant-in-Aid) 1982

TOM WESSELMANN b.1931

P 07760
Seascape Dropout 1982
Inscribed 'Wesselmann '82' b.c. and '40/50'
Woodcut, printed by Michael Berden,
Boston, published by Multiples Inc.,
New York,
21⅞ × 25 (55.6 × 63.5)
Purchased from Waddington Graphics
(Grant-in-Aid) 1982

STEPHEN WILLATS b.1943

P 07947
Wall Print 1980
Inscribed 'S. Willats' on reverse and '12'
and 'Wall Print no.80' and 'Edition
specially made for Jurgen Schweinebraden
in East Berlin during June 1980.
Edition distributed throughout Eastern
Europe'
Offset lithograph, published by
Jurgen Schweinebraden, East Berlin,
8 × 6 (20.3 × 15.2)
Purchased from the artist (Grant-in-Aid)
1983

WOLS 1913–1951

P 07948-80
Complete set of Wols' etchings
The 33 plates were made by Wols in his
lifetime: this set was printed under the
control of his widow in the mid-1950s.
Not inscribed
Thirty-three etchings and drypoints,
in range 2½ × 4 – 12⅞ × 9¾
(6.4 × 10.2 – 32.4 × 24.8)
Purchased from Reiss Cohen Inc.
(Grant-in-Aid) 1983

Appendix 1 Trustees of the Tate Gallery
1 April 1982 – 31 March 1984

The Lord Hutchinson, QC *Chairman*
The Countess of Airlie, CVO *from 21 January* 1983
Sir Richard Attenborough, CBE *until 29 December* 1982
Mr Anthony Caro, CBE *from 1 September* 1982
Miss Rita Donagh *until 17 February* 1984
Mr Francis Graham-Harrison, CB *until 14 May* 1982
Mr Patrick Heron, CBE, FBA *from 25 July* 1980
Mrs Caryl Hubbard *National Gallery Liaison Trustee from December* 1983
Mr Paul Huxley *until 14 May* 1982
Mr Peter Moores
Mr Peter Palumbo
Sir Rex Richards, DSc, FRS, FRIC *from 15 May* 1982
Mr Richard Rogers, ARA, RIBA
The Hon. Sir John Sainsbury *National Gallery Liaison Trustee until 28 June* 1983

Appendix 2   Gallery Staff

position as at 1 April 1984

THE MODERN COLLECTION

Ronald Alley, BA	Keeper (Curator A)
Richard Morphet, BA	Deputy Keeper (Curator B)
David Brown, DVM & S, BA, BSC	Curator C
David Fraser Jenkins, MA, MPhil	Curator C
Richard Francis, MA	Curator C
Richard Calvocoressi, MA	Curator D
Catherine Lacey, MA	Curator D
Christine Kurpiel	Personal Secretary

PRINT COLLECTION

Elizabeth Underhill	Curator C
Jeremy Lewison, MA	Curator E
Ian Friend, DIP AD, HDFA	Curator F
Suzanne Benney	Curator G

BARBARA HEPWORTH MUSEUM – ST IVES

Brian Smith	Curator F
George Wilkinson	Museum Technician III
Victoria Raynsford	Publications/Salesperson

MUSEUM SERVICES

Michael Compton, BA	Keeper (Curator A)

EDUCATION DEPARTMENT

Simon Wilson, MA	Head of Education (Curator D)
Patricia Turner, MEdAD	Lecturer (CuratorE)
Richard Humphreys, MA	Lecturer (Curator F)
Patricia Adams	Schools Liaison Officer (Curator G)
Richard Chapman, BA, Dip Arts Admin	Audio Visual Officer (Curator G)
Keith Skone	Film Officer (Curator G)
Susan Duncan	Personal Secretary

ARCHIVE COLLECTION

Sarah Fox Pitt, BA	Curator C
Clare Colvin, MA, Dip Archive Admin	Archivist (Curator E)
Jennifer Booth, BA, Dip Archive Admin	Archivist (Curator F)
Tamsyn Woollcombe	Personal Secretary

LIBRARY

Antony Symons, BA, FLA	Head of the Library (Curator D)
Beth Houghton, Dip AD, ALA	Librarian (Curator E)
Krzysztof Cieszkowski, MA, DLIS	Cataloguer (Curator E)
Meg Duff, BA, Dip Ed, Dip NZLS	Cataloguer (Curator E)
Elisabeth Bell, MA	Exchange Librarian (Executive Officer)
Caron Galbraith	Clerical Officer
Diana Hart	Typist

Clare Signy, BA, Dip Cons	Conservator F (student)
Paul Ackroyd, BA	Conservator G (student)
Nicole Ryder, BA	Conservator G (student)
Victoria Todd	Personal Secretary
Thomas Lye	Senior Conservation Technician (Museum Technician II)
John Anderson, Dip AD	Conservation Technician (Museum Technician III)
Marian Conway	Conservation Technician (Museum Technician III)
David Gribbin, BA	Conservation Technician (Museum Technician III)
Steven Huxley	Conservation Technician (Museum Technician III)
Kevin Miles	Conservation Technician (Museum Technician III)
Leslie Prince	Conservation Technician (Museum Technician III)
Jack Warrans	Conservation Technician (Museum Technician III)

WARDING STAFF

Robert Collier, BEM	Head Warder
Henry Izzard	Deputy Head Warder
Thomas Acott	Warder V
Edward Crane	Warder V
Dennis Smith	Warder V
John Trodd	Warder V
Stanley Washington	Warder V
Audrey Cox	Warder VI
James Cronin	Warder VI
Derek George	Warder VI
Mohamed Malik	Warder VI
John McColgan	Warder VI
David Mortram	Warder VI
Marion Sinclair	Warder VI
Ahmed Tally	Warder VI
Mahmood Tourabaly	Warder VI

WARDER VII'S

Mulammad Aslam	James Brown	George Crowley
Ernest Aylott	Felik Bryan	William Crumpler
Albert Barnard	Mohammad Bundhoo	Uriah Davis
Robert Barnard	Thomas Bushell	Amode Dowlut
Maurice Barry	Patrick Canavan	John Fenton
John Bartlett	Frank Carr	Richard Fleming
Michael Bartlett	Joseph Chance	Noel Ford
Dennis Beckett	Ally Chokowry	Michael Garrick
James Berry	Alan Clilverd	Ian Gatfield
Paul Bigrigg	Peter Clilverd	Abdolla Gaungoo
James Blumire	Robin Clilverd	Saheed Gaungoo
Haqiqat Bowry	Maurice Cockell	Marday Goinden
Bernard Brewster	Joseph Corley	Janette Gough
Stephen Brewster	John Cox	James Grant
Cyril Briggs	Marion Cronin	Leslie Gray

Reginald Hackett
Abdul Hamid
Raymond Harvey
Roy Helling
Anthony Hickey
Gloria Hird
Joseph Hook
Andrew Hunt
James Hunter
Robert Hutchins
Reginald James
Ansoobee Jaumdally
James Jerome
Joshua Johnson
Leopald Johnson
William Joyce
Sardar Khan
Nassid Kodabocus
John Kirk
Neville Kirlew
Alan Kisner
Derek Lawson
Stanley Lench
Raymond Lettin
Sentive Lisbie
Daniel MacGuire
John MacWilliams
Bashir Malik
Ghulam Malik
James Maxworthy
Andell McFarlane
James McKeever

Peter McKeever
Aonghas McKelcken
Rae Middleton
John Millington
Charles Mitchell
Henry Moore
Thomas Moran
Margot Morris
Joe Moss
Charles Murphy
Thomas Newbold
John Nichols
George Nutt
Ellen O'Donnell
Denis O'Leary
Ahmed Olia
Daniel O'Sullivan
Nehemiah Palmer
Peter Palmer
Pamela Parish
Arundbhai Patel
Kanubhai Patel
Modlukant Patel
Sanmukhbhai Patel
Vithalbhai Patel
Ronald Peachey
Herbert Peddie
Daniel Pink
Alan Preston
James Prince
Abdool Raheem
Ahmed Raheem

Rita Rippon
Joseph Roche
Edward Sandall
David Scoon
Dennis Scott
Robert Scott
Leslie Sell
Morgan Senauth
Gunwantrai Shulka
Francis Slavin
Frederick Smith
George Smith
Thomasina Smith
Thomas Smyth
George Stephenson
Henry Thandaven
William Thistle
Brynley Thomas
Phyllis Thomas
Sidney Thorpe
Goorparsad Toofaneeram
Mark Trodd
George Vitry
David Waller
Francis Wanwingkai
Terence Welch
Joyce Weller
Patrick Whelan
Leslie Williams
Robert Withers
John Young

Beatrice Jones	Housekeeper
Giuseppinna Crisca	Cleaner
Amaliese Martin	Cleaner
Antonietta Negri	Cleaner
Winifred Norbury	Cleaner
Rose O'Connor	Cleaner
Rosemary O'Donovan	Cleaner
Teresa Palombo	Cleaner
Dorothy Phillips	Cleaner
Joyce Straney	Cleaner
Janet Sullivan	Cleaner
Eva Szots	Cleaner
Vera Wilkins	Cleaner

PUBLICATIONS DEPARTMENT

Iain Bain	Manager
Brian McGahon	Deputy Manager/Accountant
Brian Lawler	Sales Manager
Stanley Bennett	Shop Manager/Stock Controller
Mollie Luther	Personal Assistant to Manager
Caroline Johnston, BA	Designer
Graham Varker-Littlewood	Assistant Accountant
Graham Langton	Copyright Controller
Sophie Hawley	Mail Order Assistant
Gilbert Gaster	Mail Order Supervisor
Peter Preston	Cashier
Ian Cameron	Head Storekeeper
Kenroy Peddie	Storekeeper
Robert Molina	Storekeeper
Rosemary Bennett	Shop Manageress
Jill Munro	Shop Supervisor
Clare Jenkins	Sales Assistant
Emma Debbs	Sales Assistant
Maggi Smith	Sales Assistant
Deidre Sharman	Sales Assistant
Susan Lawood	Sales Assistant
Ann Curtin	Sales Assistant
Angela Cameron	Sales Assistant
Kevin Driscoll	Sales Assistant
Anne Smith	Exhibition Supervisor

RESTAURANT

Paul King, MHCIMA	Manager
Elizabeth Hayward	Deputy Manager
Jacqueline Bhadha	Assistant Manager
Polly Thomson	2nd Assistant Manager

Kitchen

Michael Driver	Head Chef
Brian Gibson	Sous Chef
Colin Lansley	Chef
Elven Walcott	Chef
David Etienne	Chef
Louis Moutia	Kitchen Porter
Paul Acheampong	Kitchen Porter

Restaurant

Laura Skuce	Receptionist
Christopher Evans	Barman
Penelope Simon	Cashier
Diana Williams	Waitress
Catharine Downey	Waitress
Penelope Munoz	Waitress
Patricia Lahoud	Waitress

Margaret Kings	Waitress
Denise Lacey	Waitress
	Coffee Shop
Stella Cagneux	Supervisor
Elizabeth Wayre	General Assistant
Mary Pereira	General Assistant
Beverley Valentine	General Assistant
Angela Alexander	General Assistant
Paula Witter	General Assistant
Emily Carey	General Assistant
Marcia Buchanan	General Assistant
Yvette Taylor	General Assistant
Florence Samuels	General Assistant
Marian Williams	Book-keeper
Driss Gharbaoui	Cleaner
Zineb Gharbaoui	Cleaner
Sellam Atmani	Cleaner

Mr Robert Collier, Head Attendant at the
Tate Gallery who was awarded the B.E.M. in 1983

Appendix 3 Exhibitions

Loan Exhibitions

(Turner watercolours) **Turner and the Sea** 7 January – 27 January 1982
Landseer 10 February – 12 April 1982
Lionel Constable 24 February – 4 April 1982
(Photographic Display) **The Battersea Mural: the Good, the Bad and the Ugly**
5 March – 9 May 1982
Six Indian Painters 7 April – 23 May 1982
Graham Sutherland 19 May – 4 July 1982
Paint and Painting 9 June – 18 July 1982
Julian Schnabel 30 June – 5 September 1982
(Turner Watercolours) **Turner in the Open Air** 1 July – 31 December 1982
Giorgio de Chirico 4 August – 3 October 1982
Audio, Tape-Slide, Drawings and Performance 22 August – 8 September 1982
Jean Tinguely 8 September – 14 November 1982
Howard Hodgkin: Indian Leaves 22 September – 7 November 1982
Richard Wilson 3 November 1982 – 2 January 1983
Gordale Scar: an Essay in the Sublime 3 November 1982 – 2 January 1983
Jennifer Bartlett 17 November 1982 – 13 February 1983
Stephen Willats: Meta Filter 8 December 1982 – 10 January 1983
(Turner watercolours) **J. M. W. Turner: studies for finished watercolours** (*c.*1825–40)
2 January – 12 June 1983
Peter Blake 9 February – 20 March 1983
James Barry 9 February – 20 March 1983
Paule Vézelay 23 February – 22 May 1983
The Essential Cubism 27 April – 31 July 1983
Harold Cohen 8 June – 24 July 1983
(Turner watercolours) **Turner Abroad** 20 June – 11 December 1983
Henry Moore at 85 1 July – 14 August 1983
The Clore Gallery: Architects' Drawings 29 June – 31 August 1983
Making Sculpture 4 July – 14 August 1983
Summertime 23 August – 4 September 1983
NewArt 14 September – 23 October 1983
Reg Butler 16 November 1983 – 15 January 1984
John Piper 30 November 1983 – 22 January 1984
**Image and Process: Studies, stage and final proofs from the graphic works of
Richard Hamilton 1952–82** 14 December 1983 – 12 February 1984
(Turner watercolours) **Turner and the Human Figure** 19 December 1983 – 15 July 1984
Hans Haacke 25 January – 4 March 1984
The Pre-Raphaelites 7 March – 28 May 1984
Cedric Morris 28 March – 13 May 1984

Exhibitions drawn from the permanent collection

The Print Collection: a selection 9 March – 6 June 1982
Ben Nicholson Memorial Display 1 April – 21 May 1982
Watercolours and drawings by Rossetti 21 May – 2 November 1982
Prints and works on paper 17 August – 21 November 1982
Bequest by Mrs F. Ambrose Clark to the British Sporting Art Trust 18 August – 18 September 1982
(Archive display) **Letters from Jean Tinguely** 8 September – 28 November 1982
Eric Gill and Wyndham Lewis 27 November 1982 – 8 May 1983
The Print Room Gallery: a selection from the permanent collection 7 December 1982 – 27 February 1983
The Kessler Bequest 15 February – 29 April 1984
(Archive display) **Sir Cedric Morris and Arthur Lett-Haines** 29 March – 13 May 1984

Appendix 4 Attendance Figures

1 April 1978 – 31 March 1979	**997,568**
1 April 1979 – 31 March 1980	**1,141,471**
1 April 1980 – 31 March 1981	**1,271,485**
1 April 1981 – 31 March 1982	**975,728**
1 April 1982 – 31 March 1983	**1,254,084**
1 April 1983 – 31 March 1984	**1,301,697**

Appendix 5 Loans to the Gallery

This list is restricted to loans made during the two years 1 April 1982 – 31 March 1984 and does not include works already on loan on 1 April 1982.

*Works not still on loan on 31 March 1984

O: OIL W: WATERCOLOUR S: SCULPTURE

ARTIST	TITLE	MEDIUM	LENDER
*Philip Guston	Entrance	O	David McKee
Jackson Pollock	Summertime: Number 9A	O	Mrs Lee Krasner Pollock
Jackson Pollock	Number 14	O	Mrs Lee Krasner Pollock
Jackson Pollock	Birth	O	Mrs Lee Krasner Pollock
Naum Gabo	Torso	S	Anonymous
Duane Hanson	Florida Shopper	S	Doris and Charles Saatchi
Pablo Picasso	Compotier et Guitar	O	Douglas Cooper
*J. M. W. Turner	Temple of Jupiter Panellenius Restored	O	The Spafford Establishment
Sir Hamo Thornycroft	The Mower	S	Arthur Grogan
Henri Matisse	Interior with Black Fern	O	Ernst Beyeler
Carel Weight	Seven Deadly Sins: Sloth, Avarice, Lust, Pride, Anger, Gluttony, Envy	O	The Keatly Trust
William Blake	The Penance of Jane Shore	W	Anonymous
John Linnell	The East Side of the Edgware Road, looking towards Kensington Gardens	O	The Royal Borough of Kensington and Chelsea (Leighton House Art Gallery and Museum)
Oskar Kokoschka	Anschluss – Alice in Wonderland	O	Anonymous
Oskar Kokoschka	Loreley	O	Anonymous
Oskar Kokoschka	Marianne – Maquis	O	Anonymous
Oskar Kokoschka	Self-Portrait	O	Anonymous
Atkinson Grimshaw	Nab Scar	O	Anonymous
Frank Auerbach	Head of E.O.W.	O	Anonymous
Howard Hodgkin	In a French Restaurant	O	The artist

Watercolours from the Turner Bequest

The Trustees of the British Museum have lent further groups of watercolours for display in Gallery 13.

Subject matter has been:

July – December 1982	Turner in the Open Air
January – June 1983	J. M. W. Turner; Studies for Finished Watercolours *c.*1825-40
July – December 1983	Turner Abroad
January – June 1984	Turner and the Human Figure

Appendix 6 Loans from the Gallery

1 April 1982 – 31 March 1984

a Long Term

Public Galleries in Great Britain direct	32	
Public Galleries in Great Britain through the Arts Council	65	
Public Galleries abroad	1	
British National Collections	43	
British Embassies through the Government Art Collection	15	
Government buildings through the Government Art Collection	94	
Residencies of Colonial Governors	4	
Public Buildings in Great Britain	43	297

b Special Exhibitions

Centres in Great Britain	354	
Centres abroad	211	565
		862